THE EARTH STORY
IN THE PSALMS
AND THE PROPHETS

The Earth Bible, 4

THE EARTH STORY
IN THE PSALMS
AND THE PROPHETS

edited by

Norman C. Habel

www.SheffieldAcademicPress.com

THE
PILGRIM
PRESS
Cleveland

Copyright © 2001 Sheffield Academic Press

Published by
Sheffield Academic Press Ltd
Mansion House
19 Kingfield Road
Sheffield S11 9AS
England

www.SheffieldAcademicPress.com

ISBN 1 84127 087 3

Published in the USA and Canada (only) by
The Pilgrim Press
700 Prospect Avenue East
Cleveland, Ohio 44115-1100
USA

USA and Canada only
ISBN 0-8298-1442-6

Typeset by Sheffield Academic Press
and
Printed on acid-free paper in Great Britain
by MPG Books Ltd
Bodmin, Cornwall

British Library Cataloguing-in-Publication Data

A catalogue record for this book is available
from the British Library

Library of Congress Cataloging-in-Publication Data

A catalog record for this book is available
from the Library of Congress

Contents

Foreword

Archbishop Desmond Tutu

Planet Earth is in crisis. More and more life systems are being threatened. Scientists estimate that at least half, and perhaps as many as 80 per cent, of the world's animal and plant species are found in the rainforests. The rainforests are the lungs of the planet, producing much of the oxygen that humans and other oxygen-dependent creatures need to survive. The rainforests, alas, are still being destroyed at an alarming rate.

Resolving the ecological crisis of our planet, however, is no longer a problem we can leave to the scientists. Just as we are all part of the problem, so we are all also part of the solution. We all need to come to terms with the forces that have created this crisis and the resources within our traditions that can motivate us to resolve the crisis. One of those traditions is our biblical heritage.

It is significant, therefore, that the Earth Bible Project has chosen to take the Earth crisis seriously and to re-read our biblical heritage in the light of this crisis. The Earth Bible Team has listened closely to ecologists and developed a set of principles to re-read the biblical text from an ecojustice perspective. The concern of Earth Bible writers is not to defend the biblical text blindly, but to identify those passages which may have contributed to the crisis and to uncover those traditions which have valued Earth but been suppressed.

I commend the Earth Bible Team for including representative writers from around the globe, including the Southern hemisphere. I commend the team for confronting the biblical tradition honestly and openly in dialogue with ecologists. And, in particular, I commend the writers for daring to read the biblical text afresh from the perspective of Earth. Feminists have forced us to confront the patriarchal orientation of much of the biblical text. Earth Bible writers are now confronting us with the anthropocentric nature of much of the biblical text. We now ask: does the text devalue Earth by making the self-interest of humans its dominant concern?

I recommend you read the Earth Bible series with a critical but empathetic eye. As a critical reader you will want to assess whether writers make their case for their interpretation of the text in terms of the principles employed. As an empathetic reader, however, you will need to identify with Earth and the suffering Earth community as you read the text.

I hope that the promise of 'peace on Earth' will be advanced by this laudable project as scholars probe our heritage to understand and assist in resolving the crisis of our planet.

Editorial Preface

Norman C. Habel

> I was the Englishman overcome with enthusiasm for a barbarous place...
> I walked a little way, barefooted, and then lay down in nakedness on
> loamy earth and began to scoop it up and inhale it. The earth groaned,
> so I thought, like the beloved, caressed (Kenneally 2000).

These are the opening words on the dust jacket of Tom Keneally's
new work, *Bettany's Book*. They reflect a poetic image of how one character heard the groaning Earth in the wilds of Australia. The groaning
of Earth under the curse of human greed, heard long ago by Jeremiah,
is of quite a different kind. And the groaning has intensified for those
who can hear. Many of the writers in this volume are Earth people,
Indigenous people and prophets who hear the many voices of Earth
both in pain and in celebration.

Since this volume makes connections with the prophets, we have
included a number of articles that may be classified as a prophetic
word rather than a typical scholarly analysis of the prophetic word,
even though a scholarly analysis may inform the prophetic insight.
The first of these is the prophetic (fore)word by Norman Charles. A
Cree/Metis from Saskatchewan in Canada, Charles challenges the
academic community of writers to be accountable and to heed the
word from Indigenous peoples who know how Earth suffers from the
curses that came with colonization.

Another prophetic challenge comes from Kalinda Rose Stevenson,
who reads the harsh word from Ezekiel's God in terms of the reality
and rhetoric of the wife batterer. She hears the groaning of Earth as
the response of a woman who hears the harsh voice of Ezekiel's cruel
male God as the voice of a batterer. Keith Carley explores the uncomfortable formula of desolation for Earth used by Ezekiel to exact a
selfish and harsh justice. There seems to be little justice for Earth in the
biblical book of Ezekiel, even when God promises restoration. In this
biblical book God does promise a future, it seems, but only to vindi-
cate God's name, not for the sake of the suffering people or suffering
Earth. The message of Isaiah 65, analysed by Anne Gardner, offers a

more positive picture of hope for Earth, as do the scenarios that depict animals as an integral part of the transformed Earth community according to John Olley's study of key texts in Isaiah.

A recurring theme in a number of these studies is the deep bond or kinship between land and traditional custodians of the land that lies behind Indigenous peoples' history of mutual care/custodianship. One could dismiss the eccentric action of Jeremiah purchasing land already under Babylonian siege (Jer. 32) as the impetus for a romantic rural vision. Gunther Wittenberg in his article, however, suggests that Jeremiah's redemption of the land connects with an ancient Israelite kinship between family and land. Their future is bound up together. Laurie Braaten sees a similar bond between people and Land in Hosea 2, and discovers Land speaking for Earth. Madipoane Masenya suggests that this family–land bond is also fundamental to the life experiences of Indigenous peoples in pre-colonial Africa. By developing an eco*bosadi* reading of Psalm 127, she exposes how pursuing the traditional ideal of a large family to perpetuate the male line violates the underlying bond between human mother and Mother Earth that is necessary for sustaining the Earth community in the future.

Two readings of Psalm 104 make similar connections. Mutual custodianship and kinship with Earth are integral to Indigenous understandings of life. These two readings of Psalm 104 — the one by Arthur Walker-Jones, who worked for many years in the Pacific, and the other by Abotchie Ntreh from Ghana — represent illuminating dialogues between Indigenous cultures and the biblical text. As Native American Norman Charles declares in his prophetic word, it is time for scholars to hear the Indigenous voice both in our reading and in our relationship with Earth.

Other articles on the Psalms also challenge us as we read from the perspective of Earth. Peter Trudinger and Howard Wallace offer a fresh understanding of 'chaos waters' and Earth fertility and their possible ancient Near Eastern connections. William Urbrock's reading is a bold creative reorientation of the tradition with the voice of Earth enabling us to hear the songs of three psalms afresh. My study with Geraldine Avent challenges the tradition that a theophany — while it may be spectacular — is necessarily a good thing, especially when Earth suffers unfairly in the process.

My thanks to all contributors, including Lloyd Geering, one of the founding figures of Religion Studies in New Zealand, whose preface was part of the talk he gave to launch the Earth Bible in Christchurch.

My thanks also to the core members of the team — Vicky Balabanski, Charles Biggs, Duncan Reid, Marie Turner, Peter Trudinger, Alan

Cadwallader and Shirley Wurst, who continues to be the indispensible team editor.

I remain grateful to those who have supported the project in various ways, whether with funds, in kind or in person. The project is now located in the Centre for Theology, Science and Culture associated with the Adelaide College of Divinity and Flinders University of South Australia. The body whose financial support has underwritten the project to date is the Charles Strong Memorial Trust. This Trust is named after the founder of the Australian Church, a Christian denomination which operated from 1885 to 1955. The Trust promotes the sympathetic study of all religions and fosters dialogue between religion and other disciplines. This project is the result of a dialogue between religion, especially Christianity, and ecology. Continuing supporters of this project include Flinders University and the Adelaide College of Divinity.

A special word is in order about the logo for this series. The artist who worked with me in developing this logo and drafted its final form is Jasmine Corowa. Jasmine is a young Indigenous Australian whose art reflects traditional Aboriginal techniques of communication. Her father, Dennis Corowa, is one of the Rainbow Spirit Elders whom I supported in their publication *Rainbow Spirit Theology.* I was also privileged to edit a set of Jasmine's paintings, published in 2000 by The Liturgical Press and entitled *The Rainbow Spirit in Creation: A Reading of Genesis I.*

The logo is a symbol of Earth. The land dots are in Earth colours, forming that maze of shimmering life we call Earth community. The white dots of the sky rise above Earth. The surface of land/Earth is an open book. This is a double symbol: not only do we read land/Earth like a book (as Australian Aboriginal peoples do); when we read The Book in the Earth Bible Project also we do so from beneath, from Earth.

I appreciate the continued commitment of Sheffield Academic Press and The Pilgrim Press. I want to express my personal gratitude to the publishers David Clines and Philip Davies, who have made the academic component of the Earth Bible Project possible. The staff of Sheffield Academic Press also deserve commendation for their professionalism and patience.

Preface

Lloyd Geering

It was my pleasure to participate at Christchurch New Zealand in the launching of the first volume of the Earth Bible, *Readings from the Perspective of Earth*. And I am honoured to be invited to introduce this fourth volume.

During the last four to five hundred years, radical changes have been taking place in the way we humans view the world and understand ourselves and our cultural traditions. Our view of the universe has changed out of all recognition from that of the ancients and from that which was still universal in Europe of the Renaissance and Protestant Reformation. It has expanded both spatially and in age from what it was once thought to be. We now entertain entirely new ideas about the origin of the world and of the human race. We are much more aware today of the human origin of our cultural traditions and of what we call their religious dimension.

As part of this radical change there has been nothing less than a revolution in the way we understand the Bible. It could be called 'The Re-Earthing of the Bible'. For very many centuries the Bible had come to be regarded as a holy book sent down from heaven. Christians tended to regard it in the way Muslims regard the Qur'an, a book to be attributed wholly to the authorship of God. We now know the Bible to have had a very Earthly origin and to be a wholly human product. The Bible is a little library of books which, however inspiring we may still find them, also reflect the limited knowledge and even the prejudices of the people who wrote them.

This revolution has meant that for many people the Bible has now become a fallen idol. They reject it as having passed its use-by date. The Bible may still be the world's best-seller but the majority of people in the so-called Christian world no longer turn to it and read it regularly in the way they used to. We are in danger of falling into the heresy of the second century Marcion. So impressed was he by the message of love that came from Jesus, and so repelled was he but what he thought was the antithesis of this in what was then the only

Bible possessed by the Christians, namely, what we now call the
Hebrew Scriptures (also known as the Old Testament), that he urged
the church to abandon these Jewish books. He set out to replace the
Hebrew Bible with his own 'New Bible', which consisted of ten of the
letters of St Paul plus the gospel of St Luke (suitably edited by himself). He was actually the first to gather together Christian writings
together and to regard them as Holy Scripture (or what we now call
the Christian Scriptures, or the New Testament).

The Christian church did not follow Marcion's drastic rejection of
its cultural origins. It responded to his challenge by retaining the
Hebrew Scriptures, and adding to it its own—and more extended—
form of the Christian Scriptures. Today the Bible has not only become
a fallen idol in the popular mind but it is also coming under severe
criticism. The feminist movement has strongly condemned it for its
support of patriarchy. Some conservationists and members of the
Green movement claim that it is responsible for the current ecological
crisis because it portrays God as one who gave authority to exploit the
earth, saying, 'be fruitful and multiply...and subdue the earth'.

One of the important aspects of the biblical revolution has been the
recognition that the Bible was written by many different authors,
drawn from many different times and contexts. This means that the
Bible does not always speak with one voice. The Bible, in fact, is a
collection of voices. Some are no longer relevant, while others that
have fallen on deaf ears for centuries suddenly speak to us with new
relevance.

Those who have promoted the Earth Bible believe, following the
lead of the second century church, that we should not, in Marcionite
fashion, simply reject our cultural roots as found in the Bible; rather,
we should learn how to reinterpret them in the light of the new global
situation in which we live and in the ecological crisis we now face.

The Earth Bible is not a new Bible but a fresh way of reading and
understanding the Bible. For many centuries Christians have been
reading the Bible through spectacles tinted by the theological doctrines that developed in the post-biblical period. These placed all the
emphasis on an other-worldly form of spirituality and left the physical
Earth somewhat down-graded. That is why the interest shown by St
Francis in the trees and the flowers, the birds and the beasts along
with the natural world, generally was regarded at the time as somewhat eccentric.

Now that we are looking at the natural world very differently and
are being forced to take seriously a growing number of ecological
issues, we also find we are reading the Bible differently, as if with new

eyes. Even though many of the prophetic voices in the Bible were strongly antagonistic towards the deification of the forces of nature, seeing them in competition to the God of Israel, they still acknowledged the glory of Earth and affirmed that when God looked at everything God had made, it was very good.

The contributors to the Earth Bible are approaching the biblical texts section by section, and examining them from the point of view of Earth. In doing so they are rediscovering elements long overlooked and also bring the text under the judgement of Earth.

List of Abbreviations

AB	Anchor Bible
ABD	David Noel Freedman (ed.), *The Anchor Bible Dictionary* (New York: Doubleday, 1992)
AJT	*American Journal of Theology*
AnBib	Analecta biblica
ANET	James B. Pritchard (ed.), *Ancient Near Eastern Texts Relating to the Old Testament* (Princeton: Princeton University Press, 1950)
ANF	Anti-Nicene Fathers
BASOR	*Bulletin of the American Schools of Oriental Research*
BDB	Francis Brown, S.R. Driver and Charles A. Briggs, *A Hebrew and English Lexicon of the Old Testament* (Oxford: Clarendon Press, 1907)
BETL	Bibliotheca ephemeridum theologicarum lovaniensium
BHK	R. Kittel (ed.), *Biblia hebraica* (Stuttgart: Württembergische Bibelanstalt, 1937)
BHS	*Biblia hebraica stuttgartensia*
Bib	*Biblica*
BN	*Biblische Notizen*
BWANT	Beiträge zur Wissenschaft vom Alten und Neuen Testament
BZAW	Beihefte zur *ZAW*
CBQ	*Catholic Biblical Quarterly*
EBib	Etudes bibliques
FOTL	The Forms of the Old Testament Literature
GKC	*Gesenius' Hebrew Grammar* (ed. E. Kautzsch, revised and trans. A.E. Cowley; Oxford: Clarendon Press, 1910)
HAR	*Hebrew Annual Review*
ICC	International Critical Commentary
IDB	George Arthur Buttrick (ed.), *The Interpreter's Dictionary of the Bible* (4 vols.; Nashville: Abingdon Press, 1962)
IDBSup	*IDB*, Supplementary Volume
Int	*Interpretation*
JBL	*Journal of Biblical Literature*
JNSL	*Journal of Northwest Semitic Languages*
JPSV	*Jewish Publication Society Version*
JQR	*Jewish Quarterly Review*
JSOT	*Journal for the Study of the Old Testament*
JSOTSup	*Journal for the Study of the Old Testament*, Supplement Series
JSS	*Journal of Semitic Studies*

KB	Ludwig Koehler and Walter Baumgartner (eds.), *Lexicon in Veteris Testamenti libros* (Leiden: E.J. Brill, 1953)
NASB	*New American Standard Bible*
NCB	New Century Bible
NICOT	New International Commentary on the Old Testament
NJB	*New Jerusalem Bible*
NRSV	New Revised Standard Version
OTL	Old Testament Library
SBLDS	SBL Dissertation Series
SBLMS	SBL Monograph Series
SBT	Studies in Biblical Theology
TDOT	G.J. Botterweck and H. Ringgren (eds.), *Theological Dictionary of the Old Testament*
ThWAT	G.J. Botterweck and H. Ringgren (eds.), *Theologisches Wörterbuch zum Alten Testament* (Stuttgart: W. Kohlhammer, 1970–)
UF	*Ugarit-Forschungen*
VT	*Vetus Testamentum*
WBC	Word Biblical Commentary
WMANT	Wissenschaftliche Monographien zum Alten und Neuen Testament
ZAW	*Zeitschrift für die alttestamentliche Wissenschaft*
ZTK	*Zeitschrift für Theologie und Kirche*

List of Contributors

Geraldine Avent is a doctoral candidate at the Adelaide College of Divinity in South Australia. Her major areas of research include Psalms, Job and ecojustice hermeneutics.

Laurie J. Braaten is Professor of Old Testament at Judson College, Elgin, IL, USA. He is an ordained elder in the Church of the Nazarene, and a member of the Society of Biblical Literature, the Wesleyan Theological Society, the Appalachian Trail Conference and the Green Mountain Club. His recent publications include 'God Sows the Land: Hosea's Place in the Book of the Twelve'; and 'That God may Heal the Land: A Liturgical Context for the Book of the Twelve'.

Keith Carley is Lecturer in First Testament Studies at the Joint Theological Colleges of St John's and Trinity in Auckland and Honorary Lecturer in Theology at the University of Auckland. Among his publications are *Ezekiel Among the Prophets* and 'Psalm 8: An Apology for Domination' in The Earth Bible, 1.

Norman J. Charles, a Cree/Metis from Saskatchewan, is active in prison ministry at Rockford Institution (a minimum security men's penitentiary near Winnipeg), and helps facilitate a men's group at St Raphael Centre. He has published articles on recovery from addiction and is currently writing a book on Aboriginal self-government and exploring Aboriginal spirituality.

Anne Gardner is Senior Lecturer at La Trobe University, Melbourne. Her publications include a number of articles on women in the biblical and post-biblical tradition as well as articles on the Maccabean period. Her current research focuses on King David and Jerusalem and on the book of Daniel.

Lloyd Geering is Emeritus Professor of Religious Studies, Victoria University of Wellington and formerly Professor of Old Testament Studies at Emmanuel College Brisbane and at the Theological Hall,

Knox College, Dunedin. He is author of *Faith's New Age* (1980), *Tomorrow's God* (1994) and *The World to Come* (1999).

Norman C. Habel, chief editor of the Earth Bible Project, is Professorial Fellow at Flinders University of South Australia and Adelaide College of Divinity. His major works include a commentary on Job in the Old Testament Library, *The Land is Mine: Six Biblical Land Ideologies* and *Reconciliation: Searching for Australia's Soul*. His current research extends to ecoliturgy and ecojustice writings for the wider community.

Madipoane Masenya is a Senior Lecturer in Old Testament Studies at UNISA (University of South Africa) in Pietersburg. She co-authored *Their Story Is Ours: Biblical Women and Us. Bible Studies for South African Women*, and her essay, 'A Bosadi Reading of Genesis 16' is included in *Old Testament Essays* 2. Her current research involves a redefinition of womanhood in an African-South African context, *bosadi* biblical hermeneutics, and interpreting the Hebrew Scriptures from the perspective of traditional African cultures.

Abotchie Ntreh is Senior Lecturer in Old Testament Studies in the Department of Religious Studies, University of Cape Coast in Ghana. His doctoral dissertation was a study of the transmission of political authority in ancient Israel. His research includes reading the Hebrew Scriptures from the perspective of traditional African cultures.

John W. Olley is concurrently lecturer in Old Testament at Murdoch University, and principal of the Baptist Theological College of Western Australia. His writings include 'Righteousness' in *The Septuagint of Isaiah*, and *First and Second Kings, Then and Now*. His current research is on the text and theology of Isaiah and the Septuagint of Ezekiel.

Kalinda Rose Stevenson is an independent scholar and writer living in Walnut Creek, California. Her most significant publication is *Vision of Transformation: The Territorial Rhetoric of Ezekiel 40–48* Book Three in *Society of Biblical Literature Dissertation Series*, 154. Her current research includes Ezekiel and the land, critical spatiality, and land rights.

Peter L. Trudinger is a sessional lecturer at Adelaide College of Divinity in Hebrew Bible with a doctorate from Emory University. He has contributed four articles to the *Dictionary of Biblical Interpretation*. His major areas of research are currently in Psalms, ritual practice in Second Temple Judaism, and history of the interpretation of Isaiah.

Desmond Tutu is former Archbishop of Capetown, South Africa, and currently Archbishop Emeritus of the same city. His major publications include *The Rainbow People of God*, and *No Future Without Forgiveness*.

William J. Urbrock is Professor of Religious Studies at the University of Wisconsin, Oshkosh. His publications include 'Blessings and Curses' in *The Anchor Bible Dictionary*, and 'Sisera's Mother in Judges 5 and Haim Gouri's 'Immo', *HAR* 11 (1987).

Howard N. Wallace is Professor of Old Testament at Uniting Church Theological Hall, Melbourne. Among his major publications are *The Eden Narrative* (1985) and a number of scholarly articles. His recent research is on Psalms, especially Psalms in Christian ministry and worship.

Arthur Walker-Jones is Assistant Professor of Biblical Studies and Prophetic Ministry, Faculty of Theology, University of Winnipeg. He is the founding editor of *Koinonia* (1989) and author of 'The Role of Theological Imagination in Biblical Theology', in *Horizons of Biblical Theology*. His current areas of research include creation theologies, Genesis, post-colonialism and Indigenous cultures.

Gunther H. Wittenberg is Professor Emeritus of Old Testament at the School of Theology, University of Natal. His major publications include *I Have Heard the Cry of My People: A Study Guide to Exodus 1–15* (The Bible in Context, 1), and *Prophecy and Protest* (The Bible in Context, 2). His current research focuses on ecology, sustainable agriculture and the Hebrew Scriptures.

Shirley Wurst is an editor for the Earth Bible Project, and an Equity and Diversity Officer and sessional lecturer at the University of South Australia. Her recent doctoral thesis, entitled 'Dancing in the Minefield: Feminist Counterreadings of the Women in Proverbs 1-9', reflects her current research in feminist theory, hermeneutics, epistemology, vision-in-texts and voice-in-texts, and social justice.

Six Ecojustice Principles

1. *The Principle of Intrinsic Worth*
The universe, Earth and all its components have intrinsic worth/value.

2. *The Principle of Interconnectedness*
Earth is a community of interconnected living things that are mutually dependent on each other for life and survival.

3. *The Principle of Voice*
Earth is a subject capable of raising its voice in celebration and against injustice.

4. *The Principle of Purpose*
The universe, Earth and all its components are part of a dynamic cosmic design within which each piece has a place in the overall goal of that design.

5. *The Principle of Mutual Custodianship*
Earth is a balanced and diverse domain in which responsible custodians can function as partners, rather than rulers, to sustain a balanced and diverse Earth community.

6. *The Principle of Resistance*
Earth and its components not only suffer from injustices at the hands of humans, but actively resist them in the struggle for justice.

The principles listed here are basic to the approach of writers in the Earth Bible Project seeking to read the biblical text from the perspective of Earth. For an elaboration of these principles see Earth Bible Team 2000, 38-53.

The Voice of Earth: More than Metaphor?

The Earth Bible Team

In Volume 3 of the Earth Bible we explored where the voice of Earth is heard in ancient biblical Wisdom traditions. In that connection we wrote,

> It can be argued that applying the concept of voice to Earth is itself an anthropocentric act, making Earth into a human subject. That is clearly not our intention. We use the term 'voice' as shorthand for the diverse ways in which Earth and the Earth community may communicate. When we speak of 'body language' there is communication, even if there is no accompanying audible voice. By the voice of Earth we mean the many languages of Earth, be they gesture, sign, image or sound, that send a message — whether to humans, to other members of the Earth community, or to God.

The principle of voice, one of the ecojustice principles of the Earth Bible Project, states that Earth is a subject capable of raising its voice in celebration and against injustice. In the light of criticism by Tim Meadowcroft in a paper given at the Ecotheology Conference in Christchurch in July 2000, we believe further explanation of this — and related — principles is in order.

The significance of Meadowcroft's analysis is the way he links this principle with our hermeneutic of suspicion that biblical texts, written by humans, may well be anthropocentric. He writes:

> At this point we find ourselves falling over one of the key ironies of the project. The Earth Bible explicitly seeks to deliver the Bible from anthropocentric approaches and to discover geocentric readings instead. The purpose is to release the voice of earth from the silence into which it has been bound by both the text and our anthropocentric reading of the text. But the instrument of release itself is a thoroughly anthropocentric device, namely reader-response whereby the reader is required to adopt some *a priori* positions. At the end of the exercise, the voice of the earth continues to look suspiciously like a human creation (2000: 5-6).

In response to this criticism, we acknowledge, first of all, that we begin with the suspicion that a given text and its interpreters may suppress the voice of Earth. We make no apology for this assertion. Our experience of reading texts and their interpreters from the perspective of Earth confirms the validity of our claim. Writers in the Earth Bible Project, given a new awareness of Earth as a subject, also support this assertion.

Earth as Subject

The focus of the principle of voice is, first of all, on Earth as a subject, a non-human 'thou', an 'other' who is part of the biblical tradition. The issue initially is not precisely how Earth expresses itself, but that Earth is a subject capable of self-expression in some form. There are three grand narratives in the Scriptures—the story of God, the story of humanity and the story of Earth. In our past reading of the narratives of the Bible, however, the narrative of Earth or creation as a central subject or character has been largely ignored. To speak of God as a subject or a 'thou' does not mean that God has the same consciousness or character as humans—yet God remains a subject. Similarly, we can speak of Earth as a subject without assuming that Earth has the same consciousness or character as humans.

Voice as Metaphor

A living subject, as distinct from a lifeless object, has the capacity to communicate in some way. The voice of a subject, whether the subject is God, a biotic creature, or Earth, may be classed as a metaphor expressing the reality of communication. This metaphor is indeed anthropomorphic language—and necessarily so. Anthropomorphic language is the primary mode by which humans communicate to others to whom a significant level of independence, equality and similarity is attributed. The term 'voice' is our way of recognizing Earth as communicating as an equal but different 'thou'.

It is no less problematic to speak of the voice of Earth than to speak of the voice of God. Predication of the verb 'to speak' of Earth presents no less a hermeneutical challenge than the corresponding religious claim that God 'speaks'. The voice of Earth, on an academic level, is as hard to hear as the *bat qôl*. The metaphor of voice, however, helps us—as humans—to grasp and appreciate the reality of communication with a 'thou' other than ourselves.

An Example from Psalm 65

In the past, most interpreters have negated metaphors in which Earth or parts of Earth are given voice. A typical example of this kind of metaphor is in Ps. 65.12-13:

> The pastures of the wilderness shout for joy,
> the hills gird themselves with rejoicing.
> The pastures are clothed with flocks,
> and the valleys cover themselves with grain,
> they shout for joy, indeed they sing.

In his article on Psalm 65 in this volume, Howard Wallace reflects on the way scholars have treated this metaphor.

> Many commentators recognize the language of Ps. 65.12-13 as a metaphor, a tool of the poet. Some have spiritualized the metaphor, or resisted it by supplying a human subject to the verb in the last line... Others, such as T.K. Cheyne, have accepted it as instructive. He has commented that 'Virgil at least would not have been shocked at making nature "sing"' (1888: 179).
>
> However, the acceptance of the words of the psalmist as a metaphor does not allow us to dismiss them too quickly as simply a feature of the poetry, a matter of expression or form and not of substance.

What is the function of metaphor in texts like these? We would argue that metaphor involves the juxtaposition of two different thoughts, images, concepts that interact with each other and remain in tension with each other (McFague 1982: 37). In this text, the wilderness shouts, hills rejoice, and valleys shout for joy. The image of valleys, which we generally view as silent, shouting for joy surprises us and forces us to reflect on the connection between the two ideas. The fact that 'shouting for joy' is a human characteristic in no way negates the interaction. Wallace goes so far as to say that the

> use of metaphor in Ps. 65.12-13 does not lessen the validity of the statement that Earth has a voice with which to praise God. Rather, without the use of the metaphor the psalmist could not open our minds, let alone our ears, to hear Earth's voice. The metaphor points to a reality embodied within the physical world, one that our contemporary Western minds are not usually trained to comprehend.

Hearing Earth's Voice

The tension between the two thoughts of a metaphor, like the one discussed above, may not be experienced as a tension at all in many Indigenous cultures. The metaphor used by the psalmist may be more than a metaphor in such cultures. The psalmist's metaphor may, in fact, be taking us back to the experience of ancient peoples who have a kinship with creation that Western thinking has abandoned. Many Indigenous peoples seem to have a capacity to hear the wilderness sing and communicate in a variety of ways. For many Indigenous peoples, trees, rivers, bears and deer all have distinct voices.

In her paper on Psalm 127 in this volume, Madipoane Masenya informs us that the Bosadi woman of Africa cannot exist apart from Earth. She claims that she has been taught to listen and hear Earth's voices through close interaction with the seasons of nature and the cycles of life. We, as members of the Australian Earth Bible team, are familiar with Indigenous Australians who listen to the land and the creatures of the land—involving everything from hearing the grass grow to acknowledging the call of the kookaburra as a message of good news.

When Indigenous writers speak of Earth or land as Mother, their language seems to be more than metaphor. The land is a spiritual source, a sacred subject; it is alive. And when they address land as Mother, they are responding to their experience of Earth as kin and to the diverse voices of Earth as their relatives. In Volume 1 we cited the cry of Mary Duroux, who has heard the pain and cries of her Mother, the land, whom she described as 'crucified' (Habel 2000: 48). A further example are the words of Jack Davis (1992: 6) whose poem, *My Mother the Land*, begins:

> Mother why don't you enfold me
> as you used to in the long long ago
> your morning breath
> was sweetness to my soul
> The daily scent of woodsmoke
> was a benediction in the air.

At one level, therefore, we may wish to talk about Earth singing, moaning or shouting in the language of metaphor. At a deeper level, however, we may also grant that sensitive humans, such as Indigenous peoples, the prophet Jeremiah or the creator of Psalm 65, may be mediators of Earth's communication in a way that less sensitive Westerners may find hard to comprehend. To express the nature of that communication—a new experience, previously unknown—requires anthropomorphic language; poets have used metaphor and imagery to convey their insights to less attuned humans for centuries. As Carole Fontaine says in her article on the Song of Songs in Volume 3 of the Earth Bible:

Since poetry operates by invoking the metaphorical dimension of language, we are met with the typical features of metaphor as we encounter
each of these domains. That which is specific and well known (the
image or 'vehicle') is juxtaposed with that which is less known or more
diffuse (the 'tenor' which the vehicle explicates). In the process, the
unknown becomes known (2001: 128).

Voice in Psalms and Prophets

It is this capacity of metaphor to go beyond itself and reveal the
unknown, the latent, or the hidden that deserves recognition as we
explore the text. One task that still lies ahead is a complete classifi-
cation of the forms of language of Earth and Earth community in
biblical texts. A preliminary survey of these forms in the Psalms and
the writings of the prophets reveals a wide range of communication
modes.

In the Psalms, Earth or members of Earth community may praise
God or celebrate with singing, shouting and other forms of rejoicing
(Ps. 65.8, 12, 13). Earth rejoices (Pss. 96.11; 97.1), skies are glad (Ps.
96.11), seas roar in praise (Ps. 96.11), trees sing (Ps. 96.12) and the
works of creation give thanks (Ps. 145.10). In Psalm 148 everything
from sun and moon to sea monsters and snow is called on to praise
God. In these psalms Earth and members of Earth community are
addressed as subjects capable of responding with praise in a variety of
forms.

In the writings of the prophets, especially in Isaiah and Jeremiah,
Earth is addressed as a subject who can hear God or the prophet's
word (Isa. 1.2; 34.1; 49.13; Jer. 6.19; 22.29). Earth is portrayed as having
emotions; Earth and Earth community suffer and mourn (Isa. 24.4;
33.9; Jer. 4.28; 12.4, 11; 14.4; 23.10). Earth can obey God's commands
(Isa. 43.6; 45.8; 48.13). Earth may tremble or quake in response to
human or divine deeds (Jer. 8.16; 10.10; 49.21).

In Ezekiel there is frequent reference to Earth becoming stripped
and desolate (Ezek. 6.14; 12.19, 20; 14.15, 16; 15.8; 32.15 and more). The
use of the formula of desolation is discussed in detail by Carley in his
article. This usage, however, does not give Earth a voice in the same
way that Jeremiah and Isaiah do. Rather, Ezekiel seems to suppress
the voice of Earth and reduce Earth's community to silence. In Ezekiel
6 the prophet is told to prophesy against the mountains, who as mountains have done nothing wrong, yet the mountains have no right of
reply. They are condemned as guilty. To illustrate the force of this
injustice, Kalinda Rose Stevenson, in her article in this volume, reads
against the grain and listens to the voice of Earth as a battered woman.

Conclusion

In response to Meadowcroft's challenge, we maintain that employing the metaphor of voice is integral to the project. The metaphor of voice is more than metaphor: it opens for us a domain of reality about Earth as a subject and leads us to explore dimensions of that reality which Indigenous peoples know first-hand and some biblical writers reflect in poetic modes. The metaphor of voice is more than a rhetorical device; exploring this metaphor becomes another hermeneutical tool to enable us to move beyond the dualisms that we as a team have inherited as Western thinkers, and to begin relating to Earth as kin rather than commodity, as partner and co-creator rather than property.

Friend or Foe? Earth, Sea and *Chaoskampf* in the Psalms

Peter L. Trudinger

> They engaged in combat, they closed for battle...
> He shot an arrow which pierced her belly,
> Split her down the middle and slit her heart,
> Vanquished her and extinguished her life.
> He threw down her corpse and stood on top of her...
> The Lord trampled the lower part of Tiamat,
> With his unsparing mace smashed her skull...
> He sliced her in half like a fish for drying:
> Half of her he put up to roof the sky...
> Her waters he arranged so they could not escape...[1]

This selection from *Enuma Elish* excerpts the story of the battle between the upstart god Marduk and the mother goddess Tiamat (the primeval Ocean). Within a few decades of its discovery, the *Enuma Elish* became the central example for a proposal concerning an alternative mythic pattern of creation endemic in the ancient Near East.[2] From the myth was abstracted the *Chaoskampf* pattern, whose core consisted of the battle between the heroic deity and the forces of chaos, represented by some powerful and hostile water-being, with the victory of the god resulting in the creation of an ordered cosmos from the corpse of the vanquished enemy and the assumption of absolute rule by the god. The pattern is often seen to be confirmed in the Ugaritic Baal–Anat epic, discovered later, which also contains a description of a battle between a heroic deity and an enemy called by the twin names Sea and River, although no mention of creation is made in the surviving text.[3]

---

1. *Enuma Elish*, IV, ll. 94, 101-104, 129-30, 137-38, 140. The translation is by Stephanie Dalley (1991: 253-55). A longer description of the rearrangement of Tiamat's corpse to form the world is found in Tablet V, ll. 50-66.

2. See Gunkel 1895.

3. CAT 1.2: IV: 1-27 translation: Smith 1997: 102-104. The lack of a cosmogony in the Ugaritic material complicates the definition of 'the' *Chaoskampf* pattern. Broadly speaking, there are three possibilities: the world is constructed from the

Although the Hebrew Bible contains nothing quite like the detailed descriptions of battle which appear in the Mesopotamian and Ugaritic epics, a *Chaoskampf* pattern was nonetheless detected in the biblical writings. Like rabbits in the Australian bush, the *Chaoskampf* pattern was seen throughout the biblical writings, whenever references to a water-being and the architecture of the cosmos occurred in proximity to each other.[4]

Creation understood according to the *Chaoskampf* pattern has some unfortunate implications for Earth. In a classical *Chaoskampf* myth, as it is expressed in *Enuma Elish*, Earth, in the form it is encountered now, is dead, and, in its original mode of being, was hostile to God and inimical to harmony and order, the preconditions of life. This position clashes with all the guiding principles of the Earth Bible Project. In any formulation of *Chaoskampf*, the enemies of God are water-beings. Invariably, the major water-beings, Sea, Rivers, Leviathan, and so on, are presented as villains and suffer defeat. In other words, the *Chaoskampf* pattern precludes any intrinsic value being ascribed to a significant component of Earth community. The ramifications of such a hermeneutic hardly need be rehearsed in the Earth Bible forum. For those who would wish to associate themselves with a good God, it underwrites objectification of Earth, Sea and its large denizens, and warrants, at best, pragmatic use of their components in the name of divine order, or, at worst, an *imitatio dei* in programmes of ecological slaughter and geographical destruction. For those who are located in a tradition which privileges the biblical writings, it is a stumbling block in the path of attempts at understanding of and reconciliation with traditions that place a more positive valuation upon the Earth and Sea.

---

body of the water-being; the defeat of the water-being signals the limitation of its power and allows for the creation (or ordering) of the cosmos by some other means; or creation formed no part of the Ugaritic battle traditions (effectively a denial of the link between battle and creation). Day rejects the third option (1985: 1-18). In this essay, the term 'Chaoskampf pattern' is used rather loosely to cover any story containing the central battle–creation sequence. More detailed formulations have been proposed. As well as the discussion in Day, one should note the work of F.M. Cross, who produced an influential analysis of the mythic patterns, contrasting Hebrew and non-Hebrew forms (1973: 77-144). Arthur Walker-Jones, operating within Cross's formulation, distinguished two patterns of creation, battle and craftsman (1991). Surveys of different creation accounts may be found in Clifford 1994 and Knight 1985.

4.   Day (1985) has made a thorough study of the major biblical passages in which the battle motif is found.

In this essay the priority and pervasiveness of the *Chaoskampf* mythic pattern in the Psalms will be questioned.[5] The nexus between battle and creation will be examined closely in three psalms that might otherwise be seen to contain prime examples of the pattern in the Psalter, Psalms 74, 24 and 93 (Day 1985: 18-19). That it is possible to apply a *Chaoskampf* pattern to them cannot be denied. However, other reading strategies are also possible. The Earth Bible Project proposes an alternative hermeneutical approach that centres Earth and its components in the field of interpretation. Where a theocentric reading might start from the question 'What does this text say about God?', and an anthropocentric reading asks the same question in relation to humanity, an ecojustice hermeneutic examines first the characterization and role of Earth and its components (Earth Bible Team 2000: 38-53). It will be argued in this essay that for each of the psalms another reading strategy which centres on Earth and its components (in this case primarily water-beings, Sea, and so on) provides a more satisfactory interpretation than the *Chaoskampf* pattern in three respects:

1   in a negative sense, that there are objections to the *Chaoskampf* pattern in the context of the psalms;
2   in a positive sense, that the alternative fits the whole psalm;[6]
3   from the perspective of Earth, that the alternative allows for recognition of the intrinsic worth of Earth and its community and opens the way for them to respond to God, rather than prejudging their value and thereby silencing their voice.[7]

Psalm 74: Sea as Enemy

13 You divided the sea by your strength;
you broke the heads of the dragons of the waters.
14 You crushed the heads of Leviathan;
you gave him as food for the creatures of the wilderness.

5.   There is a large body of literature related to *Chaoskampf*. Some recent critiques have been made by Carola Kloss, who argues against Cross's pattern (1986: 42-52, 135-39); Karel van der Toorn, who rejects the theory of a cultic enactment of the creation battle (1991); and Oswald Loretz, who highlights the uncertainties inherent in the association of non-Israelite myths with Israelite psalms (1994: 281-82).

6.   Applications of *Chaoskampf* tend to concentrate on short passages. The approach adopted here attempts to provide an interpretive strategy applicable to the whole psalm and to place the *Chaoskampf* text in its literary context.

7.   That is, the strategy permits an evaluation of the text in light of the principles of intrinsic worth and voice.

15 You cut openings for spring and wadi;
you dried up ever-flowing rivers.
16 Yours is the day, yours also the night;
you established the luminaries and the sun.
17 You have fixed all the bounds of the earth;
you have made summer and winter (NRSV, *alt.*).[8]

Psalm 74 is one of the primary texts in which the *Chaoskampf* pattern of victory in battle followed by creation might be found.[9] There are similarities in expression and imagery between Ps. 74.13-14 and the battle scenes from *Enuma Elish* quoted above and also with the battle between Baal and Yamm (Sea) in the Baal–Anat epic. Ps. 74.15 is reminiscent of the creative activity of Marduk reported later in *Enuma Elish* (Tablet V, ll. 50-66). The passage undeniably juxtaposes a battle between YHWH and certain water-beings with the ordering of the creation.

Nevertheless, the parallels between the biblical account of conflict and the accounts of Marduk and Baal are flawed. In the psalm the account is brief to the point of opacity. In the other ancient Near Eastern text it is given in great detail, with motivation, weapons, strategies and gory outcome dramatically portrayed. Here is a short declaration of victory, there a difficult battle. Here there is a confusion of enemies—are there three opponents or only one with three names? There, the adversary is clear, and the fate of any retinue clarified. The shared imagery of smashed skulls cannot be pressed. A quick glance at surviving art from the ancient Near East will show quite graphically that a blow to the head of an enemy was a common representation for victory (Pritchard [ed.] 1969: nos. 295, 296, 308, 310, 360, 361). The only parallel that survives a rigorous inquest is the identity of the victim(s) as water-being(s), hardly a substantial point of contact. There are closer literary parallels to Ps. 74.13-15 in the Ugaritic material, but they take the form of lists of creatures vanquished by the gods. A good example is found in the Baal–Anat epic (CAT 1.3: III: 38-47),

---

8.   The alterations introduce consistency in translation across the three psalms excerpted here. Hebrew poetry often omits the definite article. This creates a dilemma over the translation of terms for Earth and its components, e.g., should *yām* be translated 'sea', 'Sea' or 'the sea'? Each option carries an affinity for a different characterization of the water-'being', and so expresses a different bias in interpretation. The NRSV translation is maintained here, although the definite article appears on terms for earth and water in the excerpts only twice, in Ps. 74.13 (the waters) and Ps. 24.1 (the earth).

9.   It is the first example considered by Day (1985: 21-25).

where the conquests are credited to Anat![10] Does Psalm 74 therefore preserve a tradition of YHWH as a female warrior creator? More likely, a list of defeated beings is a stereotyped form.

Given the stock nature of the list of enemies and abbreviated description of conflict, if the references to creation did not follow, then the tendency would be to read Ps. 74.13-14 as a conventional literary form attributing warrior prowess to the deity. These verses are part of a motif of conflict which supports a plea intended to call forth divine intervention against present-day enemies. They recall the paradigmatic battle of the divine warrior and so bolster other verses which ask for immediate action (Ps. 74.10, 11, 18-23).

The parallels between the creation accounts in Ps. 74 and the *Enuma Elish* are also open to question. The mood in Ps. 74.15-17 is quite different to that in *Enuma Elish*. The emphasis here is on the orderly production of the whole cosmos, with the stylistic pairing of complementary features — day–night, summer–winter, flowing–stopped — reinforcing the sense of order. The most striking difference is the lack in Psalm 74 of an explicit connection between the bodies of the enemies and the material from which the world is created.[11] Unlike the *Enuma Elish*, the passage does not describe the reorganization of any of the water-beings to form the world. Their fate appears to be far less impressive — reprocessed into food, a fate that assumes the prior existence of a created and populated world. Since it would have been relatively easy for the poet to have included a reference to the dismembered corpse in creation, the absence of a body is all the more noteworthy.

Perhaps there is irony in the juxtaposition of battle and creation in Psalm 74. The psalm most likely dates from a post-exilic period and a time when the myth of *Enuma Elish* would have been widely known. It alludes to the myth, yet lacks a key component. Does the absence of any link between the constitution of Earth and the stuff of the dead waters amount to an implicit rejection of a cosmogony of death, even an assertion of its opposite — a declaration by silence that Earth is not dead and in its genesis is not hostile to Yahweh? Such speculation

---

10.   The list starts 'Did I not smite Sea, the beloved of El?// Did I not finish off River, the great god?// I restrained Dragon and defeated him.'

11.   Ps. 74.15 is consistent with any cosmology that posits waters under the earth that can be released or stopped, regardless of the manner in which those waters came to be there. For example, it could be used as a statement about modern exploitation of artesian water resources. In some Sumerian myths, Enki, the god of underground waters, creates watercourses through non-violent sexual activity (Kramer and Maier 1989: 22-28, 47-50; Clifford 1994: 32-39).

certainly pushes the text to an extreme while remaining within the hermeneutical bounds of a *Chaoskampf* pattern.

Other hermeneutical horizons exist. How does the psalm characterize Earth? In the passage quoted, attention is focused on the divine ordering of the cosmos. This description is part of a larger motif in the psalm, one of order–disorder. The motif appears first in the description of the present disorder in land and temple (Ps. 74.3-6). So the motif pairs temple and Earth. Earth is also present in the first few lines of the psalm. In Ps. 74.2-3, the focus shifts immediately from people to homeland (*nachalah*) and then narrows to Mt Zion and temple.[12] Similarly in Ps. 74.8, interest expands from the central holy place (*mo'ed* in 74.4) to all other meeting places (*mo'ed* in 74.8) in Earth. The damage to the temple epitomizes the damage to the land and the ordering of the cosmos the ordering of the temple.[13] The abrupt and unmotivated shifts between Earth and temple suggest that the association between these two was felt to be natural. In the psalm, temple and Earth are, as it were, two personas of the same entity.

The motif of order is interlaced with the motif of conflict. Together they set up a pair of homologous relations in the psalm: between the paradigmatic ordering of the world and the need for order in the present, and between the paradigmatic victory of the divine warrior and the need for victory now. Both support the plea for action.

This close pairing of temple and Earth calls to mind another complex of traditions found in the biblical material, the so-called Zion traditions, which revolve around the city and the temple (see for instance, Levenson 1985; 1992; s.a., Terrien 1970; Alexander 1999). Among other things, these traditions hold to the central status of Zion and the temple in the cosmos. This is expressed in various ways—the mundane temple is also the heavenly palace of God; Zion is the point where heaven, land and underworld intersect; the waters under the inhabited world lie nearest the surface in the temple; the primal (and final) paradise is found there; the place stands outside of time; the temple was the starting point of creation; it is the highest point in all creation, and more. The spatial and temporal imagery portrays the temple and Zion as the centre of the web of the Earth community.

12. On the meaning of *nachalah*, translated by the NRSV as 'inheritance', but here rendered as 'homeland', see Habel 1995: 33-36.

13. While the psalm is unabashedly anthropocentric, even ethnocentric, in its aim—the people want YHWH to save them—the extent of distress is illustrated firstly and at length by a graphic description of the harm done to the land. In this there may be seen a recognition by the text that people and land are closely associated and that YHWH cares for both, c.f. the principle of interconnectedness.

Battle motifs are also part of the Zion traditions, occurring, for example, as the memory of the defence of Zion by YHWH and the confidence of future security (Psalm 48).

The complex of Zion traditions provides an alternative matrix for the thought of Psalm 74. These traditions accord with the transitions between temple and Earth that occur in the psalm. They also provide a motivation for the divine warrior to act in defence of the heavenly palace. The need for victory in the present then leads to a recollection of the mythical victories of the divine warrior over water-beings. The priority of the temple in the order of creation provides the stepping stone for the references to creation of the world. The two shifts in the two motifs to paradigmatic events result in the juxtaposition of battle and ordering of cosmos in Ps. 74.13-17. When the psalm is read in this way, the *Chaoskampf* pattern in Ps. 74.13-17 takes on a secondary status. It is derivative from the Zion traditions and generated as part of the plea for intervention. An appeal to a *Chaoskampf* pattern to explain these verses is not inescapable, although the allusion to it may be seen as a demonstration of the skill of the poet.

In the psalm, great importance is given to Earth. In the guise of the temple, it is regarded as treasured by God; as cosmos, it is a place of harmony and order. Divine concern for Earth, it is assumed, will most certainly result in intervention to control hostile forces in the present.

The water-beings do not enjoy such a happy status. They are portrayed as God's opponents, suffer horrible injury and a degrading end. They are compared with people who treat God's beloved temple–Earth as if it were only a forest for clearing. In Psalm 74, the water-beings are beyond redemption.

There are, however, remarkably few psalms in which a violent confrontation between YHWH and a water-being is so clearly stated.[14] In the majority of cases, references to water are more impersonal. These other texts do not attribute any volition or agency to water-'beings' but treat them as objects, acted upon by YHWH without confrontation.[15] In such cases it is only through an interpretive strategy, such as

14. See Pss. 74.13-15; 89.10-11. Elsewhere, opposition is implied, e.g. in Pss. 104.7; 106.9, YHWH rebukes waters and in Pss. 77.17; 114.3, 5 the water-beings flee immediately without a conflict; cf. Ps. 65.8 (verse numbers refer to the Hebrew text). In some psalms the distress of the speaker is likened to a hostile action by a water-being. In these cases the waters are attacking a human and the complaint is predicated on the assumption that YHWH can drive the source of distress away.

15. For example Pss. 33.7; 95.5; 104.6, 25; 146.6; and in the context of the Exodus: Pss. 66.6; 74.15; 77.20; 78.13, 16, 20; 105.29, 41; 106.11; 107.33, 35; 114.8; 147.18. References to water may also be used literally, in names of places, in

the *Chaoskampf* pattern or Earth Bible principles, that the water beings come alive, for evil or good. The next psalm contains an example of this.

Psalm 24: Sea as Object

1 The earth is the Lord's and all that is in it,
the world and those who live in it;
2 for he has founded it upon the seas,
and established it upon the rivers.
3 Who shall ascend the hill of the Lord?...
7 Lift up your heads, O gates!
and be lifted up, O ancient doors!
that the King of glory may come in.
8 Who is the King of glory?
The Lord, strong and mighty,
the Lord, mighty in battle... (NRSV)

When a *Chaoskampf* pattern is overlaid on this psalm, the reference to the architecture of the world in Ps. 24.2 is associated with the warrior epithets of YHWH in Ps. 24.8, 10, so that Ps. 24.2 is seen as an allusion to the outcome of a great creation battle and Ps. 24.7-10 as the triumphant return of the victor (Day 1985: 37-38). How well does this overlay fit the psalm? Several verses separate the references to the water-beings and the military prowess of YHWH. The intervening section, Ps. 24.3-6, concerns worship of YHWH, not creation or conflict. So the association of Ps. 24.2 and Ps. 24.8 is forced. Unlike Psalm 74, this psalm contains no reference to hostility on the part of the water-beings. In fact, the psalm does not attribute agency to them at all. They are not characters here, but things. Certainly the opening two verses explain YHWH's ownership of Earth on the basis of the divine creative activity, but they say nothing about the context of that activity. There is no reference to battle; a peaceful construction is quite possible. Hints of violence come later, in Ps. 24.8, 10. Here the warlike capabilities of YHWH are described quite tersely, more so than in Psalm 74. The epithets are no more than clichés. One does not have to conquer Leviathan to earn the title 'mighty', *gibbor* (cf. Judg. 11.1).

Earth is prominent in the psalm. The psalm opens with the declaration that the Earth community belongs to YHWH, its creator. A transi-

metaphors, or in stereotyped descriptions such as those indicating universal extent. Syntactically, whether the water-being is used as the subject of an active verb or not can be a marker of whether the water-being is given some degree of agency or objectified as a mere thing. Semantic considerations also play a role.

tion from Earth to Zion similar to that observed in Psalm 74 then takes
place, linking the first two sections of the psalm (Ps. 24.1-2, 3-6). The
focus moves from the world as a whole (Ps. 24.1), down to the sub-
terranean regions (Ps. 24.2) and then rises and narrows to Mt Zion (Ps.
24.3). Zion remains the setting for the rest of the psalm, as the destina-
tion of the pilgrims who seek YHWH (Ps. 24.3-6) and the implicit
location of the gates through which YHWH will pass (Ps. 24.7-10).

In Psalm 24, as in Psalm 74, the Zion traditions provide a comprehensive background for the interpretation of the psalm. It is not necessary to have recourse to a *Chaoskampf* pattern.

The call to the gates in Ps. 24.7-10 is frequently understood as an
address to the gatekeepers, rather than to the physical gates themselves. The second reading is less anthropocentric and more in the
spirit of the Earth Bible principles. It is tempting to push it further. In
the second section of the psalm, verbs implying upward movement
are used to characterize worship—the faithful ascend (*'alah*) the hill,
rise (*qum*) in the holy place, (do not) lift up (*nasa'*) their souls but lift
up (*nasa'*) a reward. In the third section, the gates are commanded to
lift up (*nasa'*) their heads. In other words, the gates are addressed in
the same style as the human pilgrims. Is this an invitation to part of
the gates to worship alongside humans as equals?

There is nothing in the psalm, however, to suggest that Sea may be
included in the worship of God.

Psalm 93: Sea Celebrates

1 The Lord is king, he is robed in majesty;
the Lord is robed, he is girded with strength
He has established the world; it shall never be moved;
2 your throne is established from of old;
you are from everlasting.
3 The rivers have lifted up, O Lord,
the rivers have lifted up their voice;
the rivers have lifted up their roaring.
4 More majestic than the thunders of many waters,
more majestic than the waves of the sea,
majestic on high is the Lord!
5 Your decrees are very sure;
holiness befits your house,
O Lord, forevermore (NRSV, *alt.*).

Once again, the movement from Earth as a whole to temple is in evidence. The second line of the psalm (Ps. 93.1c-2) starts with a reference
to the foundation of the world, and then moves to a corresponding

assertion concerning the place where God dwells, glossed here as the throne of God. In this psalm, the narrowing pattern continues one step further, moving from the throne to its occupant with the characterization of God as existent from the far past (*me^{a}olam*). The progressive narrowing of subject (world, throne, God) is matched by repeated attributions of eternal persistence albeit via synonyms (never moving, from of old, everlasting). The line builds a pyramid of permanence founded on Earth, at whose apex sits YHWH. The details of any creation event are secondary.

The following verses, Ps. 93.3-4, are amenable to interpretation as an allusion to a conflict following a *Chaoskampf* pattern (Day 1985: 35-37). The behaviour of the water-beings in Ps. 93.3 could be interpreted as depicting their challenge to YHWH prior to the battle. Ps. 93.4 would then portray the aftermath. The first verse of the psalm hails the assumption of (effective) kingship by YHWH after the battle. The defeated water-beings appear to continue to exist after the battle and even to offer a continued threat.[16] Against the application of the pattern, it ought be noted that in Psalm 93, as in Psalm 24, there is no description of the battle, only before and after shots. Also, this interpretation results in a haphazard temporal sequence through the psalm. The opening is set immediately after the battle, the second line (Ps. 93.1c-2) probably in the present of the implied speaker, Ps. 93.3 before the battle, Ps. 93.4 after it and Ps. 93.5 in the present of the speaker again.

These verses allow another interpretation. What are the water-beings doing? Their noise and actions in Ps. 93.3-4 could be understood not as hostility, but as homage. The movements of waves mimic people raising arms then falling prostrate before YHWH; the sound of the rivers and waters, cries of praise. In Ezek. 1.24 and 43.2, the 'thunder of many waters' is the audible component of the glorious appearance of God.[17] While the voices of the great water-beings may be awesome and terrifying for humans, they need not be raised in hostility to God.[18] Under this interpretation, the psalm possesses consistency in time and thought. In the opening verses, the speaking voice extols the magnificent appearance and eternal nature of YHWH. Then the

16. The sequence in Ps. 93.3 of two perfects followed by an imperfect may suggest this (Fensham 1978: 17; Tate 1990: 472). Ps. 93.4 lacks verbal forms, and is obscure anyway (Tate 1990: 473).

17. *qol mayim rabbim* (Ezek. 1.24; 43.2), *qolot mayim rabbim* (Ps. 93.4).

18. *Contra* May (1955) who argued that *mayim rabbim* in almost all its occurrences refers to enemies. The assessment that May overstated his case is a valid one (Brown 1993: 205 n. 296).

perpetual homage offered to God by the water-beings is described. Finally the eternal qualities of Torah and temple are portrayed. The psalm is a psalm of praise located in the speaker's present and weaving its acclamations together with a motif of permanence.

The psalm contains no mention that humans are present to witness this glorious theophany (apart from the implied speaker, of course). The vision is reserved for the water-beings. At last, in this third example, Sea may be freed from the bonds of chaos and may worship YHWH.

The offering of homage to YHWH by water-beings is not a concept foreign to the Psalter (Pss. 69.35; 96.11; 98.7, 8; 148.4, 7). It is an action which suggests that the water-beings are loyal servants of YHWH. There are a few other places in the Psalter where it is hinted that the waters might be more than just enemies or object; that they might be faithful servants of YHWH (Pss. 18.12; 46.5; 65.9, 10; 104.3, 26, cf. 42.8). William Brown has argued that there was a tradition that the waters played an active part in creation, assisting God (1993, esp. 249-51). This tradition is preserved in the LXX version of Genesis 1, but was edited out from the (later, mid-second-century BCE) Masoretic Text. Such an editorial process might explain the preponderance of impersonal references to water as objects in the Psalter. In any case, a sympathetic portrayal of the water-beings points to a cosmogony in direct opposition to the basic orientation of a *Chaoskampf* pattern.

Conclusion

Psalms 74, 24 and 93 are often held to contain instances of a *Chaoskampf* pattern of battle and creation. Examination of each of the psalms, however, has shown that there are inadequacies associated with this regime of interpretation. For each psalm, an alternative interpretation was proposed, one developed by starting with a consideration of Earth and its components (primarily water-beings such as Sea). In this alternative reading strategy, the Zion traditions took on importance. For two of the psalms (Psalms 74 and 24), the complex of Zion traditions provided a matrix in which to place the motifs and internal logic of the psalm. In all three there was a pattern of movement from Earth to temple which was consistent with the central role of temple in the Zion traditions as the primal kernel of the Earth community, interconnected with all other points.

It would be misleading to say that the Zion traditions replace the *Chaoskampf* pattern in the interpretation of the psalms. These two sets of traditions have much in common. The difference between them is more a matter of ordering and priority. The Zion traditions provide an alternative configuration for many of the elements found in the *Chaoskampf* pattern, one that gives a central role to a *place*, not a battle. It is a configuration more in harmony with a reading strategy that privileges the perspective of Earth. This is not to deny the existence or importance of battle imagery in the biblical material—the divine warrior motifs are too obvious for that. Rather, the presumed nexus between creation and battle is problematized.[19] Is its presence assumed too often?

The reconfiguration of traditions has benefits for Earth. In the classical *Chaoskampf* pattern, Earth is the corpse of a dead enemy of God. It can have no voice, no status, no friends. In the Zion traditions, no stigma attaches to Earth. It is free to be assessed as good and to worship YHWH, precisely the situation seen in Psalms 74 and 24 once the prejudice of a *Chaoskampf* pattern is broken. Such conclusions are steps towards the recognition of the intrinsic worth of Earth and of its voice.[20]

The pairing of Earth and temple that was observed in these three psalms deserves further consideration. To what extent does it occur in other texts (cf. Ps. 48.1-2, Hag. 1.9-10)? Can it be extended to include Mt Zion or the city itself? How does the symbolism function? In the psalms considered here, the movement has mostly been from Earth to temple. Can it be reversed? If so, possibilities for other Earth-centred readings are opened up. The pairing of temple and Earth, if it can be applied more widely as a methodological principle, can afford a way of seeing and hearing Earth in biblical texts that speak of the temple or city of Jerusalem as agents.[21]

---

19. The objection might be raised that *Chaoskampf* has been misrepresented here as a pattern, when it, like the Zion traditions, really is a complex of mythical elements which occur with varying frequencies in conjunction with each other. The objection, however, cedes the point that battle and creation need not be connected and so opens the door for Earth-oriented and Sea-oriented readings.

20. While an Earth-centred reading strategy assists the derivation of such positive conclusions, it does not force them. In Psalm 93, Earth is handled more like an object, albeit a durable one, and little is implied about its intrinsic value. The very different characterizations of Sea in the three psalms provide a more marked demonstration of the same point. Just as one text read anthropocentrically may highlight the rebellious nature of humanity (Exodus) while another text might show its faithfulness (Ruth), so too Earth-centred readings of different texts may find diverse and apparently contradictory characterizations of Earth or its components.

21. Thus one might read a story of the exile and restoration of Earth in Lam. 1 and Isa. 40–55.

Perhaps the greatest beneficiary of a move away from *Chaoskampf* is Sea, along with the other water-beings. The Psalter presents a multi-faceted picture of Sea—sometimes in conflict with God, sometimes a mere object, sometimes a loyal subject. Under *Chaoskampf*, Sea is voiceless, always the villain, fit only for death. In the absence of *Chaoskampf*, Sea, like Earth, gains an independent voice and freedom to respond to God. Sea is allowed to be a faithful worshipper of YHWH and more, to work alongside YHWH at and in creation, supporting Earth and all those who dwell in it.

> R. Aibu told a parable of a king to whom, at the very beginning of his reign, a certain legion sang a song of praise. So the king gave the legion an honor which was never to be taken away from it. Just so, when the Holy One, blessed be He, began to reign over His world, the waters were the first to sing a song of praise to Him, as is said *Above the voices of many waters* (Ps. 93.4). Thereupon, the Holy One, blessed be He, said to the waters: As ye live, I shall bestow an honor upon you, as is said *O Lord... Thou didst establish the earth upon its foundations [of water] — an honor that shall not be removed for ever* (Ps. 104.5). Hence *Yea, the world is established — it cannot be removed.*[22]

---

22. Midrash Tehillim, Psalm 93, §2; translation: Braude 1959: 125.

Rescuing Earth from a Storm God: Psalms 29 and 96–97

Norman C. Habel and Geraldine Avent

Introduction

Biblical theophanies have long been acclaimed as bold representations of God's revelation through creation or the forces of nature. Fretheim goes so far as to say that 'it is in the theophany that God's connection with the world is most clearly observed' (1984: 80). According to Hiebert, the God of Israel, who is unlimited by the natural world, is revealed by self-limitation through places, forms and powers of the natural environment (1992: 505). God is said to use everything from a small spring to a massive mountain, from a human form to a thunderstorm, to mask—yet reveal—the divine self.

One of the most frequent modes of divine self-expression, especially in archaic texts, is the thunderstorm. Wind, thunder, lightning and rain attend God's presence in the storm. Like the storm god, Baal, YHWH can even be acclaimed 'rider of the clouds' (Ps. 68.4). One of YHWH's modes of manifestation on Mt Sinai was a storm consisting of thunder, lightning and thick cloud (Exod. 19.16). According to Hiebert, the thunderstorm 'represented absolute power that could be both malevolent and beneficent' (1992: 509).

In most interpretations of these theophanies, it is assumed that God, as the lord over these storm phenomena, has a right to use them at will for whatever purposes are at hand. Little attention has been paid to the phenomena themselves as valued components of the cosmos or the effects of these phenomena on Earth or the Earth community. How does YHWH use the storm phenomena? Does Earth rejoice or suffer when YHWH exhibits meteorological prowess? Or, in terms of ecojustice principles, how does Earth fare if we read theophanies from the perspective of Earth?

In this study, we shall first read Psalm 29 in terms of the ecojustice principles of the Earth Bible Project and pose the following questions: Does the manifestation of YHWH in the storm affirm or negate Earth in this psalm? Does Earth suffer at the expense of YHWH's glorious self-revelation as the *qôl YHWH*? Subsequently we shall compare this psalm with Psalms 96–97 and explore how these hymns subvert the storm-god tradition of Psalm 29.

Earlier Readings

Since the work of Frank Cross (1950), many interpreters believe that Psalm 29 may be of pre-Israelite origin, echoing an ancient Canaanite hymn to the storm god Baal-Hadad (e.g., Holladay 1993: 20). Keel cites the following text as grounds for this claim of dependency on Baal mythology:

> Baal let his holy voice resound,
> Baal repeated the utterance of his lips [in the echo of the thunder]
> His voice rang out, and the earth trembled:
> The hills of the earth leapt
> The enemies of Baal crept into the woods (1978: 212).

Regardless of the precise connection with Canaanite prototypes, Psalm 29, as it now stands, is an expression of YHWH's manifestation in a storm theophany. It is no longer the voice of Baal, but the voice of YHWH, whose thunderous cries of self-expression in creation demand our attention (Habel 1964: 86).

Most readings of this psalm have, in our opinion, made a number of questionable assumptions about the function of YHWH's revelation in the storm. The first group assumes that this psalm is a hymn of victory similar to the Song of the Sea (Exod. 15.1-18). The language of the storm is thought to express YHWH's prowess in battle leading to YHWH's enthronement as a victorious monarch. The demonstration of YHWH's glory and might are viewed as military in nature (Craigie 1972: 145). Cross goes so far as to say that this text reflects the genre of the divine warrior returning from battle to his newly won mountain (1973: 156).

A close reading of the psalm, however, reveals that there is no specific enemy, either historical or mythic, no battle, no acclamation of YHWH as warrior (as in Exod. 15.3), and no mountain as the spoil of victory (as in Exod. 15.17). A display of power and a recognition of kingship do not necessarily imply victory in combat. In this psalm, the focus lies on the demonstration of the deity's overwhelming power in the storm. YHWH is hailed as the storm god, the storm king par excellence.

The second questionable assumption is that this psalm is a demonstration of YHWH's advent as lord over creation (Gillingham 1994: 209). Ps. 29.11, referring to YHWH's enthronement upon the flood, is cited as evidence that the psalmist is referring to the submission of the cosmic waters to YHWH and the acclamation of YHWH as king over creation (Day 1985: 58).

Once again, we would suggest that the flood is here the locus of YHWH's throne, not a cosmic foe. In Canaanite texts, El, as king and father of the gods, dwells in the midst of the watery deeps, not because he has conquered them, but because they are his domain (Pope 1955: 61). Nor is YHWH depicted as a creator. YHWH neither effects nor sustains any part of creation in this psalm. Nowhere does YHWH bring fertility, blessing or life to Earth. Psalm 29 exalts YHWH as an overwhelming storm god, not as creator or provider.

Rather than read the text focusing on themes extrinsic to the text— creation, conquest, fertility—we will concentrate our analysis on the central motif of YHWH as storm god and the impact of God, as storm, on the rest of nature.

A Storm God Spectacular

The structure of this hymn to YHWH, the storm god, is relatively simple:

> vv. 1-2: call to praise the storm god, YHWH
> vv. 3-9a: portrayal of the storm/storm god in action
> vv. 9b-10: acclamation of YHWH's kingship
> v. 11: plea for the people

The opening verses are striking because they call upon the *bene 'elim* (sons of El/God) to hail YHWH's manifestation in the storm. Neither Earth, nor the wider Earth community, including Israel, is called upon to acclaim YHWH's glorious appearance. The applause for YHWH's storm theophany comes only from above, from celestial beings called the sons of God. Regardless of the precise reading of this term (*bene 'elim*), the accolades that YHWH receives are from a heavenly entourage, presumably the council of divine beings. The perspective of the viewer is ostensibly from above—with the cheering celestial onlookers.

The language used to anticipate this appearance highlights the overwhelming splendour of the event. This appearance is hailed as a storm god spectacular, a magnificent solo performance. This perform-ance is not a sky show, however, but an Earth show, a demonstration of the forceful power of the storm god on Earth below, a panoramic display that the celestial cheer squad can observe by looking down from the heavens above.

A key term in this call to hail YHWH as the storm god is *kabod* (glory). Elsewhere in the Hebrew Bible, the *kabod* often refers to the visible manifestation of YHWH's presence. In the priestly writings, the glory assumes the visible form of a mobile cloud filled with fire (Exod. 25.24-17; 40.34-38; cf. Lev. 9.23; 1 Kgs 8.10). Ezekiel *sees* the glory in all its mystery and majesty (Ezek. 1.28; 3.23; 10.4). The English rendering 'glory' is often taken to mean great honour or majesty, thereby losing some of the visual force of the original. The verbs and imagery associated with *kabod* emphasize not only the majestic but also the visible dimension—the glory is a mysterious visible manifestation of YHWH, something awesome and other, but something seen.

It is not surprising that when the grand display of this storm god's power has taken place, the response of the celestial onlookers is encapsulated in one universal chorus: 'in his temple all cry "glory!"'. In the storm, YHWH's self-manifestation is made visible for all the heavenly watchers to behold. There is no reason to believe that the divine beings called to praise God in the opening verses are different from those worshippers who respond in Ps. 29.9b. The temple in this verse therefore is not the temple of Jerusalem, but the heavens themselves, the celestial abode of YHWH, as in Ps. 11.4 (cf. Isa. 66.1). These are presumably the heavens/skies YHWH stretches out like a sacred tent (Ps. 104.2) beneath which the storm god appears (Habel 1972). Translated into contemporary idiom, the celestial viewers cry 'great show, YHWH'.

The climax of this spectacular storm show is the acclamation that YHWH is 'enthroned over the flood' (Ps. 29.10). The term for flood (*mabbul*) occurs only here and in the flood story of Genesis. There is no evidence in the context to suggest that the psalm is referring to this particular ancient tradition. Some scholars argue that the flood refers to the conquered enemy of YHWH (Kloos 1981: 641), perhaps the figure of Yam (Sea) in Canaanite mythology. YHWH, it is argued, is acclaimed as king because of victory over the waters of chaos in much the same way that the storm gods Baal and Marduk are acclaimed as kings after their victories.

We would argue, however, that the focus of Psalm 29 is on the storm as the demonstration of YHWH's power and rule rather than the conquest of foes—whether mythic or cosmic. As mentioned previously, no specific enemy or battle is described in the advent of YHWH as storm god. Moreover, the acclamation of YHWH as king is found in many psalms where the focus is not on victory or conquest (Pss. 97.1-5; 99.1-4). One obvious progression of thought in Psalm 29 is that a flood of waters results from the advent of the storm god on Earth. Over the raging storm waters, YHWH, the storm king, reigns and the heavenly entourage celebrates.

The Force of the Storm

One of the remarkable features of this storm theophany is the close identification of the deity with the storm. Here the clouds are not YHWH's chariots, nor are the winds YHWH's messengers (Ps. 104.3-4). Here YHWH does not use the thunder as a vehicle to communicate (Exod. 19.19) or the flashes of lightning as weapons of war (Ps. 18.14). Here the storm is YHWH's self-manifestation. This psalm is not the portrait of a spectacular storm sent by God; it is the portrayal of a spectacular storm god in action.

The expression *qol YHWH* is usually rendered 'the voice of YHWH', and associated with thunder as a dominant dimension of the storm (Kraus 1988: 348). In this psalm, however, the expression *qol YHWH* does not refer to a loud noise, but to the storm itself. The *qol YHWH* breaks and shatters, twists and batters; the *qol YHWH* is the storm in action. Nowhere does the parallelism of the poem point to the *qol* as thunder or a comparable component of the storm cloud noise. The *qol YHWH* is parallel with YHWH or with 'the God of glory' (Ps. 29.3), the visible manifestation of the deity. The *qol YHWH* is a poetic designation of the storm theophany, not the thunder as but one component of the storm.

How is this storm/storm deity depicted? What is the result of this storm god's show on Earth below? First, following the cue of the call to praise in the opening verses, the storm is described as powerful and spectacular in appearance (Ps. 29.4). And, as we might expect, the storm god thunders onto the scene (Ps. 29.4). The thundering commences over the waters, perhaps the waters of the West—the Mediterranean. These waters become 'many waters', an expression that suggests turbulent seas or the rising waters of raging rivers.

When the storm moves from the waters to the land, the full force of the storm becomes apparent. It shatters the cedars of Lebanon (Ps. 29.5). The advent of the storm does not provide rain or sustenance for the cedars. Rather, the mightiest trees of the forest are broken into pieces, as the intensive form of the verb *shbr* (to break) implies. The storm flattens the forests in its path. The mountains of Lebanon and Sirion are so convulsed by the storm that they seem like a young wild ox leaping into the air (Ps. 29.6). As the storm progresses, flames of fire flash forth to continue the devastation—perhaps a reference to forest fires that sometimes accompany storms.

The storm moves from the forest to the wilderness or desert. Instead of the image of shattering, we meet a threefold use of the verb 'to writhe' (*chwl/chyl*). The storm causes the deserts and their inhabitants

to writhe in agony under the onslaught of the wind (Ps. 29.8-9a), until
the vegetation is stripped bare (*chsp*) as the locusts strip olive trees
bare (Joel 1.7). There is no rain for the parched desert. Instead, the
aftermath of the storm is a path of devastation, evidence of the passage of something like a tornado. In the wake of this destructive storm
deity, the Earth community suffers while the choir of heaven cries
kabod — great show!

A Plea for Peace

There are two dominant voices up to this point in the poem — the
voice of the celestial choir and the *qol YHWH*, the voice which is the
storm god in action. Beneath the sevenfold barrage of the *qol YHWH*,
the voices of Earth and the Earth community are effectively silenced.
They neither praise God in chorus with the choir above nor cry out in
anguish at their cruel treatment by the storm god. They are rendered
insignificant in the face of God's thunderous self-manifestation.

The final verse of the psalm, however, may suggest another voice
calling in the aftermath of the storm. The text reads:

> May YHWH give strength to his people;
> May YHWH bless his people with peace (translation mine).

In the wake of the storm the psalmist does not respond in praise to the
resultant scene of devastation and royal power. Rather, the cry of the
psalmist seems to be a not-so-subtle reminder to YHWH not to forget
God's people. A demonstration of devastating storm power on Earth
is nothing but egotistical theocentrism if there is no ensuing blessing
for the people of Earth.

It is precisely the use of the term for strength (*'oz*) by the celestial
chorus in the opening verse that the psalmist reinterprets in the
closing verse. The psalmist pleads for a show of strength that results
in blessing not bluster, peace on Earth, not parading of power. This
pleading is tantamount to a call for YHWH to surrender the role of
storm god and become a god of peace for the people. The psalmist
does not plead directly for Earth, but in pleading for blessing and
peace (*shalom*) implies an interconnected world in which God, creation
and humanity work in harmony.

Even if this verse is rendered as a statement rather than a petition, it
stands in tension with the preceding verses — an ironic postscript. To
declare that YHWH will bless people with peace seems to be belied by
the violent nature of YHWH's self-manifestation in the storm. The
theophany as such includes no signs that YHWH comes to bless with

peace, but rather depicts YHWH as overwhelming with meteorological power.

Rescuing Earth

If the closing voice in Psalm 29 is that of a single psalmist pleading for the people in the face of a storm god on the rampage, the voices in Psalms 96–97 are those of the entire Earth community responding in praise to the manifestation of YHWH's presence. These psalms, we would argue, rescue Earth from the overpowering storm god of the earlier psalm.

On a literary level, the dependency of the second text on the first (Brueggemann 1984: 144) is immediately evident from the following comparison.

Psalm 29	*Psalm 96.7–97.6*
1a Attribute to YHWH, sons of gods	96.7a Attribute to YHWH, families of the peoples,
1b attribute to YHWH glory and strength.	96.7b attribute to YHWH, glory and strength.
2a Attribute to YHWH the glory of his name.	96.8 Attribute to YHWH, the glory of his name.
2b Worship YHWH in holy array.	96.9a Worship YHWH in holy array.
8a The voice of YHWH makes the wilderness writhe (*chul/chyl*).	96.9b Tremble (*chul/chyl*) before him all the earth.
9a The voice of YHWH makes the oaks writhe (*chul/chyl*)	97.4 The earth sees and trembles (*chul/chyl*).
9b and strips the forests bare.	96.12 All the trees of the forest sing for joy.
9c In his temple all cry 'Glory!'	97.6 The skies declare his righteousness, and all the peoples see glory.
10 YHWH sits enthroned over the flood.	96.10 Say among the nations, 'YHWH is king! YHWH sits enthroned as king forever. The world is established. It will never be moved.'
	97.1 YHWH is King! Let the earth rejoice!

The incorporation of key terms, images and idioms from Psalm 29 into the hymn encompassing Psalms 96 and 97 represents more than the appropriation of common liturgical expressions or storm motifs. The orientation of the second hymn, we contend, subverts the orientation of the first. The second hymn rescues the silenced Earth from the dominating storm god of the first.

The deliverance of Earth from the storm god of Psalm 29 is apparent when the following transformations of the tradition in Psalms 96–97 are considered:

The storm god of Psalm 29 becomes the creator of the skies/heavens to be revered above all other gods (Ps. 96.4-5). These skies are specifically God's sanctuary where celestial manifestations appear to bring rejoicing rather than terror.

The glory (*kabod*) of YHWH revealed as visible in the storm of Psalm 29 is beheld by all people as a theophany that reveals YHWH's advent in righteousness and justice (Ps. 97.2-6). A violent thunderstorm becomes a manifestation of righteousness—a life-restoring presence.

The cry of 'glory' from the celestial onlookers at the great storm show is transformed into a unified proclamation of praise by those on Earth and in heaven (Ps. 97.6). Glory is now seen in life-giving righteousness, not in destructive thunderclouds.

Earth is battered by the advent of the storm god in Psalm 29; Earth responds with awe before the advent of YHWH in the second hymn (Ps. 96.9; 97.4-5). In Psalm 29 Earth is reduced to a battered object; in the second hymn Earth becomes a subject, a 'thou' who rejoices and celebrates.

The verb *chul/chyl*, in context, seems to imply a response of writhing anguish when the storm god strikes in Psalm 29, but a response of trembling wonder when YHWH appears bringing justice (Ps. 96.9; 97.5). By using the same terms as the psalmist in Psalm 29, but in a different context, the second psalmist cleverly shifts the focus to praise rather than anguish.

Earth and the Earth community are totally silenced in Psalm 29, while in Psalms 96–97 Earth is summoned to 'sing to YHWH' (Ps. 96.1), 'worship YHWH' (Ps. 96.9), and 'rejoice' (Ps. 9.11; 97.1). Before the thundering storm king the voice of Earth is suppressed; before the king of righteousness the voice of Earth is liberated.

The restoration of Earth's voice in Psalm 97 is especially powerful. The skies, the land and the seas all exult in celebration (Ps. 97.11). All life in the seas responds with a rapturous roar (Ps. 97.11). The fields and forests stripped bare and left desolate before the storm god (Ps. 29.5-9) now sing for joy in celebration before YHWH's advent. Instead of a storm deity demonstrating his might with unwelcome force, the god of Psalms 96–97 is welcomed as a god of righteousness by all the Earth community—the peoples, the inhabited world (*tebel*) and Earth itself (Ps. 96.13).

Conclusion

A comparison of these psalms would tend to support the claim that within ancient Israel, there was a diverse worshipping community that not only embraced the voices of the Earth community in its celebration, but also dared to transform those worship traditions which silenced and hence devalued Earth. An even more radical feature of this transformation is the subversion of a theocentrism that exalts the power of God at the expense of the Earth community. The hymnic celebration of Psalms 96–97, by subverting this ancient storm-god tradition, challenges the validity of a theophany that is a destructive display of divine might. A theophany incorporating the forces of nature that does not bring blessings to Earth and evoke songs of joy from the Earth community is not worthy of the name.

In terms of the ecojustice principles reflected in our approach, Psalm 29 devalues Earth by treating it as a domain for divine power plays, while Psalms 96–97 acclaim the participation of—and consequent valuing of—the entire Earth community in a rich response to YHWH's advent. It is especially obvious that the first psalm negates and silences the voice of Earth while the second makes the voices of Earth and the wider Earth community central to the focus of its call to celebrate. The principle of interconnectedness may not be articulated in terms of contemporary ecology, yet it is clear that the worshipping parties in Psalms 96–97 form a community united in celebration, a community that includes everything from the fish of the sea and the trees of the forest to the skies above and all peoples below.

Jubilate Deo omnis terra: God and Earth in Psalm 65*

Howard N. Wallace

Introduction

In Psalm 65 the psalmist would have us listen as the pastures and valleys joyously raise their shouts and songs of praise to God. Earth has a voice with which to respond to the gracious acts and gifts of God. In so doing, it takes its place alongside human worshippers in the temple and throughout the whole world, in giving praise.

But there are many ways in which Earth's song of praise is stifled. It happens in our present world through deforestation and the subsequent increase in salination of the land. It happens when the International Whaling Commission rejects a proposal for a sanctuary in the South Pacific, as it did in July 2000. In the Western world in recent centuries we have helped silence Earth's song as we have viewed the human relationship with Earth in subject–object terms. The relationship has been dominated by attitudes of consumerism and exploitation of resources. We have even perceived God's relationship with Earth in service of our human self-image.

Biblical interpreters have also stifled accounts of the joyous song of Earth. They have often placed stress on history as the sphere of God's revelation and activity.[1] This is understandable given the Hebrew Bible's own emphasis on this. But in the process, questions of YHWH and Earth have not been addressed sufficiently. Discussions on the fertility of Earth have often focused on the worship of Baal and the problem of syncretism and apostasy (e.g. in relation to 1 Kgs 17–19; Hos. 2).

The interpretation of Psalm 65 has not been spared in this situation. The last section of the psalm (Ps. 65.9-13),[2] and in particular the final

---

* The quotation in the title of this paper, *Jubilate Deo omnis terra*, is taken from the Vulgate: Ps. 66.1. The sentiment is nevertheless apt for Psalm 65.

1. See e.g. Kraus 1986: 62 or some earlier works on Hebrew Bible theology, such as G.E. Wright 1952 or von Rad 1965.

2. Verse numbers for Psalm 65 and other passages will follow the custom set out in NRSV and other translations.

image of the pastures and valleys joyously praising God (Ps. 65.12-13), has often been treated briefly in the interest of other issues such as the unity or context of the psalm, or the place of humans in the psalm.[3] Thus the matter of the relation of God to Earth and its fertility has not been treated fully. Earth's voice has been silenced even when the biblical writers would have it shout loudest.

In Ps. 65.12-13, the psalmist speaks of Earth having a voice with which to praise God. My aim is to see how this section of the psalm fits within the whole, to ask what the psalm yields in terms of understanding Earth's praise of God, and what contribution this might have for present faith and theology. I will begin with a translation and analysis of the psalm before moving to the broader discussion of God and Earth in the psalm. Some attention to the unity of the psalm in particular is important in this regard.

Translation of Psalm 65

To the director. A psalm of David. A Song.
1 To you silence[4] is praise, O God in Zion;
and to you vows are fulfilled, [2] O hearer of prayer.
All flesh will come to you.
3 When sinful deeds are too great for us;
our transgressions you pardon.
4 Blessed is the one whom you choose and bring near.
He will inhabit your courts.
May we be sated on the goodness of your house,
on the holiness of your temple.
5 With awesome deeds in righteousness you answer us,
O God of our salvation;
O confidence of all the ends of the earth
and the distant seas.[5]

---

3. See e.g. Delitzsch 1871: II, 229-30; Weiser 1962: 466; A.A. Anderson 1972: 471-72; Kraus 1989: 26-31; and Tate 1990: 143.

4. The Hebrew text reads *dumiyyah*, 'silence'. The sense of this has often puzzled interpreters. Some have understood it in terms of resignation or a silent acceptance of God's rule (e.g. Cheyne 1888: 176; Delitzsch 1871: II, 226; Tate 1990: 137) or as closeness to God (Levine 1995: 222). The LXX and Syriac have read the consonants *dmyh* as coming from another root *dmh*, 'to be like', translating it in the sense 'to be right, fitting'. This reading is reflected in the NRSV, REB, NJB and JPSV translations. However, MacLaren (1895: II, 248) notes that the LXX emendation requires imposing 'a somewhat unusual meaning on the word gained'. I will retain the Hebrew reading.

5. The word *yam*, 'sea', is in the singular followed by a plural adjective. Rather than change it to read 'peoples' with the Syriac or 'islands' following Kraus

6 Who establishes the mountains in his strength,
who is girded with might,
7 who stills the roaring of the seas,
the roaring of their waves,
and the turmoil of the peoples.
8 The inhabitants of the ends (of the earth)
are in awe of your signs;
You make the east and west[6] sing for joy.

9 You visit the earth and give it abundance,
You enrich it greatly;[7]
The stream of God is full of water;
You provide their grain, for thus you prepare it.
10 You saturate its furrows, you press down its ridges,[8]
you soften it with showers, you bless its growth.
11 You crown the year of your goodness,
and your tracks drip fatness.
12 The pastures of the wilderness shout[9] for joy,
the hills gird themselves with rejoicing.
13 The pastures are clothed with flocks,
and the valleys cover themselves with grain,
they shout for joy, indeed they sing.

Unity and Structure of Psalm 65

The psalm divides into four sections:

vv. 1-2: Introduction
vv. 3-4: God and the temple in Zion;
vv. 5-8: God and the cosmos;
vv. 9-13: God and Earth.

(1989: 27), I suggest seeing *yam* as a scribal error (haplography) for the plural *yammim* 'seas'.

6. Reading *motsa'e* as the 'places of the morning and evening', i.e. the east and the west where the sun rises and sets, rather than what comes forth in the morning and the evening. The resulting phrase is a merism indicating the whole world, in parallel with 'the inhabitants of the ends (of the earth)'.

7. The adjective *rabbat* is used adverbially, 'greatly' (cf. Pss. 120.6; 123.4; 129.1-2 and possibly Ezek. 24.12).

8. Reading *rawweh*, 'saturate', and *nachet*, 'press down', as infinite absolutes rather than as imperatives and translating as continuous present tense parallel with the next line.

9. The Hebrew reads *yira'pu*, 'they drip', with the same verb as in Ps. 65.11. This verb needs an object which some presume to be 'fat' from the previous line (cf. Tate 1990: 138). I read *rua'*, 'to shout for joy', with others (e.g. Kraus 1989: 27) instead of *r'p*, presuming the latter to be the result of dittography. Reading *rua'* in Ps. 65.12a makes this line parallel with the following line.

Some commentators have questioned the place of Ps. 65.9-13 in the whole psalm.[10] In its present form, the integrity of the whole cannot be doubted. The psalm opens with a declaration of the universal praise of the 'God, in Zion' who is the one 'who answers prayer' (Ps. 65.1-2). This praise consists of 'silence' and the fulfilment of vows (Ps. 65.1-2a).[11] The outcome is that 'all flesh' will come to God (Ps. 65.2b). Each line in the Hebrew begins with the words 'to you', clearly emphasizing that this praise is offered rightly to God.

The introduction to the psalm presents two difficulties. First, how is silence praise? The word *dumiyyah*, 'silence', and its related word group, is often used in prayers. Baumann (1978: 264) considers that in the context of prayer,

> [if] silence is the basic meaning of the words, it is silence caused by the powerful impress of an impending or actual calamity or by the expectation of coming salvation, and that is what gives it its specific nuance.

He further notes that *dumiyyah* can imply 'quiet expectation' (Pss. 39.2; 62.1) and the idea of silent waiting connected with salvation (Lam. 3.26; cf. 3.49). In my view, Ps. 22.2 provides the closest parallel for the sense of *dumiyyah*, 'silence', in Ps. 65.1. The NRSV translates *dumiyyah* in Ps. 22.2 as 'rest', but the sense is clearly not just rest from troubles. It refers to the peace given by God's answer to prayer. This reference also occurs in the context of praise (Ps. 22.3). Thus, we can understand 'silence' in Ps. 65.1 not in a passive sense of resignation but in a sense of confident expectation.

The second matter concerns the phrase 'all flesh' in Ps. 65.2b. Ps. 65.3-4 focuses on human worship in the temple and could imply that 'all flesh' is to be read in that context only. However, the strong interconnections between the different sections of the psalm, which I will indicate, suggest that the phrase includes not only the chosen (Ps. 65.4) but also 'the inhabitants of the ends [of the earth]' (Ps. 65.8) and the flocks that cover the pastures (Ps. 65.13).[12] Moreover, given the fact that Earth itself has a voice with which to sing praise to God (Ps. 65.12-13), 'all flesh' would seem to envelop the entire Earth community, both people and nations as well as Earth itself. In this regard we

10. E.g. Kraus (1989: 27-28) and Briggs (1907: II, 80-85).

11. In light of the latter part of the psalm, the vows have been seen in relation to a time of sowing and/or a time of drought (e.g. A.A. Anderson 1972: 464). On the other hand, the reference to vows being fulfilled could make the more general point that God answers prayer.

12. The phrase 'all flesh' can be used to refer to all living creatures, human and animal, e.g. Gen. 9.11, 15-17; Lev. 17.14; Num. 18.15; Ps. 136.25.

note that' *'erets*, 'earth', occurs only twice in the psalm, referring once to the whole world including peoples (Ps. 65.5; contra Kraus 1989: 30), and once to Earth blessed with abundant fertility by God (Ps. 65.10).

The second section (Ps. 65.3-4) focuses on the temple in Zion. It emphasizes the gracious movement of God towards the people in terms of forgiving the sins that overwhelm them and in bringing God's chosen near to the temple. Some scholars have suggested that the language of Ps. 65.4 refers to priests only,[13] but Ps. 65.2b and the last two sections of the psalm indicate that in the whole psalm a far wider group of worshippers is envisaged. It is unlikely that Ps. 65.4 would speak only of priests (see also A.A. Anderson 1972: 467-68; Tate 1990: 141-42). The section ends with a desire by the psalmist to be 'sated on the goodness of [God's] house, on the holiness of [God's] temple' (Ps. 65.4). In the immediate context, the parallel between 'goodness' and 'holiness' suggests that 'goodness' is a quality of the temple. On the other hand, the lack of specificity invites a connection with the reference to 'goodness' later in the psalm (Ps. 65.11). Moreover, the root *śb'*, 'to be sated', refers to satisfaction, or even a sense of 'excess', in many ways (BDB, 959). Both words, therefore, suggest a connection between worship in the temple and the abundant fertility described later in this psalm.

The third section (Ps. 65.5-8) focuses on God as saviour and 'confidence of all the ends of the earth'. Ps. 65.5 and 65.8 provide an *inclusio* for the section with verbal and thematic connections.[14] However, while there are parallels between these verses, there is also movement. Ps. 65.5 focuses on God as the salvation and confidence of the people, while Ps. 65.8 speaks of the response of the inhabitants of Earth.[15] Ps. 65.5 and 65.8 also connect this third section to the other sections of the psalm. The statement 'you answer us' in Ps. 65.5 recalls the description

13. E.g. von Rad (1965: I, 405 n. 49). The verbs 'choose' and 'bring near' occur together in passages dealing with priests (e.g. Num. 16.5).

14. Ps. 65.5 and 65.8 both refer to 'the ends (of the earth)' and contain the Hebrew root *yr'*, 'to fear', in the words 'awesome deeds' and 'are in awe' respectively.

15. Mowinckel (1962: I, 162) sees the inhabitants of the earth (Ps. 65.8) as 'demonic powers of the *tĕhôm* around the earth'. He presumes Ps. 65.7c to be a later addition. However, this need not be the case. The statement in Ps. 65.5b, which sees God as the 'confidence of all the ends of the earth', surely presumes a positive relationship between God and the peoples. Given the *inclusio* involving Ps. 65.5, 8, it seems more likely that the individuals referred to in those verses are not demonic in either dimension of the term, that is, opposed to God or non-human.

of God as 'hearer of prayer' in Ps. 65.2 and the stilling of the seas and
the turmoil of the peoples recalls the 'silence' of Ps. 65.1. On the other
hand, the mention of the east and west singing for joy in Ps. 65.8
points forward to the joy and song at the end of the psalm.

It is not immediately clear what is referred to by the terms 'awesome deeds' and 'salvation' (Ps. 65.5), and 'signs' (Ps. 65.8). It could be
argued that they indicate events in the history of Israel, as the terms
are used elsewhere to describe events associated with the exodus.[16]
However, within Psalm 65 the terms most probably refer to other than
historical events. By virtue of the structure of this section of the psalm,
they are closely associated with the matters described in mythic language in Ps. 65.6-7, namely establishing the mountains and stilling the
seas. God sets the foundations of the cosmos and brings order to it.[17]
These matters thus constitute the 'awesome deeds' and 'signs'. But
further definition is possible. I mentioned above that Ps. 65.5 and 65.8
not only provide an *inclusio* for this section of the psalm, but link it to
other sections. With these connections in mind, the 'awesome deeds',
'salvation', and 'signs' can also be understood in terms of God's answering prayer and 'visiting' Earth to bestow abundance upon Earth.

While the content and a change in Hebrew verb forms[18] distinguish
the final section of the psalm (Ps. 65.9-13), it has several connections
with the earlier sections. In Ps. 65.9-13, the psalmist returns to the
sphere of Earth with an account of God's granting an abundant harvest. The psalmist praises God in Ps. 65.9-11 by describing God's
blessing of abundant fertility. This echoes the desire to be sated in Ps.
65.4. The word 'goodness' in Ps. 65.11, referring to abundant fertility,
also connects the last section of the psalm to the second, where 'goodness' is used in relation to the temple (Ps. 65.4). There may be a further
link between this final section and the second section in the reference
to 'the stream of God' (Ps. 65.9c). Some scholars see this as a reference

16. The phrase 'awesome deeds' refers to the events at the Reed Sea in Ps.
106.22, while the word 'signs' is associated with the plagues in Egypt in Pss. 78.43;
105.27 and 135.9. The mythic language of stilling the seas is also used in the
exodus context (e.g. Ps. 114 and Isa. 51.9-11).

17. The language is familiar from other contexts. God establishes the
mountains in Pss. 90.2 and 95.4, and stills the roaring of the seas in Pss. 74.12-17;
77.17-21; 89.9-12; 93.3-4; 107.29.

18. The form changes to the perfect and could suggest that thanks is given in
Ps. 65.9-13 for some past harvest. In this case a separate origin is supposed for the
section (e.g. Kraus 1989: 30). However, this does not address the final form of the
psalm. Reading in the latter context I prefer to retain a continuous present in
translation for the verbs in Ps. 65.9-13.

to rain or channels for rain (e.g. Kissane 1953: 278-79; A.A. Anderson 1972: 470-77), but it could also refer to a Jerusalem cultic tradition that sees the sanctuary as the source of water for the land (thus Kraus 1989: 31; cf. Ps. 46.4; Isa. 33.21; Joel 3.18; Ezek. 47 and Zech. 14.8). Ps. 65.9-13 is also connected to the third section (Ps. 65.5-8) through the references to water and rain and to mountains/hills. In addition we note the use of the verb *kwn*, 'to establish', used in Ps. 65.6 where God establishes the mountains, and in Ps. 65.9 where it appears twice.[19]

In Ps. 65.12-13 the psalmist's praise joins with the joy of Earth. These verses begin and end with statements expressing joyous exclamation and singing. Ps. 65.12 speaks of the pastures and hills rejoicing, while in Ps. 65.13, the flocks and crops are described as clothing for the pastures and valleys. The fact that the two verses are parallel makes it clear that an abundance of flocks and crops is the means by which the pastures and hills rejoice. Thus the final section ends in a similar way to the second and third sections. Each concludes by recounting a response to God's action: the worshippers desire to be sated on the goodness of the temple in Ps. 65.4; the inhabitants of Earth are in awe of God's acts in Ps. 65.8; and Earth shouts for joy in Ps. 65.13.

Thus, while each of the sections of Psalm 65 has a distinct emphasis, they are intricately connected in the present form of the psalm. The whole psalm stands as a unity. The statement of God's founding and ordering action in the cosmos is at its centre, both structurally and conceptually. The 'God in Zion' is 'the confidence of all the ends of the earth'. Earth itself, in terms of abundant fertility in Ps. 65.9-13, joins in this universal praise of the God in Zion, the one who answers prayer.

God and Earth

The present form of the psalm raises an important question. How does the psalmist see Earth as relating and responding to God?

There are several statements on the relation between God and Earth in the final section of the psalm. First, God is the source of Earth's life and abundance.[20] Ps. 65.9-11 emphasizes this, with God as the subject

---

19. In Ps. 65.9 God provides the people with grain, literally 'you establish their grain', and God prepares it, literally 'you establish it'.

20. The Hebrew verb in Ps. 65.9 translated 'visit' (*paqad*) often carries with it the notion of 'attending to' things necessary. Ps. 80.14 provides a parallel to the use of the verb in Ps. 65.9. The statement 'have regard (*paqad*) for this vine' in Ps. 80.14 (NRSV), in which the vine is used as an image for Israel, is parallel to the statement

of each of the verbs describing the process of bringing fertility to Earth. Earth is the recipient of each action in these verses. God provides grain, tends and waters Earth, and blesses the growth. The harvest, which is rich and abundant and 'drips fatness', comes as the result of God's goodness (Ps. 65.11).

If we accept the unity of the psalm, then further points can be made. The third section (Ps. 65.5-8), which has connections with both the preceding and following sections, establishes the mythic background for the rest of the psalm. It contains the declaration that God is the one who orders the cosmos, the one who establishes the mountains and stills the seas and the peoples. God is the one who can pardon sins and grant abundant fertility.

I also noted above several connections between Ps. 65.9-13 and the second section (Ps. 65.3-4) which focuses on the temple. One of these concerns the word 'goodness' (Ps. 65.4, 11). Both temple and Earth reflect the 'goodness' of God. The connection is reinforced if we understand 'the stream of God' (Ps. 65.9) as issuing from the temple. The word 'sated', in relation to the goodness of the temple (Ps. 65.4), could also allude to the abundant fertility in Ps. 65.9-13. These connections draw together Earth's abundant fertility and the worship in the temple.

Another connection concerns the movement within the last three sections of the psalm. In each God moves outward towards creation: in terms of forgiveness when sin overwhelms the people (Ps. 65.3), in terms of establishing the mountains and stilling the seas (Ps. 65.6-7), or in giving fertility to Earth (Ps. 65.9-11). In each there is a corresponding movement back towards God: as God brings the chosen near to his temple (Ps. 65.4), as the inhabitants of the Earth stand in awe and 'east and west sing for joy' (Ps. 65.8), or as Earth responds in joyous praise (Ps. 65.12-13). The sections thus detail how 'all flesh' comes to God (Ps. 65.2b). The coming together of worshippers and God in the temple, the inhabitants of Earth standing in awe of God's signs, and the coming together of God and Earth in abundant fertility, complement each other. In each case intimacy is the result of God's initial movement towards creation. Thus, the presence of God in the temple, and the 'awesome deeds' in ordering creation, are continuous with the work of God in and with Earth.

When we consider these three sections in conjunction with the introduction (Ps. 65.1-2), we see that the God who does these things is the God in Zion, who hears and answers prayer. The abundant

in Ps. 80.18 'give us life' by virtue of the chiastic arrangement of Ps. 80.14-18. Cf. also Job 10.12.

fertility of the final section (Ps. 65.10-14) is an answer to prayer. But also the parallel responses at the end of each of the last three sections suggest that abundant fertility is not only the answer to a prayer by worshippers, but is itself Earth's 'prayer of praise' to God. This prayer is the gift of God to Earth. Just as worshippers in Ps. 65.3-4, who are forgiven and brought near to God, break forth with a desire for the goodness of God's house, so Earth is enriched by God's gift of abundant fertility and breaks forth into joyous praise. In each case, God's gift makes the response of worship possible. God's dealing with Earth is not simply a response to human worship. The psalm suggests that while the two are intricately related, God's dealing with Earth and its response of jubilant praise have their own integrity in the context of all creation. Earth has its own voice. As in the case of human worship, Earth lifts its voice in a song of praise in response to the gracious actions and initiative of God.

The present form of Psalm 65 raises another question. What is the relation of this psalm to the greater context of the ancient Near East and other aspects of Israelite religion? Do we hear of the voice of Earth raised to God in prayer anywhere else in the Hebrew Bible or other ancient Near Eastern literature?

A number of texts from Syria-Palestine bear witness to the perceived relationship between the gods and the fertility of Earth. This is particularly so in relation to the Canaanite/Syrian storm god Baal. In one Ugaritic text, Asherah, consort to the high god El, praises the latter's decree that a temple should be built for Baal. She cries:

> And now indeed
> may Baal appoint the season of his rains,
> the season of his storm.
> The sound of his voice from the clouds,
> his hurling lightning to the earth (KTU 1.4.v.6-9).[21]

In a second text El has a vision of Baal, who has been dead, returning to life. Part of the vision reads:

> let the heavens rain oil,
> the wadis run with honey (KTU 1.6.iii.6-7 and 12-13).[22]

While the motif of the fertilizing rain of Baal is present in a number of texts, and is associated on occasion with Baal's enthronement in his

---

21. Cf. the translations of Gibson (1977: 60-61); Wyatt (1998: 101); and Cross (1973: 149). The text numbering of Dietrich, Loretz and Sanmartín (*KTU*) is adopted here.

22. Cf. Gibson 1977: 77; Wyatt 1998: 136-37; and Cross 1973: 151.

new temple, in none of the Ugaritic texts is there any expression of joy
on the part of nature (Kloos 1986: 46-47). In the second example cited
above, the rain of oil and the flow of honey in the wadis are signs for
El in his dream that Baal has returned to life after having been killed
in his battle with Death. In other words, they are not independent
expressions of joy on nature's part at the news of Baal's return, but
rather the outworking of Baal's renewed work of fertilizing Earth (cf.
also Kloos 1986: 47 n. 105).

Another Ugaritic passage from the story of Kirta describes Baal's
dispensation of fertility to Earth. The tablet is badly damaged around
this passage but enough is clear to read in part:

> Pleasant for the earth is the rain of Baal,
> for the field, the rain of the Most High.
> Pleasant for the wheat in the furrow,
> for the emmer in the ploughed field (KTU 1.16.iii).[23]

I would compare also the description of Adad, the north Syrian
storm god, in the Tell Fekheryeh bilingual inscription:

> who rains down richness,
> who dispenses pasturage and watering grounds
> for the peoples of all the cities...
> controller of the rivers,
> who makes the entire world prosper,
> merciful god, to whom it is good to pray.[24]

In the Canaanite/Syrian texts cited above a number of motifs recur
in various combinations. These include temple building and fertility.[25]
The last two texts cited bear particular similarities to Ps. 65.9-10 in
terms of describing the way the storm god fertilizes Earth, and, in the
second case, in the link with universal claim and hearing prayer. However, none of the passages cited mentions any response from Earth
itself. The motif of the joy of nature is absent from all of them. That
motif can be found in a number of biblical texts beside Ps. 65.12-14. It
is clearly evident in Pss. 89.12; 96.11-12; 98.7-8; and Isa. 35.1-10.[26]

---

23. For other translations and more detailed discussion of the relevant column,
see Gibson 1977: 98; Parker (ed.) 1997: 35-36; and Wyatt 1998: 231.

24. Ll. 2-3 of the Aramaic inscription. *Editio princeps*: Abou-Assaf *et al*. 1982: 61-
62. Dion also notes the ascription of these attributes to Adad and Marduk in Assyrian texts (1991: 52 n. 36).

25. Kloos (1986: 48-49) makes a similar observation but does not include
temple building separately.

26. Possibly also Ps. 97.1, although the reference to the earth and coastlands
could refer to people rather than to the physical locations.

However, these texts do not refer to it in the context of the fertility of Earth, as in Psalm 65.[27] On the other hand, psalms other than Psalm 65, which do deal with fertility, do not include the motif of the joy of nature (e.g. Psalms 67, 85 and 126).

Thus, Psalm 65 is unique. That is not to say it is unrelated to texts describing the theophany of Baal.[28] It contains motifs discussed above, especially temple and fertility. The motif of the joy of Earth constitutes the response to God's action in the final section. Psalm 65 is, therefore, not a haphazard linking of parts, nor one based on catchwords alone. Rather, it appears to have been developed with full awareness of the motifs of the storm god theophany. It fully exhibits the theological perspective of the tradition but goes beyond that.

This suggests that a theological stream speaking of the relation of Earth and its fertility to Israel's God may have taken its place within the larger Israelite religious tradition.[29] Such a stream may well have drawn on wider Canaanite or Syrian traditions while bringing its own interpretation to bear on them. Israel's God was not just a god of history, present, or noticeably absent, at times of community salvation or crisis. Its God was also one of fertility, of Earth and its cycles of barrenness and abundance. In Psalm 65, God is not 'immanent in nature' (Frankfort and Frankfort 1946: 363), as was the case in Egypt or Mesopotamia, but infuses Earth with its own life and receives praise in the fulfilment of that life. God's ordering of creation is the foundation for the life and joy of Earth. Earth's produce is its response, its 'shout for joy', at the life-giving presence of God.[30] This 'shout', which according to Ps. 65.13 consists of the flocks clothing the pastures and the grain covering the valleys, cannot be heard in the way the song of joy from the inhabitants of 'the ends of the earth' can in Ps. 65.8. The silence mentioned in Ps. 65.1 could be seen in relation to Earth's 'shout' in Ps.

27. In this sense Kloos (1986: 50-52) does not make significant distinction within the biblical material, although to be fair to Kloos, his main focus is on Psalm 29 and not on fertility as such.

28. I assume here that there is relative homogeneity throughout Syria-Palestine in the myths, associated motifs and iconography of the storm god. Cf. also Dion 1991.

29. Mowinckel (1962: I, 162-63) sees the context of this theological tradition as the festival of YHWH's enthronement.

30. Just how strong this tradition was within Israel and what its development entailed needs further investigation. Psalm 65 would firmly associate this tradition with the temple, although whether that means official support is difficult to say. The tradition also does not appear to be exclusivist in its stance if Psalm 65, with its inclusion of '(all) the ends (of the earth)', is an indication.

65.13. Just as the silence of worshippers in the temple needs to be understood in terms of confident expectation, so the 'silence' of the fields needs to be heard for what it is: Earth's confident expectation in God, its 'shout for joy'.

Our Response

Psalm 65 both challenges and encourages us to see our relationship with Earth, and its relationship with God, in ways different to those we have inherited. The psalmist assumes an intricate connection between the activity in the sanctuary, the orderliness of the cosmos and the nations, and the fertility of Earth. God's gracious action towards each part of the creation gives rise to the joyous response of each part: worshippers, peoples, Earth. All this was part of the psalmist's world-view, which saw connections many in our own world no longer see, or no longer trust.

First, the psalmist attributes a voice to Earth. The psalmist sees Earth as a living entity capable of giving praise to God. This praise arises in the same way that human praise does: in response to God's gracious, life-giving acts. The psalmist asserts a fundamental continuity between God's regard for the 'chosen', the peoples at the ends of the earth, and Earth itself. There is likewise continuity and connection between the responses of each in praise. Earth's voice harmonizes with the joyous song of 'east and west' and joins the silent praise of the peoples. Earth's voice is a voice in prayer offered to the one who, according to the psalmist, hears prayer and answers.

Many commentators recognize the language of Ps. 65.12-13 as metaphor, a tool of the poet. Some have spiritualized the metaphor (e.g. Weiser 1962: 465-66), or resisted it by supplying a human subject to the verb in the last line (so Delitzsch 1871: 231). Others, such as Cheyne, have accepted it as instructive. He has commented that 'Virgil at least would not have been shocked at making nature "sing"' (1888: 179). However, the acceptance of the words of the psalmist as metaphor does not allow us to dismiss them too quickly as simply a feature of the poetry, a matter of expression or form and not of sub-stance. Metaphors not only have decorative or rhetorical qualities but have cognitive qualities as well.[31] Complex metaphors, such as we have in Ps. 65.12-13, depend on the interaction of two concepts or thoughts, and what we know about each of these helps us organize

---

31. For comments on the nature of metaphor see e.g. Black 1962: 46 and Newsom 1987: 189.

our thinking or reorganize it in relation to the other (Black 1962: 38-43). The use of the metaphor in Ps. 65.12-13 does not lessen the validity of the statement that Earth has a voice with which to praise God. Rather, without the use of the metaphor the psalmist could not open our minds, let alone our ears, to hear Earth's voice. The metaphor points to a reality embodied within the physical world, one that our contemporary Western minds are not usually trained to comprehend. The psalmist helps us hear Earth's praise of God in the abundant fertility of the world around us.

Secondly, the psalmist's association of pastures, valleys and so on with joyous song invites a broadening of our understanding of what we understand as praise and what can praise God. Praise in this context is not a rational enterprise or response to events. The richness of the metaphor in Ps. 65.11-13, as well as the reference to mythic events in Ps. 65.5-8, broadens the possibility of praise beyond the rational, linguistic, conscious human endeavour. It allows for what can only be expressed in the imagination or in mythic language. Furthermore, the psalm suggests that praise is not necessarily linked to human worship alone. In Ps. 65.11-13 Earth sings and shouts for joy in its abundant fertility. It sings for joy in following its life cycle. Life itself, which is lived in fullness, wholeness and peace, is an offering of joy and praise to the God whose gift that life is. Praise is embodied in the very life of Earth and its community. Human praise is but a part of the chorus. We are challenged to recognize that and to be lost in the wonder of the life of the world around us. We are challenged to reassess our doctrines of creation and give Earth space to voice its praise to God. Brueggemann comments on the end of Psalm 65 in this vein:

> Have we come to such a profane understanding of reality, such a reduction of creation to commodity, that we are incapable of speaking in this way? The problem is not that we are scientific and believe in secondary causes, but that we are autonomous and believe in no cause beyond self. Such a doxology as this serves to keep life securely in the context of creation-imagination and prevents the reduction of life around us to commodity (1984: 136).

Finally, if Psalm 65 calls us to reassess our doctrines of creation, it suggests that this process begin in worship. I speak here not in terms of worship that supports or arises out of human domination of Earth, but of praise, and lament when appropriate, in concord with that of all the Earth community. God's dealing with Earth and its response of jubilant praise have their own integrity in the context of all creation. The integrity of the human voice of praise depends on the recognition of the integrity of Earth's voice of praise. The human propensity to reduce Earth to object status, both in relation to God and to human-kind, or to perceive human existence only in terms of the historical, is basically a failure to see humankind as part of the Earth community (cf. Knierim 1995: 236). B.W. Anderson states:

> Interpreting the creation faith within the context of worship tends to shift the accent from the creation as event in the beginning to a relation-ship in the present, from the initiating act of the Creator to the crea-ture's dependence on the creator... Outside that relationship, which defines human nature or 'personhood', one leads an unauthentic and finally meaningless existence (1994: 211).

The voice of Earth would have us understand praise in terms of life lived in joy and thankfulness to God. In this at least, Earth's voice utters wisdom that needs to be heeded.

The Earth Song in Psalms 90–92

William J. Urbrock

Introduction

Recent scholarship on the Psalms has reflected a revived interest in the development and overall shape of the Psalter. Partly in response to the alternative sequencing of psalms that is preserved in manuscripts from the ancient community at Qumran, scholars have re-examined the significance of the traditional editorial arrangement of our Psalter into five books. Special attention has been given to: (1) the psalms that open and close the collection or that stand at the 'seams' between the five books; (2) other editorial framing and organizing mechanisms that appear to produce connections between certain sub-groupings of psalms; and (3) the significance of the editorial super-scriptions, both as regards groupings of psalms and as regards the idealized portrait of King David conveyed by the psalm headings.

Psalms 90–92 in the Traditional Arrangement

Psalms 90–92 introduce the fourth book (Psalms 90–106) in the traditional five-book division of the Psalter and appear to stand at a crucial juncture in the overall scheme of the collection. Studies by Gerald Wilson (1985; 1993), David Howard Jr (1993), J. Clinton McCann (1993), and others, have called attention to the pivotal position of Psalm 90, the only composition in the entire Psalter attributed to Moses, and to the change of mood in the fourth book. The heavy concentration of Davidic superscriptions in the first two books (see Childs 1971; Cooper 1983; Mays 1986) focuses attention on the ups and downs of David's personal fortunes and the successes and misfortunes of the Davidic dynasty. Later, Psalm 89 closes the third book with a climactic lament over the rejection of the Davidic 'messiah' and a poignant plea for the restoration of the divine promises to David's line.

The fourth book, however, opens with not a word about David or his dynasty. Rather, the superscription of Psalm 90 shifts attention to Moses: 'A Prayer (*tepillah*) for Moses, the man of God'. It is as if

Moses, whom tradition remembered as the great intercessor for Israel (see Exod. 33.12-16; 34.9), himself takes up the plea of Psalm 89, but here on behalf of the entire people, not just the Davidic monarchy. Thus, a focus is set for all of the fourth book, whose seven references to Moses (in Psalms 90, 99, 103, 105 and 106) offset only one elsewhere in the Psalter (Psalm 77). The concentration of references to Moses and his leadership during the wilderness era seems to invite readers to meditate on the days of Israel before David had ever come on the scene and Israel had not yet entered Canaan—days when YHWH alone was Israel's monarch. Indeed, a central theme in the psalms of the fourth book is heralded by the proclamation 'YHWH *malak!*' ('YHWH reigns!'), a theme which James Luther Mays (1994: 32) identifies as 'the organizing confession of the Psalter'.

Howard (1993: 110-12) has demonstrated the close alliance of Psalms 91 and 92 with Psalm 90. The three psalms share several key lexical terms as well as language and themes from the Wisdom tradition. More significant, however, is the overall message conveyed when one reads the three psalms in sequence. The poignant intercession of Moses in Psalm 90 appears to be answered by the strong assurance of Psalm 91, which guarantees refuge and protection for all who seek shelter in the divine (see Creach 1996: 94-95). This message of hope, in turn, appears to elicit the heartfelt thanksgiving and joyful praise expressed in Psalm 92. The new focus of the fourth book, first provided by Psalms 90–92 and carried through to Psalm 106, may be intended as an answer to the trauma of exile and dispersion after the Babylonian overthrow of Jerusalem, the temple, and the Davidic monarchy in the early sixth century BCE. As Creach observes, Book IV appears to invite readers to 'recognize the limitations of the human condition, and especially human rulers, and seek refuge in Yahweh' (1996: 99-100).

Theocentric, Anthropocentric, and Terracentric Hermeneutics

When we read these three psalms, therefore, through the interpretive lenses provided by the editors of the Psalter, we read according to the usual double focus, theocentric and anthropocentric, that is the default setting, as it were, in the Hebrew Bible. The anthropocentric focus concentrates our attention on the short but troubled life of humanity (Ps. 90.3-6, 10[1]); human sin and folly, which call forth the anger of God

---

1.   Citations follow the NRSV versification.

(Pss. 90.7-9; 92.6-9); and the utter dependence of mortals on the compassion and favor of God (Ps. 90.13-17) that might allow the pious and
their works to flourish (Pss. 90.17; 92.12-14) and might call forth their
praise and thanksgiving (Ps. 92.1-4). The theocentric focus concentrates
our attention on the majestic nature of God, who is everlasting and
most high (Pss. 90.1-2; 91.1, 9; 92.1, 8), just and upright (Ps. 92.15);
whose dominion requires punishment of the wicked (Pss. 91.8; 92.7, 9)
and protection of God's 'servants' (Ps. 90.13, 16) from every sort of
danger (Ps. 91.3-13); and who can be moved by intercession and
prayer to 'turn' (Ps. 90.13) from anger to compassion so as to satisfy
the faithful with a long and fruitful life (Pss. 91.16; 92.12-14).

How might we read these three psalms from the perspective of
Earth? I suggest we employ an earthist or terracentric interpretive
strategy on three fronts. (1) I propose terracentric superscriptions for
these psalms, so as to provide alternative templates for interpreting
their form and message. These superscriptions invite us to make an
imaginative leap, allowing Earth, as well as humans and God, to take
center stage in these psalms. (2) I suggest we attend especially to the
Earth Bible Project's guiding ecojustice principles of interconnectedness, voice, and resistance. A reading of Psalms 90–92 attentive to the
principle of interconnectedness may display how Earth and all its
children together are time-bound in their flourishing and perishing.
Furthermore, a reading attentive to the principles of voice and resistance allows us to hear Psalms 90–92 as a magnificent Earth song. In
this song Earth joyfully celebrates its divine birth and calling, laments
over its suffering at the hands of God and humanity, cries out for
justice and renewal, and expresses confident hope for its future deliverance and restoration. Such a reading does not silence the voices of
God or humanity; it does, however, give voice to the third party present in these psalms but often not heard, Earth itself. (3) I suggest
some ways in which these psalms could be read in conversation with
the earth sciences and with some recent developments in ecotheology.

A Note on Terminology

While it is common to picture Earth as female (as in the e.e. cummings
poem below), one could equally well follow an ancient Egyptian view
which considered Earth the masculine counterpart (*Geb*) to the feminine sky (*Nut*). Joseph, I think, puts the matter correctly in his discussion with Potiphar in Thomas Mann's *Joseph in Egypt* (1938: 254): 'But
the bottom of the world and the tree of life are neither male nor
female, rather both in one'. In this paper I choose neither female nor
male but non-gendered pronouns for Earth. Similarly, while the

biblical translations reflect the masculine titles and pronouns for God in the Psalms, I use non-gendered terms in the discussion.

The Earth Song in Psalms 90–92

O Sweet Spontaneous
O sweet spontaneous
earth how often have
the
doting
    fingers of
prurient philosophers pinched
and
poked
thee
, has the naughty thumb
of science prodded
thy
    beauty   . how
often have religions taken
thee upon their scraggy knees

squeezing and
buffeting thee that thou mightest
    conceive
gods
    (but
true

to the incomparable
couch of death thy
rhythmic
lover
    thou answerest

    them only with

            spring)

                                        e.e. cummings (1923)

Outline: A Song in Three Parts
   Psalm 90: A Prayer of Earth, the Child–Body of God, Lamenting the Passing of
   Species
   Earth acknowledges God, the eternal mainstay (vv. 1-6)
   Humans acknowledge their ephemeral nature (vv. 7-12)
   Earth prays for divine favor and renewal (vv. 13-17)

   Psalm 91: For Earth. A Miktam. (To the tune of Do Not Destroy)
   An anonymous fossil-like inscription recites

a protective incantation for Earth (vv. 1-13)
God, the divine mainstay, affirms the
     protective charm (vv. 14-16)

Psalm 92: A Psalm. A Song of Earth. For the Sabbath Day
Earth, the child–body of God, praises God and
     celebrates its renewal (vv. 1-11)
Earth blesses its righteous children and
     acknowledges the eternal rock (vv. 12-15)

The Editorial Superscriptions
As discussed above in the introduction, Psalm 90 carries a superscription that focuses our attention on Moses and his role as Israel's great
intercessor. Although Psalm 91 carries no superscription in the Hebrew
Bible, the Septuagint preserves an alternative tradition that entitles the
psalm 'A Praise Song, for David' (*ainos oides toi dauid*). Psalm 92 is
titled 'A Psalm (*mizmor*); a Song (*shyr*) for the Sabbath Day'.

In the outline above I played editor and revised the superscriptions
for these three psalms so as to massage readers towards a terracentric
perspective. Such a move, which involves only a minimum of interpretive daring, may yield rich insights for an Earth-reading of these
psalms. Below, I comment first on the superscription and then on the
body of each psalm. I include my own translation of Psalm 90 (anno-
tated in Urbrock 1974: 10-13) and use the NRSV translation for Psalms
91 and 92.

Psalm 90: A Prayer of Earth, the Child–Body of God, Lamenting the Passing of Species

The Superscription
The superscription serves to introduce both Psalm 90 and the entire
Earth song in Psalms 90–92.

It alludes first to the title of the important Christian ecological
theology written by Sallie McFague (1993). McFague argues persua-
sively for a paradigm shift in our view of Earth and the universe that
takes into account what contemporary science reveals to us about cosmic evolution, our ancient Earth made of star-stuff, and humanity as
one climactic product of the evolution of life on Earth. McFague (1993:
vii) proposes a model of our universe as God's body and of Earth as
our true home, the planet to which we belong as surely as all the other
life forms that have evolved here (1993: 56-57). This organic panen-
theistic model affirms the inhering of Earth and the universe in God
and insists that God is intimately involved in all the fortunes, for good
and evil, for life and death, through which the universe, Earth our

home, and all the living, including humanity, must pass (1993: 176-77). As 'citizens of planet earth', one species among millions of others in our common home, our first loyalty must be *to* Earth itself, our first care and central concern must be *for* Earth itself, and our primary role must be as partners *with* Earth in working for the common well-being (McFague 1993: 108-12). This is the 'planetary agenda', the 'universal vocation of planetary well-being', to which all of humanity is now called (McFague 1993: 11).

McFague's ideas find resonance in a report of the World Council of Churches to its 1991 general assembly in Canberra, Australia, and in the writings of US ecotheologian Jay McDaniel, Brazilian theologian Leonardo Boff, Hong Kong-born churchwoman Kwok Pui-lan, and others. As reported in Brockelman (1997: 41) the WCC report pictures God as 'the creator who "bodies forth" all that is' and states that '[i]n the light of the incarnation the whole universe appears to us as God's body'. Similarly, McDaniel (1997: 121-22) 'commend[s] to Christians and others' an imaging of God which suggests that 'the universe itself is the very body of God and that the ultimate unity of the universe is itself a life'. Boff (1994: 244) challenges us to develop a 'new planetary conscience' which recognizes Earth's dignity and rights, derived from its existence for millions of years independent of human beings. Kwok (1994: 109) proposes an 'ecological model' of God, which recognizes that 'God, human beings, nature are interdependent and interrelated, just like the three interconnected arrows of the familiar symbol for recycling'. Indeed, James Gustafson (1994: 44-45) reminds us that even John Calvin, convinced that 'Nature is the theatre of the power and glory of the Divine', once wrote: 'I confess, of course, that it can be said reverently, provided that it proceeds from a reverent mind, that nature is God'. Calvin did add reservations, lest God and God's works be confused.

Secondly, the superscription alerts readers to one of the most distressing symptoms of Earth's transformation at the present time: the systematic destruction of habitats that are home to numberless as yet unidentified species of plants and animals. The 'Vital Science' feature written by William Stolzenburg in the September–October 2000 issue of *Nature Conservancy* (p. 10) magazine presents a detailed summary:

> More than half the world's abundance of species lie within the bewildering realms of the largely uncharted tropics, more than 99 per-cent of them yet to be documented. What is best known about them is that they are rapidly disappearing. The world's tropical forests are falling under the saw and going up in smoke at the rate of about 11 square miles a day, its species disappearing at a conservatively estimated three per hour. Any would-be rescuers had better flag them and quickly.

The Body of the Psalm

Lord!

> A mainstay (*ma'on*) you have been
>> For us from age to age!
>>> Before the mountains were born,
>>> Or you brought forth the Earth and the world,
>> Yea, from aeon to aeon!
> You,

God! (Ps 90.1-2)

Reciting in elegant poetic chiasmus, Earth addresses God, speaking for the universe of which it is a part, for itself, and all its inhabitants, acknowledging its place within the divine milieu. Earth recognizes God as the mainstay (*ma'on*; see Dahood 1968: 172 n. 3; 322 n. 1) who, like a birthing mother, brings forth and sustains all from aeon to aeon. Earth also reminds us of its ancient heritage, recalling the great times of orogenesis (mountain building) which have changed its face as the child–body of God many times during its more than 4.5 billion years of existence. Here, we may be reminded of such magnificent Palaeozoic events (from the late Silurian through Permian periods) as the Caledonian, Acadian, Alleghenian, and Hercynian orogenies that raised the Old Red Continent along the northern margin of Europe, created great mountain ranges along the eastern and southern margins of what is now North America, birthed a great mountain range across southern Europe, raised the land in England, and, finally, marked the assembling of Pangaea about 250 million years ago (Levin 1991: 309, 337-70; Hardy 1999: 38, 72-73).

> You return humankind to the dust:
> 'Return, human children!'
> For a thousand years in your eyes—
> Like yesterday just passes!
> Or like a watch in the night!
>
> If you pluck them, they are (like) a sleep.
> In the morning like grass (which) shoots up—
> In the morning it sprouts and grows;
> By evening it wilts and withers (Ps. 90.3-6).

Earth's voice, although still addressed to God, alerts humans to their reality as ephemeral creatures, rising from the dust of Earth like grass and soon returning to Earth. Perhaps Earth also wishes to remind its people in North America of the vanishing of the great prairie grasslands. Writing, the 'NWF View', in the August–September 2000 issue of *National Wildlife*, Mark Van Putten, President and Chief Executive Officer of the National Wildlife Federation, notes that 70 per cent of the former short-grass and mixed-grass prairies are gone, while only 1 per cent of the former tall-grass prairie now remains (p. 7). Scattered remnants of the latter comprise North America's most rapidly disappearing ecosystem, leaving hundreds of grassland species threatened or endangered. Indeed, grassland bird species are experiencing the most precipitous decline of any wildlife population in North America.

> Truly, we perish by your anger;
> By your wrath we are dismayed.
> You have set our iniquities before you,
> (The sins of) our youth in the light of your countenance.
>
> For:
> All our days turn 'round under your fury;
> We bring our years to an end like a sigh!
> Our span of years is seventy years,
> Or, perhaps, at most, eighty years;
> But most of them are toil and trouble.
> Yea! They pass by quickly, and we vanish.
>
> Who experiences the brunt of your anger,
> And your fury like those who fear you?!
> Teach us so to number our days
> That we may gain a heart of wisdom (Ps. 90.7-12).

In these verses humans join Earth's prayer by acknowledging their short span of life, nearly infinitesimal compared to that of Earth or of the eternal mainstay. Dare we suggest that here humans also acknowledge that, as a species, they may one day disappear from Earth altogether? Peter Hardy observes that

> [i]t is true to say that no species has remained unchanged over geological time and that the vast majority have become extinct in a few tens or hundreds of thousands of years. It should be apparent from this, although there may not be much to be done about it, that the human species is no more likely to live forever than any other (1999: 134-35).

In these verses we might also hear technologically sophisticated humankind mindfully acknowledging that, since the 'youth' of our brave new age of technology, we have hastened the passing of species at an accelerating pace by our wanton consumption and destruction of life-supporting resources. More than a decade ago, Sean McDonagh (1990: 74-106) lamented the senseless destruction of the rainforests in the Philippines and wondered what it would be like 'when the trees are gone'. Moreover, on ethical and religious grounds, he identified the injustice we are inflicting on future generations of life on Earth as we bring about large-scale extinction of species, thus sterilizing Earth and compromising the integrity of creation (McDonagh 1990: 88). This is the 'ecological sin' spoken of by Boff (1994: 244-45):

> The biblical precept 'You shall not kill' (Exod. 20.13) may also refer to biocide and ecocide for the future. We are not permitted to create environmental and social conditions that produce disease and death for future living creatures, human and non-human.

Finally, we may read Ps. 90.11-12 as a prayer for wisdom precisely by those who 'fear' God and wish to honor Earth as God's child–body. It is they who have a heightened awareness of divine wrath and fury for their participation, both knowingly and unknowingly, in the widespread human abuse of Earth and their fellow-creatures. The humble request, 'Teach us to number our days', might be read as expressing readiness to end the quest to continually prolong our human life span, at whatever cost. 'Teach us' rather to identify more closely with the rest of the Earth community and accept our limited share in the cycles of life that Earth fosters.

> Turn, YHWH!
> How long?
> Take pity on your servants!
> Satisfy us in the morning with your loving kindness!
> Then we will exult!
> Then we will rejoice!
> All our days!
> Make us happy for as many days as you afflicted us,
> As many years as we experienced misfortune.
> Let your work appear to your servants,
> And your majesty to their children!
> And let the favor of the Lord our God be upon us!
> And the work of our hands let him sustain for us!
> Yea, the work of our hands, sustain it! (Ps 90.13-17)

As at the beginning of the psalm, Earth now speaks again for itself and all its inhabitants, human and non-human, all of whom are God's servants in one way or another. Earth prays that divine loving kindness (*chesed*) and favor (*no'am*) will bring about a renewed future for all these servants. Does Earth's talk of 'affliction' and 'misfortune' directed by God remind us of past upheavals and extinctions during Earth's more than 4.5 billion years of life, long before humanity appeared on the scene? Additionally, might Earth be asking in particular for respite from the afflictions so often visited upon it and the rest of its creatures by the dominating and exploitative ways of humankind? Earth asks for a new kind of shared present, one in which the work of God, the work of Earth, and the work of everyone in the Earth community might together achieve a greater 'happiness' for all. Here we are reminded of the ecojustice principle of interconnectedness, which highlights Earth as a community of interconnected living things mutually dependent on each other for life and survival.

Psalm 91: For Earth. A Miktam. To the Tune of Do Not Destroy

The Superscription

As a third alternative to the Hebrew Bible (no superscription) and the Septuagint ('A Praise Song, for David'), I propose this superscription 'For Earth. A *Miktām*'. While the meaning of *miktam* is disputed, the Septuagint's translation *stelographia* suggests that we read this psalm as if it were some sort of inscription, as Patrick Miller also suggests in his notes to Psalm 16 in the Harper Collins Study Bible (1993). The other *miktams* editorially identified in the Hebrew Psalter are Psalm 16 and the grouping of Psalms 56–60. Like Psalm 91, all of these compositions convey assurances of deliverance from enemies and death for those who take refuge in the divine.

The additional note, 'To the Tune of *Do Not Destroy*', forges a strong link to one *miktām* in particular, Psalm 57. This psalm bears a similar superscription, and, like Psalm 91, duplicates the picture of the faithful seeking refuge in the shadow of the divine wings, which offer protection from arrows, snares and lions.

I suggest we read Psalm 91 as a sort of inscription, preserved like a fossil in the ancient rocks, addressed to Earth. Its words remind us of aeons past and promise repeated renewal for Earth and life on Earth despite widespread upheavals and extinctions over the millennia.

The Body of the Psalm

> You who live in the shelter of the Most High,
> who abide in the shadow of the Almighty,
> will say to the LORD, 'My refuge and my fortress;
> my God, in whom I trust'.
> For he will deliver you from the snare of the fowler
> and from the deadly pestilence;
> he will cover you with his pinions,
> and under his wings you will find refuge;
> his faithfulness is a shield and buckler (Ps. 91.1-4).

Here an anonymous speaker addresses Earth. The voice could be that of a long-extinct archaeocyathid from the Palaeozoic Cambrian, the earliest abundant reef-building animal on earth (Levin 1991: 382), or a similarly extinct ammonoid cephalopod, one of the millions that flourished during the Mesozoic Age, which Levin has dubbed the 'Age of Ammonoids' (Levin 1991: 475). Or, from the Mesozoic 'Age of Reptiles', these words could be spoken to Earth by one of the thousands of dinosaurs that roamed the lands and whose relatives, the pterosaurs, plesiosaurs and ichthyosaurs filled the skies and waters.

Whatever fossil creature we hear speaking, its opening sentences reaffirm and extend the message proclaimed at the beginning of the Earth song: God, the 'mainstay...from age to age' (Ps. 90.1), is also 'refuge' and 'fortress' in times of 'deadly pestilence' (Ps. 91.2-3). This Most High, the almighty One of the mountains (*shadday*, Ps. 91.1), like a great bird protecting its young under its 'pinions' and 'wings', or like a warrior armed in 'shield and buckler', surely will deliver Earth and all who seek shelter in the divine presence (Ps. 91.3-4). This message of reassurance seems to be given in reply to the fervent prayers of Earth and its children in Ps. 90.13-17 for divine favor and sustenance and for the revelation of God's 'work' and 'majesty' during a time of renewal.

> You will not fear the terror of night,
> or the arrow that flies by day,
> or the pestilence that stalks in darkness,
> or the destruction that wastes at noonday.
>
> A thousand may fall at your side,
> ten thousand at your right hand,
> but it will not come near you.
> You will only look with your eyes
> and see the punishment of the wicked.
>
> Because you have made the LORD your refuge,
> the Most High your dwelling place (*ma'on*),
> no evil shall befall you,
> no scourge come near your tent.
>
> For he will command his angels concerning you
> to guard you in all your ways.
> On their hands they will bear you up,
> so that you will not dash your foot against a stone.
> You will tread on the lion and the adder,
> the young lion and the serpent
> you will trample under foot (Ps. 91.5-13).

The anonymous fossil creature continues to address Earth. As we humans listen in to these verses, however, the impressive imagery of terror and pestilence, scourge and destruction, threatening beasts and serpents, conjures up many of our worst fears. Set over against the picture of protecting divine 'angels' or messengers (Ps. 91.11-12), the war-like scene of arrows and plague and of thousands falling to left and right (Ps. 91.5-8) is reminiscent not only of human battles but of demonic forces that seem always ready to attack life on Earth.

Dahood (1968: 331) has suggested that the combination of 'arrow' and 'pestilence' may be a symbolic reminder of Reseph, the Canaanite god of pestilence, who was sometimes called 'lord of the arrow'. One is reminded, too, of the famous seventh-century BCE Aramaic amuletic plaque from Arslan Tash in Upper Syria, with its figures of a winged sphinx, a she-wolf, and an axe-wielding god, accompanied by incantations against the 'fliers', 'lamb-stranglers', and the god Sasam (Cross and Saley 1970). Cross and Saley note that all these threatening powers are night demons who go abroad in darkness. Furthermore, they remark that both the content and shape of the plaque argue for its function as a protective device to be hung up in the doorway of a house. The parallels to 'the terror of the night' (Ps. 91.5) and the assurance that no 'evil' or 'scourge' (demon?) will approach the tent (Ps. 91.10) in Psalm 91 are striking.

In light of these considerations and in view of our superscription 'To the Tune of *Do Not Destroy*', we may interpret the fossil-like Earth-inscription that is Psalm 91 as a sort of protective charm or incantation for Earth. Life forms may come and go, 'A thousand may fall at your side, ten thousand at your right hand' (Ps. 91.7), but Earth itself shall remain. Only a poetic conceit? Jack Horner has reported on a rock bed about 1.25 miles long by 0.25 miles wide in Montana that contains nearly 30 million bones representing some ten thousand individual Maiasaura (see Levin 1991: 488). A thousand may fall, ten thousand, but Earth itself shall remain.

Timothy Weiskel (1997: 12) notes that professional journals representing all the earth sciences warn that

> we are currently in the midst of a global 'extinction event' which equals or exceeds in scale those catastrophic episodes in the geological record that marked the extinction of the dinosaurs and numerous other species.

Thomas Berry (1997: 214) has gone so far as to suggest that we have entered 'the terminal Cenozoic'. In view of the unprecedented manner by which human agency is bringing about the widespread destruction of species at what may be the end of our age, would we be amiss in identifying the demonic figures of Psalm 91 and the 'wicked' destined for punishment (Ps. 91.8) as being precisely ourselves? Such an identification would accord with the ecojustice principle of resistance by acknowledging human injustices to Earth and hearing ancient voices from Earth which struggle against them. Perhaps the 'wicked' today are all of us, whenever we refuse to recognize the ecological signs of the times, whenever we allow the few to monopolize and destroy natural resources, whenever we refuse to re-examine and reform our own habits of over-consumption and waste. By contrast, perhaps today's angelic guardians (Ps. 91.11-12) of Earth are also all of us, insofar as we awaken to the critical threats to the existence of thousands of life forms—ourselves included!—and as we enter the lists creatively to forge new dreams and new directions, along with Earth and our fellow creatures, for future life. Here I echo the warning and invitation put forth by Jose Pepz M. Cunanan (1994: 27):

> Those who would venture into the field of environment and development should be forewarned that this is not a neutral and sanitized area… these are grounds full of traps and pitfalls, confrontations and conflicts. These are minefields filled with risks and dangers.
>
> [Nevertheless,]…the last decade of the twentieth century and the ushering in of the twenty-first century are golden moments when the renewal and transformation of society, humanity and of the earth can take place. It may be our last chance, and so, by God's grace, we have to make the most of it.

Otherwise, a thousand may fall, ten thousand—humanity as well— but Earth itself shall remain.

> Those who love me, I will deliver;
> I will protect those who know my name.
> When they call to me, I will answer them;
> I will be with them in trouble,
> I will rescue them and honor them.
> With long life I will satisfy them,
> and show them my salvation (Ps. 91.14-16).

This portion of the Earth song concludes with a response by the divine mainstay that echoes the charm-like incantation in the previous verses. God promises protection and rescue in times of trouble and an *'orek yamim*, a 'length of days' ('long life', Ps. 91.16) to Earth and all who call upon the divine name. The phrase is reminiscent of the conclusion of Psalm 23, which looks forward to a return to God's house for an *'orek yamim*, and of the conclusion of Psalm 93, which affirms that holiness befits God's house for an *'orek yamim*. Similarly, in Psalm 91 the promise is for a 'length of days' within the 'shelter of the Most High' (Ps. 91.1) and the 'refuge' of the divine mainstay (*ma'on*, Ps. 91.9, cf. 90.1). On Earth's timescale, this 'length of days' could mean additional millions or billions of years, long after our current ecological crisis has become as distant a memory as that of the fossil-creatures we have imagined speaking to us in Psalm 91. In terms of the timescale of *Homo sapiens*, which so far appears to have covered less than a million years, dare we hope for another million?

Psalm 92: A Psalm. A Song of Earth. For the Sabbath Day

The Superscription
Except for the interpolation 'A Song of Earth', the superscription is that which appears in the Hebrew Bible. In thinking of the Sabbath day, we may also keep in mind the Sabbath year described in Leviticus 25. According to this priestly teaching, every seventh year was to be set aside so that 'the land shall observe a Sabbath for the LORD' (Lev. 25.2). During this Sabbath year, there would be no sowing or pruning, reaping or ingathering; the land would enjoy 'a year of complete rest' (Lev. 25.4-5). Only what the land yielded on its own during this special year was to be eaten as food by humans and by animals domesticated and wild (Lev. 25.6-7). Not to worry, since the land was bound to bring forth a triple yield, a sign of divine blessing, during the Sabbath year (Lev. 25.20-21)! A startling idea!

In view of our superscription for Psalm 90 at the beginning of the Earth song, with its reminder of the devastation of species, a more fitting way to afford a Sabbath rest for Earth in our time might be to engage in various efforts of environmental restoration. This was suggested for the rainforest in the Philippines by McDonagh (1990: 93-105), who urged co-operation between local communities, schools, churches, governments, and international banking agencies in supporting reforestation as one of several initiatives to heal the exploited land. McDonagh cited similar sentiments expressed in the pastoral letter, 'What is Happening to Our Beautiful Land?', circulated in 1988 by the Roman Catholic bishops of the Philippines (1990: 105-106).

It may surprise many of us to learn that reforestation/tree-planting Eucharists are currently being celebrated regularly by some independent churches in Africa. M.L. Daneel (1994) reports on Zimbabwe's ecumenical earth-keepers' movement, formalized in 1991 as the Association of African Earth-Keeping Churches (AAEC). He also reproduces portions of a Eucharistic tree-planting liturgy, during which communicants receive the sacramental bread and wine while holding seedlings in their hands. Subsequently, church leaders and congregation plant the seedlings in 'holy soil', which has been prayed over and sprinkled with holy water. Finally, Daneel notes that in this tree-planting Eucharist a close identification is made between Christ's body and the abused and barren soil. In this way, Christ joins the ancestors as guardian of the soil and as the soil itself. Hence, in

Christian terms, Daneel (1994: 262) notes that '[r]eplacing the trees in sacramental recognition of the lordship of Christ—the ultimate guardian, who reigns over yet suffers within the stricken earth—brings life and celebration to creation'.

Such a Eucharist appears to embody the Earth Bible Project's ecojustice principles of resistance, by acknowledging human injustices to Earth and linking the suffering of Earth with the suffering of Christ, and of custodianship, by enacting a mutually sustaining and renewing partnership between Earth, God and people.

The Body of the Psalm

> It is good to give thanks to the LORD,
> to sing praises to your name, O Most High;
> to declare your steadfast love in the morning,
> and your faithfulness by night,
> to the music of the lute and the harp,
> to the melody of the lyre.
>
> For you, O LORD, have made me glad by your work;
> at the works of your hands I sing for joy.
> How great are your works, O LORD!
> Your thoughts are very deep! (Ps. 92.1-5).

In this final psalm of the three included in our Earth song, Earth again finds its voice. In a manner reminiscent of the singing of morning stars and divine beings at Earth's beginning (Job 38.7), Earth breaks forth into praise of the most high. Singing to the accompaniment of lute and harp and lyre, Earth declares that God indeed has demonstrated the 'steadfast love' (*chesed*) prayed for in the opening part of the Earth song (Ps. 90.14) and the 'faithfulness' (*'emunah*) promised by the ancient voices in the second part (Ps. 91.4, *'emet*). Earth, which had prayed that God prosper 'the work of our hands' (Ps. 90.17, *ma'aseh yadenu*), now sings to God, joyfully acknowledging 'the works of your hands' (Ps. 92.4, *ma'aseh yadenu*) and extolling the greatness of 'your works' (Ps. 92.5, *ma'aseka*) and the depths of 'your thoughts'. It is as if Earth recognizes that its own birth and eventual demise (on the scale of billions of years), as well as the rise and extinction of life-forms on Earth (on scales of millions of years or less), constitute a divine work eminently praiseworthy, if incomprehensible.

> The dullard cannot know,
> the stupid cannot understand this:
> though the wicked sprout like grass
> and all evildoers flourish,
> they are doomed to destruction forever,
> but you, LORD, are on high forever.

> For your enemies, O LORD,
> for your enemies shall perish;
> all evildoers shall be scattered.
> But you have exalted my horn like that of a wild ox;
> you have poured over me fresh oil.
> My eyes have seen the downfall of my enemies;
> my ears have heard the doom of my evil assailants (Ps. 92.6-11).

Earth continues its praises in poetic images reminiscent of those in Ps. 90.1-2, 5-6 at the beginning of the Earth song: God's eternal exaltation (*marom le'olam*, Ps. 92.8) stands in stark contrast to the ephemeral grass-like flourishing of the wicked (Ps. 92.7). Reassured by the promises that Earth's own 'eyes' would 'see the punishment of the wicked' (Ps. 91.8), Earth takes up the refrain that 'all evildoers shall be scattered' and that, indeed, 'My eyes have seen the downfall of my enemies'. Earth can afford to take the long view: eventually, its despoilers are themselves destroyed. This reminder of Earth's resistance and resilience, is sobering for us, especially if, as I suggested in my discussion of Psalm 91, we ourselves, Earth's own people, may nevertheless be counted among Earth's enemies.

Finally, we may hear in Ps. 92.8-11 Earth's triumphant assertion that it is indeed to be feared and respected as the child–body of God. The bold juxtaposition of the climactic tricolon in Ps. 92.9 with Ps. 92.11 bespeaks Earth's conviction that its enemies are also God's enemies. The even bolder juxtaposition of Ps. 92.8 and 92.10 bespeaks Earth's confidence that, just as God is exalted on high (*marom le'olam*), Earth is ever renewed and exalted by God like a wild ox (*tarem kir'em*). The alternating or interlaced juxtapositions (Ps. 92.8 with 92.10 and 92.9 with 92.11), along with the poetic assonance and alliteration (Ps. 92.8, 1), underscore the imagined identifications.

> The righteous flourish like the palm tree,
> and grow like a cedar in Lebanon.
> They are planted in the house of the LORD
> they flourish in the courts of our God.
> In old age they still produce fruit;
> they are always green and full of sap,
> showing that the LORD is upright;
> he is my rock, and there is no
> unrighteousness in him (Ps. 92.12-15).

Earth was blessed by the protective incantation of Psalm 91. Now, as Earth brings its song to a close, it speaks a word of blessing to the 'righteous'. We may take the 'righteous' to be those who, unlike the 'wicked' of Ps. 91.8 but like the angelic guardians in that psalm, recognize their solidarity with Earth and seek to co-operate with Earth and their fellow creatures.

The terms of the blessing are especially striking if we read them alongside the picture of the devastated forests discussed earlier. Here the picture is not of devastation but of luxuriant growth. The righteous are compared to great trees that flourish year after year, bearing fruit into a ripe old age. Moreover, they grow and flourish 'in the house of the LORD...in the courts of our God'. Here Earth itself may be considered the sanctuary in whose sacred courts the righteous flourish. Such an image expands the picture of the land of Israel/Judah as the divine sanctuary (Exod. 15.17; Ps. 114.2) to include the entire expanse of Earth.

In fact, date palms (Ps. 92.12a), which yield one of Earth's most storable and nourishing foods, may grow 100 feet tall. They first start bearing fruit at the 'old age' of about 35 years, producing an average annual yield of some 125 pounds (Jacob and Jacob 1992: 807). Cedars of Lebanon (Ps. 92.12b) are those that produced the panels for Solomon's Temple in Jerusalem (1 Kgs 5.6-10). These magnificent trees, prized for their durable and fragrant wood and their aromatic resin and oil, may live up to 3000 years, truly an 'old age' (Jacob and Jacob 1992: 805).

The picture of the flourishing date palm and cedar of Lebanon may evoke for us a larger scene that encompasses the wonder of trees, especially fruit-bearing trees, and the even wider expanse of flowering plants. During the Palaeozoic era, long after the Earth's beginning, the first unquestioned remains of vascular plants, the psilophytes, appear in the Middle Silurian (over 400 million years ago). Forests of lofty, leafy trees had developed by late in the Devonian (over 350 million years ago), while seed-producing, pollinating, but non-flowering plants (the gymnosperms) developed by the late Palaeozoic (over 245 million years ago). Plants with both seeds and flowers (the angiosperms) first evolved late in the Mesozoic Era (Levin 1991: 374-75). In his classic work, *The Immense Journey*, Loren Eiseley celebrates 'How Flowers Changed the World' (1957: 61-77). First came the pine and spruce forests with their 'primitive wooden cone flowers' (1957: 67). Much later, however, occurred 'that far-off Cretaceous explosion of a hundred million years ago that changed the face of the planet' (1957: 69-70). It was then that true flowering plants, with their 'fantastic little seeds skipping and hopping and flying about' (1957: 72), began to make possible Earth as we now live in it. 'The weight of a petal', remarks Eiseley, 'has changed the face of the world and made it ours' (1957: 77).

Speaking as an eco-feminist, Chung Hyun Kyung (1994: 178), cele-brates how trees, rooted deeply in Earth yet thrust upward into the freedom of sky, 'provide shelter and shade for the life and growth' of all sorts of creatures. Their 'fruit gives food for the body and [their] flower gives food for the soul', while their dying leaves help re-create the soil. 'This cyclic, rhythmic process of creating, nurturing, healing and re-creating life', she concludes, 'symbolizes the aspirations of the cosmic spirituality of eco-feminism'.

The very last word in our Earth song, however, is not about trees but about the Rock (Ps. 92.15). In a powerful poetic inclusion, the eter-nal mainstay, addressed at the beginning of the Earth song as the one who birthed the mountains and brought forth Earth and the world (Ps. 90.2), is here acclaimed as the eternal rock, 'upright' and without trace of 'unrighteousness', hence forever trustworthy.

Conclusion

David Hallman (1994: 6), speaking for many others, has noted that 'we are in the early stages of a profound conceptual shift in theology'. He argues that the Bible has much to contribute to this shift:

> listening to the word of God with ears sensitive to the ecological crisis is exhilarating. God has not abandoned us. God is speaking powerfully and poignantly through scripture if we are prepared to hear the mes-sages.

In our terracentric reading of Psalms 90–92 as an Earth song in three parts the 'word of God' has been listened to as a word of Earth, God's child–body. The reading has been sensitive to the Earth Bible Project's ecojustice principles of voice, resistance and interconnectedness. Earth has found a voice and has reminded humans of their limited life-span as a species, prayerfully acknowledged dependence upon the divine mainstay, and confidently proclaimed solidarity with the divine rock. Ancient fossil-like voices have chanted a charm-like protective incan-tation for Earth, resisting the enemies of life and indicting human agency in bringing about the onset of a massive extinction of life-forms on Earth. Finally, the entire Earth song has celebrated the inter-connectedness of all life-forms on Earth, whether extinct, now living, or yet to evolve. The song has presented Earth as the child–body of God and humans as both demonic and angelic insofar as they destroy or foster the welfare of the entire community of life on Earth within the shelter of the most high.

In Psalm 90, the first part of the Earth song, Earth offered a prayer for the prospering of 'the work of our hands', the realities of suffering and death notwithstanding. Perhaps, as we mature and learn to co-operate with God and Earth more intelligently and more wholeheart-edly in 'the work', God and 'sweet spontaneous' Earth together will answer us 'only with spring'.

Psalm 104: A Celebration of the *Vanua*

Arthur Walker-Jones

Introduction

The traditional labelling of Psalm 104 by biblical scholars as a 'creation psalm' introduces into its interpretation Western dualisms that have been destructive to Earth. Living for six years amongst the cultures of Oceania helped my own recognition of the relativity of European culture and the possibility of more Earth-conscious interpretations. The regional, ecumenical, theological college at which I taught in Fiji had as part of its mandate the promotion of Pacific contextual interpretations and communicating the unique insights of Pacific Islanders to the world. In what follows I would like to honour the wisdom of the cultures of Oceania by allowing it to critique and supplement Western interpretations of Psalm 104 (Sugirtharajah 1996: 20-27). Since indigenous peoples and Earth have both fallen on the wrong side of Western dualisms and their exploitation is interrelated (Primavesi 1991: 24-64), it seems appropriate to pay special attention to indigenous knowledge in reading Psalm 104 from the perspective of Earth.

After an introduction to the Fijian understanding of Earth, the discussion will follow to some extent the flow of Psalm 104 while discussing God in Earth (Ps. 104.1-9, 32), Earth as living, intrinsically valuable, and interconnected (Ps. 104.10-30), and Earth celebration (Ps. 104.31-35).

Vanua

What Fijians write and say about the *vanua*, normally translated 'land', is illustrative of their relationship to Earth. This word, and the cultural understandings that it represents, reaches across Oceania through all the Polynesian cultures and into some Melanesian cultures. It is *fenua* in Maohi Nui,[1] *fanua* in Samoa,[2] *fonua* in Tonga, and *hanua* in the

---

1. Maohi Nui (Great People) is the indigenous name for French Polynesia. Tahiti is just one of many islands.
2. See the discussion of the Samoan understanding by Iutisone Salevao in the first volume of the Earth Bible (Salevao 2000: 221-25).

Solomon Islands, to name just a few. Micronesians have told me that although they do not have the same word, they have similar cultural sentiments regarding land. According to Fijian theologian and church leader Sevati Tuwere, as a symbol, *vanua*'s 'place in the overall worldview of the Fijian people cannot be over-emphasized' (1992: vii). Fijian anthropologist Asesela Ravuvu says *vanua* has physical, social and cultural connotations (1987: 14). Physically, it refers to a person's village, district or country, including farmland, forest, fishing grounds, and all the birds, animals, vegetation and physical elements of the place (Tuwere 1992: 20). Socially, *vanua* can refer to all Fijians or meetings of various smaller groups. The people are referred to as '*lewe ni vanua* (the inner part of the land). Without the people, the *vanua* is like a body without a soul' (Tuwere 1992: 21). Culturally, *vanua* also refers to the beliefs, values and practices of people of a particular place or Fiji as a whole. The spirits of ancestors and ancestral gods are present and active in the land. These have power and can bring bless-ing or curse depending on whether or not a community lives accord-ing to the beliefs, values and practices of the *vanua*. In my experience, natural events such as cyclones can be interpreted as the result of human sin or injustice. *Vanua* 'can refer alternatively to the social and physical environments, or to the supernatural world, or to all the elements which make life occur' (Ravuvu 1987: 15). Unlike Western dualisms that separate God, humanity and Earth, all things are active, interrelated and interdependent in their support of the life of the *vanua* and thus can be active in resistance to injustice.

As reflected in the Fijian concept of *vanua*, the cultures of Oceania place a greater emphasis on communicating than does the dominant global culture. During Ravuvu's eight months of fieldwork in Fijian villages he observed the 'frequent, almost continual, occurrence of ceremonial events' (1987: 3) that consumed considerable time, effort and resources (1987: 329-35). These ceremonies emphasize co-opera-tion, mutual support and kinship ties in the *vanua*.

Moreover, this kinship and mutuality includes Earth. Ancestors and ancestral gods are in the land and many ancestral gods or totems are flora or fauna. The Fijian myth of origins, recounted by both Tuwere (1992: 29-36) and Ravuvu (1987: 263-68), like *vanua*, exhibits a remark-able absence of the dualisms that are the ideological basis of European exploitation of women, indigenous people and Earth. The original, ancestral god of the Fijians is Ratu-mai-Bulu (Chief from Earth) or Ratu-mai-Bula (Chief from Life). The naming of the original, ancestral god 'Chief from Earth' and the interchange of 'Earth' and 'life' indi-cate that Earth is the source of life. Ratu-mai-Bulu is part snake and part human. In the myth, Ratu-mai-Bulu gives birth to human twins who in turn give birth to sea snake twins. The mother and sea snake twins hide in Earth and turn into plants and trees that become the main ancestors of Fijians. Gods, humans, snakes, trees and plants intermingle. The dualisms of god–human, human–animal, human–nature are absent and replaced by intermingling and kinship within Earth community. This is similar to the ecojustice principle of interconnectedness, but goes beyond an understanding of ecological interconnectedness to a personal feeling of identification and relationship.

While these cultural beliefs and practices do not necessarily prevent Pacific Islanders from exploiting the environment, they do give them a feeling of kinship with Earth that can function in resistance to exploitation. Tuwere quotes Sanaila of Levuka, Wailevu, as saying

> land for me is like a mother. When the soil is thrown carelessly all over the place when one has already dug a wild yam, it hurts because it is part of me (1992: 23).

Abraham Toroi from Bougainville told me that local people's shock and horror at the destruction caused by the large open-pit mine was one of the reasons for the civil war in Bougainville. The cognate of *vanua* in many Pacific languages means 'womb' and is connected to the belief that Earth is our mother. Celine Hoiore of Maohi Nui told me that in the debate over French nuclear testing, the reason people gave for opposing underground nuclear testing was that they should not treat their mother that way: 'We would never sell our mother'. The Tahitian church played a significant role in opposing nuclear testing, and the churches, through the Pacific Conference of Churches, have been united in their opposition to nuclear testing. The churches have been active on other environmental issues such as mining, logging and global warming. Given the general passivity and deference to authority of Polynesian cultures, I think this political activism on environmental issues indicates the affinity Pacific Islanders have for Earth. The traditional Pacific understanding of Earth community, thus, has significant similarities to ecological science's understanding of the web of life and provides resources for resisting environmental destruction.

My intention is not to idealize Fijian culture. As both Tuwere and Ravuvu note, the *vanua* is patriarchal. Colonial and neo-colonial discourse, however, tends to emphasize positive aspects of the dominant culture and negative aspects of the subject culture. My intention is to counter this tendency by affirming positive aspects of Fijian culture that are similar to the ecojustice principles of the Earth Bible Project. Thus Earth has intrinsic worth because gods and ancestors are in

vanua and gods, ancestors, people, flora and fauna are mutually interrelated and interdependent in their support of life. Earth is also a living
subject and able to communicate and resist evil. In the sections of the
paper that follow, therefore, a *vanua* reading of Psalm 104 notices first,
God in Earth and as Earth; second, Earth as alive, interconnected, interdependent and intrinsically valuable; and third, Earth as able to raise
its voice in celebration of life and in resistance to exploitation.

God in Earth

The separation of God from nature intrinsic to much Western theology has facilitated the colonization of women, indigenous people and
Earth. With characteristic clarity C.S. Lewis expresses the traditional
separation when he says:

> To say that God created Nature, while it brings God and Nature into
> relation, also separates them. What makes and what is made must be
> two, not one. Thus the doctrine of Creation in one sense empties Nature
> of divinity (1958: 80).

According to Lynn White (1967: 191): 'For nearly two millennia
Christian missionaries have been chopping down sacred groves, which
are idolatrous because they assume spirit in nature'. Removing divinity from nature 'made it possible to exploit nature in a mood of indifference to the feelings of natural objects' (1967: 189).

This separation of God from nature seems in practice to have been
inadequate for Fijians. According to Ravuvu:

> The Christian God is referred to by the people as *kalou vakayalo* (spiri-
> tual god) and is…invoked for spiritual benefits generally such as being
> admitted to the afterlife Kingdom of God. The ancestral gods referred to
> as *kalou vakalago* (temporal or bodily god) continue to be placated for
> temporal advantage, and are represented in the person of a chief among
> his [or her] people (1987: 258).

He goes on to describe temporal 'advantage' as 'prosperity and fertility' (1987: 258). Fijians consider the Christian God supreme because
of 'the technology, power and knowledge of the West', and Christian
ministers 'denounce the chief's relationship with the ancestral gods'
(Ravuvu 1987: 255). In the ceremonies Ravuvu documents, participants pray to both the Christian God and ancestral gods. They refer to

> the ancestral house platforms (*yavutu*) where the ancestral gods (*Kalou
> vu*) are still believed to dwell. Being close at hand, and accessible to
> their worshippers, their cooperation and assistance are sought, and they
> are placated so the wishes of the people may be fulfilled (1987: 254).

One of the reasons for the continued functioning of traditional religions is that ancestral gods are more accessible and present in the *vanua*.

Biblical scholars have long recognized Israel's extensive borrowing of Canaanite mythic patterns (Albright 1968: 159-68). Some have declared this imagery secondary because of its 'foreign' origin (von Rad 1984: 61). The tendency was to contrast Canaanite nature religions with Israel's historical faith. This interpretation rests on a Western dualistic separation of God and nature, and nature and history. A case could equally well be made on the basis of texts such as Psalm 104 that Israel recognized and accepted wisdom and revelation in the indigenous Canaanite understandings of the presence of God in Earth.

Scholars recognize ancient Near Eastern influence on various parts of Psalm 104. Jörg Jeremias points to thunder as the voice of God in Ps. 104.7 and the trembling of Earth in Ps. 104.35 as examples of what he calls a 'storm theophany' (1977: 19-24). In addition, storm imagery for God seems especially prevalent in the first strophe (Ps. 104.1-4). God is wrapped in light (Ps. 104.2), has a chariot made of clouds and rides on the wings of the winds (Ps. 104.3). Hermann Gunkel (1895: 91-99) included Psalm 104 as evidence in the Hebrew Bible of the influence of the Mesopotamian myth *Enuma Elish*, which he called a *Chaoskampf* (battle against chaos). More recently, Hans-Joachim Kraus labels the second strophe (Ps. 104.5-9) 'conquest of the primeval flood' (1989) and cites the work of Otto Eissfeldt (1953). In the central part of Psalm 104, scholars have also noticed similarities to the Egyptian hymn to the sun and the encyclopaedic lists of Egyptian natural science (Kraus 1989: 298).

One of the benefits of the work of Frank Moore Cross is that he perceived an ancient Canaanite mythic pattern (1973: 162) that ties many of these elements together. Elsewhere I have argued that this Canaanite mythic pattern comes into Israel in a tradition that is identifiable in a large number of psalms and other passages by its consistent genre, language and religious function (Walker-Jones 1991: 54-112). The tradition appears first in victory songs[3] and then spreads to hymns such as Psalm 104[4] and other genres[5] (Walker-Jones 1991: 87-100). While space does not permit an explanation of this tradition-historical analysis in its entirety, the language and content can be outlined in three parts as follows:

---

3.   Exod. 15; Judg. 5; Ps. 18.7-15. For similar texts see also Ps. 68.7-9; Deut. 33.2; Hab. 3.3-5.

4.   Pss. 8.4; 104.7-8; 114.3-4.

5.   Pss. 24.2; 46.7b; 76.3-8; 89.9-12; 74.12-17; 114.5-8; 77.16-20.

1. March. The divine warrior approaches from a place, accom-
    panied by the divine assembly and portrayed as a thunder-
    storm. Thunder is God's voice and lightning bolts are God's
    arrows. God rides on clouds accompanied by light, fire and
    rains. Earth and mountains shake.
2. Battle. God comes against the historical enemies of Israel,
    especially in early poetry and Zion theology, and the mytho-
    logical enemies Sea, rivers, many waters, Leviathan, Rahab,
    Tannin, and the deep. God's rebuke (*gᵉr*) scatters sea and
    mountains.
3. Monarchy. God as monarch founds (*ysd*) and establishes (*kwn*)
    Earth. God's presence in the divine temple on the divine
    mountain causes Earth to respond with fertility (Walker-Jones
    1991: 66).

The language and pattern of this tradition are present in Psalm 104.
God appears as a storm god 'wrapped in light' and riding on clouds
and winds (Ps. 104.2-3). Flame and fire[6] are God's servants. Flame and
Fire are minor gods in the Canaanite pantheon that here appear as
part of the divine assembly. Thus Ps. 104.1-5 contains typical elements
of the 'march' in the above outline of the tradition. Ps. 104.5-9 contains
typical elements of the second movement in the pattern, the 'battle'.
The deep and the waters cover Earth. They flee from God's rebuke
(*gᵉr*) and thunderous voice. The third part of the pattern is mentioned
in the introduction to this second strophe. God has founded (*ysd*)
Earth. The last strophe, Ps. 104.31-35, returns to the first part of the
pattern in the mention of the Earth trembling and mountains smoking.
The central three strophes of Psalm 104 are a lengthy expansion of one
aspect of the third part of the pattern—fertility. An important point to
note in relation to the use of Fijian wisdom for interpretation is that
Psalm 104 itself makes use of indigenous theology. The language and
pattern of this ancient myth structure Psalm 104.

The violence of this mythic pattern in its ancient Near Eastern forms
is foreign to the ecojustice principle of mutual custodianship and makes
one suspicious of the ideological uses to which it might be put in both
the ancient and modern worlds. In Mesopotamia, the god Marduk
defeats and butchers the mother goddess Tiamat to make the parts of

---

6.   The MT 'a flaming fire' is problematic because the gender of 'flame' does
not match the normal gender of 'fire' and singular 'flaming fire' does not agree
with the plural 'his servants'. Commentators either understand this as asyndeton
(Dahood 1970: 35) or suggest that a waw (and) has dropped out (Kraus 1989: 297).
In either case the translation is then 'fire and flame'.

the world. In Canaan, the god Baal defeats the god Sea in order to establish his rule and the fertility of the land. In Babylon and Canaan the mythic pattern legitimated monarchy, empire and Asiatic modes of production that exploited peasants and land for the benefit of the nobility. The monarch, as the representative of the god, established order and fertility. In the Hebrew Bible the mythic pattern becomes part of the ideological justification for the monarchy. This link is clear in Psalm 18 where a monarch gives thanks for the storm god intervening against enemies of the monarchy and in Ps. 89.25 where the hand of the monarch rules over the waters of chaos. These ancient ideological uses should make us suspicious of contemporary uses to which the pattern might be put. Modern European culture continues to have imperial ambitions even in the neo-colonial era and often sees itself as at war with Earth. I recently saw an advertisement from an agricultural magazine that showed a military tank pulling a herbicide sprayer with the following caption: 'it's war out there'. A god's conquest of a part of nature that is designated as evil and chaotic, the sea or serpents, easily legitimates human conquest of an Earth that is perceived as chaotic and evil. In contrast, as the Fijian myth of origins indicates, Fijians consider sea snakes their ancestors, and allow their children to play with them even though they are deadly poisonous. Moreover, while Pacific Islanders recognize the ugly moods of the sea, they are at home on the sea and value it as a daily source of food essential for life.

It is significant then that in Psalm 104 monarch and war are noticeably absent. This contrasts with other uses of the tradition that are clearly associated with the earthly monarch or God as monarch. Moreover, Sea and Leviathan are not the primeval enemies of God and humanity as in some biblical texts (Ps. 74.14; Isa. 27.1). Leviathan is a fellow creature made to laugh and play.[7] In Ps. 104.7-9, the picture of the deep scrambling up mountains and down valleys to get back behind the line God has set between land and sea could be humorous. Far from dangerous dragons, Leviathan and the deep seem to be frisky pets in need of training. Traditional Western interpretations, influenced by a dualistic separation between God and Earth, have tended to hear this transformation of the tradition as a reflection of the power of God; an ecological interpretation may, however, hear in this variation of the tradition a closer, friendlier relationship within Earth community.

---

7.   NRSV has 'sport'. The Hebrew word can mean play, laugh, dance.

While the monarchy and war are noticeably absent, the centre and largest part of the psalm (Ps. 104.10-30) is dedicated to fertility and life. The rainstorm God waters Earth (Ps. 104.10-13). Claus Westermann has argued that salvation as a theme in the Bible has been emphasized to the neglect of blessing. Concretely, blessing refers to fertility, but more broadly to everything that contributes to prosperity and success. Whereas salvation speaks of singular interventions by God, blessing speaks of ongoing, providential care by God (Westermann 1978: 3-4). Psalm 104 celebrates the providential care of God—the provision of water, food, shelter and the spirit of life—that Fijian culture finds lacking in Western Christianity. Towards the end of this central part of Psalm 104, God is also present in Earth as spirit (Moltmann 1985).

> When you take away their breath (*ruach*), they perish.
> And to their dust they return.
> When you send forth your spirit (*ruach*), they are created.
> And you renew the face of the land (Ps. 104.29b-30; translation mine).

If death is not viewed as something evil,[8] but as a natural part of the cycle of life, then it is possible to see here a reference to God's involvement in the cycle of life. The same Hebrew word *ruach* is used both of the 'breath' of all creatures and the 'spirit' of God. God and creatures share the same breath, the same spirit. The cycles of seasons and generations are like the inhaling and exhaling of God. Although the principles of the Earth Bible intentionally avoid God language, one of the reasons for the intrinsic worth of Earth in both Fijian culture and Psalm 104 is the presence of God or gods in Earth. In Psalm 104 God is present in Earth as spirit providing blessing, fertility and life.

In some ways Psalm 104 reverses the curse of Gen. 3.14-19.[9] In Gen. 3.14 the serpent crawls on its belly, eats dust, and is at odds with humanity, but in Ps. 104.26 the serpent Leviathan is created to play in the ocean.[10] In Gen. 3.17 the land is cursed because of humanity, but in Ps. 104.30 the face of the land is renewed. In Gen. 3.17-18 the land produces thorns and thistles and humanity has to work and sweat just

---

8.   Death causes 'worry' for creatures (v. 29a) but that does not have to mean that it is evil. Anxiety about death is a natural part of the desire for life, but life also requires the death of the old to make way for the new.

9.   I would like to thank Norman Habel for the suggestion that Psalm 104 reverses the curse and for his many other editorial suggestions that have greatly improved this paper.

10. Gen. 3.14 speaks of a *nachash* (serpent) and Ps. 104.26 speaks of *liwᵉyātān* (Leviathan), but Isa. 27.1 calls Leviathan a serpent (*nachash*).

to get food, but in Psalm 104 earth produces plants to serve up food, wine and oil for humanity's enjoyment. In Gen. 3.19 humans die and return to the dust of the land, but in Ps. 104.30 the same spirit (*ruach*) that brooded over the creation in Gen. 1.2 now creates (*br'*) each new generation and renews the face of the land.

If we ask when this psalm in its present form was most likely written, the Babylonian exile comes to mind. Much similar Earth theology seems to come from this period.[11] Having come from arid hill country to the fertile lands around the Tigris and Euphrates rivers, the Israelites would have been impressed by the fertility, abundance and goodness of the land. The psalm celebrates this goodness. Against the Babylonian imperial claims that their technology and their gods were the source of this goodness, Psalm 104 claims that the presence of Israel's God in the land is the source of all life.

In addition to speaking of God's presence in the Earth, this ancient mythic pattern also uses Earth metaphors to speak of God. The guiding ecojustice principles of the Earth Bible Project (Earth Bible Team 2000) do not address metaphors for God. Feminists have critiqued male images for God as patriarchal and sought to recover female images for God from the Bible and elsewhere. Similarly, I would suggest that the predominance of human images for God is anthropocentric, rests on European dualisms, and supports the exploitation of Earth. McFague's view that every metaphor 'is and is not true' (McFague 1982: 19) suggests that anthropomorphic metaphors are untrue in some ways and natural metaphors are true in some ways. At the very least the rainstorm metaphor in this psalm speaks of God's presence in Earth, providing the water and food that sustain life.

Earth is Alive

Earth, with its diverse cast of characters, is a central actor in Psalm 104; humanity has only a bit part. The name of God occurs only twice at the beginning of the psalm (Ps. 104.1), once in the centre (Ps. 104.24) and seven times in the final section (Ps. 104.31-35). In the centre of Psalm 104, while God is the unnamed subject of some of the verbs, Earth, or parts of Earth, is often the subject of the verbs and clauses. Earth thus becomes a major actor in the drama.

---

11. Gen. 1 and Second Isaiah come to mind. I use Earth theology rather than the more common Creation theology because 'Creation' has separated God from the Earth and we need at this point in our history to ask whether these texts actually speak of God's presence in Earth.

In the Fijian worldview human beings belong to the land. Accord-ing to Tuwere:

> One does not own the land: the land owns him. [Humanity] and land are one. [They] derive [their] name and therefore [their] basic constitu-tion as...human being[s] from the *vanua* which means both turf and people. 'Title' reverses this: the land belongs to [human beings]. [Hu-man beings have their] title and therefore the *right* to use it in any way [they] want. Herein lies the basic difference between the Fijian view of the land and the European (1992: 34; original altered to make text inclusive).

Personally, I am suspicious of the Earth Bible's principle of mutual custodianship (Earth Bible Team 2000: 50). Like ecofeminist Heather Eaton (2000: 69), I fear that mutual custodianship is stewardship in sheep's clothing. The principle is, however, a movement in the right direction and is similar to a Fijian understanding of Earth. Humans bring *vanua* to life, but they belong to *vanua*. The land needs them and they need the land. They are dependent on the land for identity and life.

Contrary to the principle of mutual custodianship, the relationship between Earth and humanity is not mutual in Psalm 104. First, Earth has no need of humans as partners and humanity has no special role as custodian. Unlike Gen. 1.26-29, here there is no mention of creation in the image of God, no special, royal role, no dominion. Humanity is not created in the image of God. Humanity is just one among many species and plays a small part in the sweep of the psalm. In the second section (Ps. 104.10-15), where three of the five or six references to humanity occur, humanity is clearly dependent on Earth. A chiasmus defines and structures this section.

```
wild animals
        in the mountains
                birds in branches
                        Earth satisfied
                                grass for animals
                                        bread,[12] oil
                                        bread, wine
                                but plants for people
                        trees satisfied
                birds in trees
        in the mountains
wild animals
```

12. NRSV has 'food' here, but the Hebrew word is the same as is later trans-lated 'bread'.

The *geographical* movement of the form and content of the poetry is indicated by the above arrangement of the chiasmus in the form of a V or valley. The poetry moves from the mountains down into the wadis and valleys and then back up into the mountains. Rain falls in the mountains to quench the thirst of wild animals, birds and trees, then flows into the valleys to irrigate plants for animals and people. The poetry then climbs back up the trees and mountains that provide homes for birds and wild animals. Humanity shares the valleys with all other animals (Ps. 104.14). The Hebrew word translated 'animals' can refer to wild or domestic animals and collectively to all. Earth provides the food, wine and oil for humanity's physical and mental well-being. Humans are dependent on Earth.

Moreover, Earth and many of its inhabitants have independent, intrinsic worth. Humanity is surrounded in the larger structure by birds and wild and remote animals. God and Earth provide water, food and habitats for them independent of human beings. Springs provide water for wild animals and wild asses (Ps. 104.11). Trees provide nesting sites for birds (Ps. 104.12, 17). The mountains provide habitat for wild goats and rock badgers. Much of the flora and fauna that feature in the psalm have little use for humanity. They are wild (Ps. 104.11, 18, 20) and dangerous (Ps. 104.21, 26). All of them are imbued with the spirit of God (Ps. 104.29-30) and cause God to rejoice (Ps. 104.31). Even animals dangerous to humans have intrinsic worth. Lions seek their food from God. In the wisdom of God, lions are nocturnal and humans are diurnal; lions are in their dens when humans are at work. But lions also have their time and God feeds them (Ps. 104.19-23). Similarly, Leviathan is not a primeval monster, but was created by God to laugh and play in the sea. Even dangerous animals and sea serpents have a time and a place and thus a right to exist. The picture the poetry paints is like the Chinese prints inspired by Buddhist spirituality in which humanity is a small part of an impressive landscape. Humanity is part of a much larger landscape in which all parts have intrinsic value.

According to James Lovelock (1982), the way in which the complex interactions of the atmosphere, oceans and living things all combine into one organic system whose balance supports life is best understood not mechanically, but as a large organism, a living planet. Psalm 104 paints a similar picture of Earth. First, Earth is alive. Winds are messengers and fire and flames are servants (Ps. 104.4). Springs water wild animals (Ps. 104.11). Birds sing (Ps. 104.12). Earth is satisfied (Ps. 104.13) and makes grass sprout for cattle and herbs for humanity

(Ps. 104.14). The trees are satisfied (Ps. 104.16).[13] Birds build nests (Ps. 104.17). Mountains belong to goats (Ps. 104.18). Forest animals creep out at night and lions pray to God for their food (Ps. 104.20-21). The sun knows when to set (Ps. 104.19). Like the animals of the forest, sea creatures wait on God who provides their food on time (Ps. 104.27). All of them worry when God is hidden and they perish (Ps. 104.29). Earth trembles (Ps. 104.32). Earth is full of living things; all things considered animate or inanimate, including Earth itself, are alive.

Moreover, the repeated elements of the poem create connections and relationships that are suggestive of modern ecology's understanding of the web of life. For example, water, essential for life, flows through Psalm 104. God appears as a thunderstorm in the first section and sets a boundary so that the waters of the ocean will not flood Earth (Ps. 104.1-9). In the second section (Ps. 104.10-18), God provides springs in the valleys (Ps. 104.10) and rain in the mountains (Ps. 104.13). In the fourth section (Ps. 104.24-30), the sea abounds with life (Ps. 104.25). Especially in an arid climate, water would have been perceived as essential for life. Springs provide water for wild animals (Ps. 104.11). Earth that is satisfied with rain makes grass and plants grow (Ps. 104.14).[14] These provide food for cattle and people (Ps. 104.14). Water satisfies trees (Ps. 104.16) that in turn provide nests for birds (Ps. 104.17). The mountains also provide habitat for wild goats and rock badgers (Ps. 104.18). Although only select species are mentioned, the emphasis of the poetry is clearly on the number and diversity of species. Earth is 'full' of 'all' the 'manifold' creatures (Ps. 104.24). These are 'innumerable'. They are 'both small and great' (Ps. 104.27). The emphasis is on the number and diversity of species. The repetitions that tie Psalm 104 together, therefore, are suggestive of a diverse, interdependent and interconnected Earth community.

Earth Celebrates

Praying, feasting and singing are characteristic of the frequent community ceremonies in Fijian villages mentioned by Ravuvu in the first section of this paper. Community celebrations are characteristic of

13. That the trees are the subjects of an active Hebrew verb is obscured by the NRSV translation 'are watered'.

14. Most translations and commentaries take God as the subject of the participle so that God brings forth grass and herbs. This would agree with hymnic participles elsewhere in the psalm where God is the subject. However, Earth could also be the subject. This would agree with Genesis where Earth 'puts forth' vegetation (1.10) and brings forth living creations (1.24).

Fijian culture and Pacific cultures generally. A *vanua* reading of Psalm 104, therefore, notices the celebration by and of Earth community that builds to a climax at the end of the psalm.

In the central section of the psalm (Ps. 104.10-30), eating and drinking are recurring themes, and prayer and celebration anticipate the praise of the final section. Gushing springs quench the thirst of wild animals. Water satisfies Earth. Plants provide food for people and animals. God fills all creatures with good things. In Ps. 104.21 lions pray to God for their food and in Ps. 104.27 all creatures pray for their food.

Beauty, humour and celebration accompany this prayer and feasting, and anticipate the final section of the psalm. Within the structure of the poem, Ps. 104.12 seems to be purely aesthetic. It paints an idyllic picture of birds singing in tree branches that arch over streams of water. The singing of the birds foreshadows the praise of God at the end of the psalm. In Ps. 104.15, food, oil and wine from Earth make people happy. They strengthen and gladden human hearts and make their faces shine. Even Leviathan laughs and plays in the sea.

The end of Psalm 104 erupts in an imperative call to praise (Westermann 1981: 122-35). This final section (Ps. 104.31-35) is replete with jussives, cohortatives and an imperative. The second and third person verbs of the central section give way to first person verbs. Who is the 'I' of this final strophe? Since Earth with its numerous and diverse inhabitants is the main character in the psalm, the 'I' could be the voice of the Earth. Or, at least, in the context, the 'I' is a person who speaks on behalf of the abundant and diverse life of Earth community. Earth calls on God to join in the celebration in Ps. 104.31. Ps. 104.31 asks God to 'rejoice' in Earth and in Ps. 104.34 Earth 'rejoices' in God. An Earth community that includes God rejoices together.

The 'works' celebrated in Ps. 104.31 pick up an earlier exclamation of praise for God's 'works' in Ps. 104.24. In the context of Psalm 104, God's 'works' (Ps. 104.31) are God's provision of water, food, homes, and the rhythms of night and day, work and rest (Ps. 104.10-23). The 'works' of God are the creation of numerous, diverse species (Ps. 104.25). These works include creatures that are threatening to humans, such as lions and Leviathan, and the natural cycles of death and renewal (Ps. 104.29-30). In this context, the 'sinners' of the final verse are those who would block or kill the abundant life and beauty of which the poem speaks. God and Earth sing together a song that rejoices in abundant life and resists exploitation.

In summary, both Fijian culture and Psalm 104 speak to the ecojustice principles of the Earth Bible Project in a number of ways. First,

Western dualisms between God and nature, and humanity and nature, are noticeably absent. In the concept of *Vanua* and in the Fijian myth of origins, gods, humans, plants and animals are all interrelated and interdependent. Similarly, in Psalm 104 humans are one aspect of Earth community, a dependent part of Earth. Rather than separating God from nature, Psalm 104 uses an indigenous tradition: God as rainstorm provides water, food, fertility, blessing, joy and life in Earth. The tradition is considerably less violent and hierarchical than in other biblical and ancient Near Eastern forms, and in several ways reverses the 'curse' of Genesis 3. All this indicates a friendlier relationship with Earth. Second, the Fijian understanding of people as the soul of the land and dependent on land for life and identity is similar to the principle of mutual custodianship. Psalm 104, however, has no custodial role for humans and focuses instead on their psychological and physical dependence on Earth. Third, the intrinsic value of Earth in Fijian culture and Psalm 104 is in part due to the presence of God, or gods, in Earth. In addition, Earth is neither background nor object but an organic, living, central subject of Psalm 104. Fourth, both Fijian society and Psalm 104 speak of the interconnectedness of all things in different ways. In Fijian culture this is expressed in terms of community and kinship. In Psalm 104 an Earth community that includes God shares the same water and the same divine spirit and celebrates together. Fifth, in both Fijian culture and Psalm 104, Earth is capable of speaking and resists human injustice. In the context of Psalm 104, the 'I' of the final strophe is Earth community celebrating all that supports life and calling for the removal of 'sinners' who exploit and kill Earth community. Thus, indigenous wisdoms, ancient and modern, can help us move beyond Western, dualistic readings towards Earth readings of Psalm 104 that recognize Earth community breathing, drinking, eating, praying and singing together.

The Survival of Earth: An African Reading of Psalm 104

Abotchie Ntreh

Introduction

In this paper, I plan to demonstrate that when Psalm 104 is read from a predominantly African perspective, the psalm reveals an impulse and a call for the survival of Earth. This perspective also reflects the principle of mutual custodianship affirmed by the Earth Bible Project: Earth and members of Earth community, including humans, are to take care of each other according to the laws of interdependency implanted in creation and recognized by traditional African societies. If this principle had been followed in the past, life on Earth would continue to be richly satisfying for all creatures.

This paper also claims that collaboration between a minority view in Africa and a Western concept of 'civilization' has tended to over-power traditional African views of Earth to the detriment of Mother Earth and human life in it. It is still possible to say, however, that as long as humans continue to live on planet Earth, it is not too late to amend the way we treat Earth and foster the survival of all species. This paper, therefore, is a call back to the ancient biofriendly values of our forebears as a way to reverse the deterioration of Earth and all living things on it. This call, I would argue, is evoked by the impulses of Psalm 104 and is consistent with the principles of the Earth Bible Project.

The Majesty of God in Creation (Psalm 104.1-4)

Africans believe that Earth is the creation of God. They extend glori-ous appellations to God in praise of God's creative activity. Most of these appellations are the same as those showered on the king as a representative of God. What is showered on the king is actually meant for the one he represents—God.

Apart from the common belief among many African peoples that God created light, the sun and the moon, many African societies see the sun as the manifestation of God in person. John S. Mbiti pointed out that for many African people the words for God and sun are the same: the name *Ruwa*, among the Chagga of Tanzania; We among the peoples of the Ashanti hinterland of Ghana and Ivory Coast; *Chein* among the Luo of Kenya; and *Kazooba* among the Ankore of Uganda. The Nandi of Kenya use *Asis* for God and *asista* for sun. Other African societies ascribe divinity to the sun (Mbiti 1989: 52). Thus the expression 'wrapped in light as with a garment' (Ps. 104.2a) may be understood as a manifestation of God's power, eminence and nature.

Among most African peoples God is the source of light (Mbiti 1989: 4). This is not surprising since God is closely associated with the sun. Mbiti writes: 'The Nuer and Shona believe that God is revealed or manifested in lightning'. The association is so close that the Bambuti of the Congo, the Banyarwanda of Rwanda, and the Igbo and the Yoruba of Nigeria accord lightning divine status (Mbiti 1989: 53-54). From an African perspective, the expression 'wrapped in light' may refer to the fact that just as a human being cannot look at the sun with the naked eye, so God is incomprehensible to humans except when God is made known in the visible light that the human eye can tolerate.

According to the psalmist, YHWH stretches out the heavens like a tent (Ps. 104.2). Many Africans hold the view that the heavens were the first to be created by God (Mbiti 1989: 54). Among some African societies, the names for God are associated with the heavens. For example, one Shona name for God is 'the Great One of the Sky'; another is 'the One above'; a Tiv name for God, *Aondo*, means 'heavens, sky' (Mbiti 1989: 54). The heavens are perceived as God's dwelling place. This is also true of Ga cosmology, in which the immortal God is believed to be dwelling in the sky and mortal humans on the Earth (Kilson 1971: 135; Mbiti 1989: 52, 95). In this ideology there is a separation between the sky and Earth.

The waters that surround the heavens—the source of floods feared in Mesopotamian myths (Eichrodt 1967: 93)—become, in this psalm, the place where God locates the beams of chambers. Who can establish beams on waters? Only a God whose ways are incomprehensible! God not only establishes the beams of palatial chambers on the heavenly waters above; God also rides the clouds and winds that bring these heavenly waters to rain down on Earth (Ps. 104.3).

Wind and fire are identified as messengers or servants of God. This idea is common among African peoples (Mbiti 1989: 32). It is understandable that the wind is said to be a messenger of God, since rain is normally preceded by winds. Fire is called a 'minister of God' by this psalmist (Ps. 104.4), like a person in God's service to achieve God's

purposes. Some Africans see the fire in lightning as that which God
uses to achieve destructive purposes when angry (Mbiti 1989: 52).

YHWH is Lord Over the Waters (Psalm 104.5-9)

If the first stanza of this psalm focuses on the God's creative actuality,
the rest of the psalm emphasizes the survival or securing of Earth. In
creation, God places Earth on its foundations and makes it secure.
Earth is not hanging precariously in space; rather, like a solid building
that is properly planned and built, God sets Earth on its foundations.
So Earth cannot be shaken. This idea has been recognized as parallel
to Mesopotamian and Egyptian thought (Weiser 1962: 66; Toombs 1971:
290-91).

This perspective is a little different from the general African worldview. However, the foundations can be understood to refer to boundaries on Earth. The Hebrew word *mākôn* means a fixed or established
foundation, place or site (Exod. 15.17; Ezra 2.68). This being so, it is
possible to understand this section of the psalm from the African perspective that lands are fixed territories. Members of a community are
identified by the fact that the land of their abode has been fixed for
them by God and is not to be sold. Not only must Earth be secure for
life to continue, but lands as the core of Earth are to be fixed for the
good of the Earth community.

The point also needs to be made that the Hebrew word *'ereṣ*, 'Earth',
can also be translated as 'land'. Land (a piece of Earth) is seen as fixed
for families, clans and people, and is never to be sold without consent
to those outside the family or clan or people to which it belongs. Land
can only be alienated with the consent of its heirs. This is the way that
harmony is preserved among members of a given group of people.
This practice is also a way of ensuring that the Earth is not shaken;
that is, peace is maintained (Beattie 1968: 192; Fortes 1987: 248-49;
Shorter 1973: 26-27; Boulaga 1981: 182; Whiteman 1984: 215). The
Earth can be shaken, however, if territorial boundaries are not respected. Changes to the land-tenure system in Africa that make land
an economic commodity are a threat to the fixed boundaries for peoples and communities. When land becomes an economic commodity,
African people feel the foundations of Earth have been shaken.

According to the Tallensi of northern Ghana, the created Earth is
alive. Fortes writes: 'The Earth is impersonal, but "alive" (*bonvor*), that
is, a controlling agency in the lives of men [*sic*]' (Fortes 1987: 255). If
the Earth is 'alive' then it stands to reason that it can be 'killed'. After
God created Earth as a living entity, God covered Earth with the deep

—the sea of the abyss. In the Genesis account of creation, the deep is seen as already existing before creation and may be viewed as opposed to God's creative activity, and a threat to the life of Earth. Here, however, the deep is at the mercy of God. It is a tool in the hand of God. It poses no threat to God.

The assertion that the 'waters stood above the mountain' suggests that the sky above the mountain is pregnant with water—that is, mountains are seen as the source of rain. God assigned mountains as the locus from where rains originate for the good of creation. This water, which may have been perceived in the ancient Near East as a force that threatens the stability of the Earth, is here seen as a valued creation of God whose activities are contained: God determines the limits beyond which the waters cannot go. If God does not set limits these waters could again flood Earth. The flow of these waters is in response to God's dictates (Anderson 1981: 720-21). The survival of Earth is a priority of God.

The psalmist also announces that 'at the sound of your thunder they take to flight' (Ps. 104.7). In most African societies God's voice is heard in the sound of the thunder (Kilson 1971: 138); some African societies perceive the thunder as divine (Bascom 1969: 84; Mbiti 1989: 53). Most Africans believe that when God speaks no one can respond (Kilson 1971: 137-39). What the psalm teaches here is that at the sound of the thunder, the waters (rain) above the mountains flee. This may be a reference to the thunder that immediately precedes the falling rain. At God's bidding the rains are no longer a threat to human life. In this sense, then, God uses thunder to command the rainwaters that can cause destruction to flee to their assigned place. Most African peoples regard rain as one of the greatest gifts of God for humanity. God's purpose for rain is the preservation—not the destruction—of Earth.

YHWH Sustains Earth (Psalm 104.10-18)

Ps. 104.10 declares: 'You make springs gush forth in the valley'. According to the Ga of Ghana, after God had created the sky, God created Earth and the waters that run on this Earth; these waters are all gathered together into rivers and ultimately make the sea (Kilson 1971: 60). When God gives humanity that greatest gift of rain (Ps. 104.13), it fills the valleys. This supply of rain is seen as one of the most important activities of God (Mbiti 1989: 41, 47). This rain is in contrast to the destructive waters that flee in response to God's voice in the thunder. So when humans are in need of rainwater they pray to God for it (Mbiti 1989: 32). Sometimes religious specialists in this field pray on behalf of the entire community. Rainmakers are recognized in most African communities as people who can bring the will of God into fruition by bringing rain to communities (Wagner 1978: 211, 220). Water then seems to gush forth in the valley when it rains on tops of mountains.

The Ga and the Nuer associate the rainwater so closely with God that they say God is falling in the rain (Mbiti 1989: 53; Kilson 1971: 59). It has also been seen in modern environmental studies that clean water is essential to the survival of life (Turner 1970: 49; Kraft 1996: 29). The rivers that are filled by the rainwater also become a means of transport. When travellers come to a river they take some of the water from the river and offer it as sacrifice to God (Mbiti 1989: 78). Water sources also support agriculture and fisheries in Africa. This happens when the rain refreshes the streams and waters the land. It brings food to the freshwater fish and rejuvenates vegetation that supports animal and human life. The forest and the rocks in the mountain also become the habitat for some birds and animals (Ps. 104.18). Thus the life cycle is set in motion and sustained by the falling of rain.

The rainwater softens the soil and renews the forest. It also becomes the source of water supply for all the animals that live in the forests along the valley. The foliage of the forest becomes the home for all sorts of birds. Plants also yield their produce as food for animals. Food plants, animals and birds are also intended for human consumption. Thus by the gift of rain the whole cycle of life on the Earth is perpetuated: each part of the cycle is dependent on other parts for survival. All this is possible because the rules of nature that God has ordained involve patterns of interdependency. In this process life is ordered and perpetuated. Living things are given their various strategies for existing and their roles in preserving life on—and with—Earth. The psalmist, and indeed the African peoples, want us to realize that human life is intertwined with plant life, animal life and more. All parts of Earth—the entire Earth community—are mutually interdependent.

The forests help to preserve the water-bodies. Traditionally, it was thought that spirits dwelt in rivers and streams. Thus, African peoples were taught not to tamper with the domain of the spirits (Mbiti 1989: 84). Among most African peoples some forests are designated as sacred groves. Thus they are the preserve of God and religious functionaries. In this way such forests are preserved from common usage. The same is true of places that are believed to be the abode of the divine. The consequence of contravening this belief was inimical to human life and comfort. However, with the advent of 'civilization' on the African continent, this African worldview was branded primitive and superstitious. Thus Africans learned to give up this notion. This Western view was also reinforced by other African maxims that seem to support the beliefs of the colonists. For example, the Akan of Ghana say that:

> It is the human being that counts;
> I call upon gold, it answers not;
> I call upon cloth, it answers not;
> it is the human being that counts (Gyekye 1996: 25).

These factors have caused African peoples to violate the taboos that they once used to protect animals and the environment. However, the long-term effects are there for all to see. These water-bodies give drink to animals and humans. The trees along these water-bodies become the homes of the birds and animals. Some of these birds and animals become food for humans. A break in this interplay between plant, animal and human life is a break in the survival of all these lives.

When God no longer sends the gift of rain to Earth, as God used to do, this is understood as a consequence of the violation of the laws of God in living interchangeably with plants and animals. This is so because traditional African peoples, like the psalmist, see everything in the light of their relationship to God and God's laws of interaction among living things. Therefore in times of drought, the Africans call on rainmakers to seek help from God to bring rain. These rainmakers and other religious functionaries turn to God for a more effective performance of their duties (Mbiti 1989: 72). They make propitiatory sacrifices to God on behalf of the people; God listens to the rainmakers when the wrongs committed by humans have been corrected.

YHWH Orders the Heavenly Bodies (Psalm 104.19-23)

In Psalm 104 the psalmist stresses that God does not only take an interest in the small things—God is also interested in the heavenly bodies (Weiser 1962: 668-69). The psalmist elaborates on the way God ordered the heavenly bodies. As in the creation story in Genesis 1, the moon is perceived as having been given the function of helping humans to determine the seasons. The moon is also perceived as a child of God. Thus just as African children do what their parents want, so the moon, as God's child, acts according to the bidding of God. Again, among the Balese of the Congo, 'the moon is God's left eye'; and the Nuer believe that 'God shines through or in the moon'; others, like the Banyoro of Uganda, the Bushmen of South Africa and the Katab and Kagoro of Nigeria, 'hold religious ceremonies monthly, especially when a new moon appears' (Mbiti 1989: 52). When the new moon appears, the Ga of Ghana exclaim that life will continue as a result of it. Thus the moon has a very important place in the life of African peoples. The moon signifies the continuity of life and marks the seasons and times.

The same is true of the sun. The psalmist goes on to say that the sun knows its time for setting. The sun is seen as another child of God. If the moon is God's left eye then the sun is the right eye (Mbiti 1989: 47, 52).

Together with the moon, the sun determines seasons and times for which activities have to be performed. We know that the proper amount of sunshine is important for the normal growth of food crops and even for the survival of life on Earth. Thus the sun and the moon are not independent bodies that do whatever they like. As God's children, they are messengers or servants. They do that which God expects. The sun gives light in the day and the moon gives light in the night. By God's design the day is normally used by humans with the light of the sun and animals come out in the night (Ps. 104.20). It does seem to be God's design for humans to do their work during the day, in the light of the sun (cf. Ps. 127.2). This is the period during which humans are able to see their way to do their work. It seems that this duration within which humans are to do their work is enough for their survival. In this way humans coexist with wild animals. Animals also preserve themselves from humans who may be ready to hunt them for food. This is one strategy God has instilled in nature to help preserve animal species (Ps. 104.20-23).

In this process even the wild beasts of the forests may not find it easy to get their prey. They frighten their prey by roaring. This is the way they seem to seek their food from God. According to the psalmist, it seems, work was not meant to be perpetual; it was not meant to produce food for export. However, with economic demands for certain food items from certain sections of Earth, work periods and patterns have changed. This causes humans to continue to work unceasingly, and Earth is given no rest: humans continuously exploit the resources of Earth. This is bad for Earth in many ways. It depletes Earth of nutrients. This forces humans to resort to the use of chemical fertilizers that tend to be detrimental to Earth.

Consistent with this idea of preservation of animal life on Earth is the idea of taboo and totem. Long before modern science began to talk about preservation of plant and animal species, Africans have been preserving both through the notion of totems. Some African peoples regard certain animals as sacred and therefore do not eat these animals. In totemism, 'social groupings are identified by an emblem or totem, which is often also a food avoidance, sometimes reinforced by magical sanctions' (Shorter 1973: 61-62, 164). The point needs to be made that this is also true of plants and other inanimate objects that are regarded as totems of a group. In this regard the people of the group see themselves in a special kinship relationship with the animal, plant or object in the totemic system. Africans, by this means, protect these animals, plants and objects (see Tylor 1958: 318-24; Beattie 1964: 71, 74; Mbiti 1989: 102; Whiteman 1984: 122). The purpose of this concept has been captured by Ikenga-Methuh in the following words:

> The main objective of an African is to live a life in harmony with humanity and with nature... He [sic] feels himself in intimate rapport and tries to maintain harmonious relationship with the animal, vegetable, and other elements and phenomena in the universe (Ikenga-Methuh 1987: 78).

It is interesting to note that most of the animals or plants that are designated as totems are not prolific in the areas in which such designations are made. If these animals and plants happen to be located in any particular forest, that forest is also designated a sacred grove, because it is the habitation of sacred animals and plants and hence is not accessible to all. This is one way our forebears preserved animals, plants and forests. However, today this way of thinking has been designated as primitive and superstitious. Sadly, most educated Africans have moved away from the ways of our ancestors, to our own detriment and to that of Earth.

YHWH and Creation (Psalm 104.24-30)

In Ps. 104.24-30, the psalmist praises God's marvellous works on Earth, and in the sea. All the living things in the sea, including Leviathan, are said to be God's handiwork. In the ancient Near East, Leviathan was believed to be one of the sea monsters that rivalled God; here this monster is reduced to a plaything of God. This view is very strange for Africans who know no creature can rival God.

African peoples who live by water-bodies believe that there are deities that inhabit these waters. These water-bodies are believed to be presided over by beneficial divinities. Thus they are treated with great reverence. Some of these water divinities are worshipped. However, all these divinities are subject to God. They have appointed priests who perform elaborate rituals for them (Mbiti 1989: 54; Opoku 1978: 60-61). What this means is that Africans who live by the sea abhor any violation of the sanctity of the sea. Some African peoples have sacred days on which they give rest to the sea. On these days, they do not go fishing. By this means the sea is thought of as having an opportunity to replenish itself.

The psalmist sees the expanse of the sea and believes that the living things in it are innumerable. This notion is also present in the minds of most people, including many African peoples, today. Thus they tend to act as if nothing they do can affect the sea and creatures that live in it. With this notion it is not too surprising that when humans learn how to overcome the fear of the monstrous creatures in the sea, they tend to exploit these creatures. Since they are believed to be innumerable, humans do not entertain the notion that they could become extinct. Thus, we exploit all other living things as much as we can, including things of the sea. The point is again stressed that Leviathan, the wild beast that was supposed to be a threat to God, is here seen as a thing with which God plays. This is consonant with the belief of most African peoples that all the creatures of the sea are created by God, and therefore they are all subject to God's tender care and — in this Psalm — may also be present, like Leviathan, for God's enjoyment.

The psalmist says that all the living things of the sea receive their sustenance from God. This is possible because God continues to send forth God's spirit who creates and renews life (Ps. 104.30; Gen. 2.7; Job 12.10; Eichrodt 1967: 48). Since Africans perceive God's presence in all things, when there is a famine or lack of anything, it is taken for granted that a law of God in the life cycle might have been violated. God only turns away in anger when the laws governing the survival of these creatures have been violated. This brings hardship upon all living creatures. Calamities — such as drought, epidemics and floods — seem to be beyond the human activities; they are therefore attributed to God or other spiritual beings. However, this perception is nuanced by the notion that if God causes these calamities then they are God's punishment for human mischief (Mbiti 1989: 44).

To push the issue further, one may then say that human activity is the ultimate reason why such calamities occur. Humans violate the laws of nature and God turns away so that humans are left to face the consequences of their actions. Invariably the view of primal religions is that God does everything. However, since there is this notion of human complicity, it is clear that the problem of survival is also linked to humans and their actions. Since humans have destructive tendencies, it is clear that all living things have to depend on God not only for their sustenance but ultimately also for their survival. However, if humans do not work with God in preserving life on Earth according to God's ecosystems, human survival is itself in jeopardy.

Although human origins are not explicitly discussed in this psalm, it is also clear that when humans die they return to where they came from—Earth (Ps. 104.29). In Gen. 2.7 it is clear that humans are created from the dust of Earth. This is consonant with the African treatment of Earth described earlier. The Ibo of Nigeria regard Earth as a mother and a goddess who gave humans all that they have and without whose gifts they would be lost (Opoku 1978: 57). Thus Mother Earth is the most loved deity and the one who is closest to the people. 'Offerings are also made to her during the planting season and when the fruits are reaped' (Opoku 1978: 58). The Akan of Ghana believe that all humans emerge from the bowels of the Earth and that death is a return to the Earth. Thus before a grave is dug, a libation is poured to ask for permission to dig a hole so that a child of Earth may be buried in her womb (Opoku 1978: 56-57). Thus it is clear that although everything good that comes to humans is ultimately from God, it is through Earth that they are made possible. Our origin, sustenance and ultimate exit depend on Mother Earth. It thus behoves us to treat her with ultimate care so that she reciprocates even more care and benevolence to us. When all this is done in the proper manner, it is possible to give the final praise to God.

An Oath to YHWH (Psalm 104.31-35)

The rest of the psalm is again an acknowledgment of the benevolence of YHWH. God is praised as the king par excellence. God's glory is sung again as it was at the beginning of the psalm. The psalmist ends the psalm in the same manner in which it began. God's power in creation is again resounded. Furthermore, the psalmist prays that God's handiwork should continue in the way in which God meant it to. When humans take a closer look at Earth and the way God has created Earth community to help perpetuate human life, the psalmist asserts that we cannot but praise God. Every living being should show appreciation for what God has done for all creatures. In this section of the psalm the psalmist prays for long life in order to continue to give praise to God; the psalmist believes that only the lips of living persons can praise God—the dead cannot praise God.

The psalmist's desire to see God's will done in the land of the living causes the psalmist to pray for the extinction of the wicked whose actions contradict the dictates of God. This is not merely a prayer of the psalmist. Many traditional African prayers include blessings and curses. The blessings are for well-wishers and the curses for ill-wishers. These curses certainly include banishing and even death, if that is the only way for good to prevail and Earth to survive. It is also a self-fulfilling prayer. If our actions towards and with Earth make God — and Earth—happy, we receive the blessings of God. On the contrary, if our actions are in contrast to God's desires, God—and Earth—may retaliate.

Conclusion

I have highlighted the fact that the predominant traditional views of African peoples concerning Earth are positive and reflect the principle of mutual custodianship: when we take care of Earth it takes care of us. That principle also seems to be reflected in Psalm 104 where we discover God using Earth to care for us. However, 'civilization', together with a few African sayings that promote the belief that human life is the ultimate and the most essential reality on Earth, have distorted the traditional norms and values of African peoples towards Earth, with the result that Earth is continually being destroyed. And the danger is that if the trend continues, life on Earth will be become impossible. I contend, therefore, that Psalm 104 calls us back to the wisdom of our forebears, to learn and to apply their values towards Earth—both for its survival and our own.

Shorter writes:

> every religious outlook must be grounded in a positive attitude towards the natural environment, because it is only this world of nature which can speak to us of a divine order and of a hope of ultimate wholeness... Human beings have their history and their immense technical achievements, but they deceive themselves if they think that these release them from dependence on natural elements. Furthermore, they deceive themselves if they imagine that their own achievements in history reflect innate meanings of nature (Shorter 1985: 21).

To save Earth and ourselves we need to return to the time-tested norms of African traditional religion and the values of Psalm 104, and marry them to the new scientific methods that are ecologically sound.

An Eco*bosadi* Reading of Psalm 127.3-5

Madipoane Masenya (ngwana' Mphahlele)

Introduction

Being born in ancient Israelite and traditional African cultures is tanta-mount to being born in family cultures, cultures that set great store by large family sizes. Children, particularly sons, are highly valued in these cultures. To have many children is to be wealthy. The expression 'sons are a heritage (*nachalah*) from the Lord' (Ps. 127.3) reminds one of the Northern Sotho proverb: *a ba tswalwe ba ate gobane mo-na-le-pelo ga a tsebjwe* (literally: let them be born, let them increase, because one who has a [long] heart is not known). The present article is aimed at re-reading and re-hearing Ps. 127.3-5, informed by my experiences as an African-South African woman who is Earth-conscious. I want to investigate whether the Israelite and African worldviews in terms of procreation and the value placed on children can be empowering for African women if read from an eco*bosadi* perspective.

As a point of departure, I will make a brief comment on what I have termed an 'eco*bosadi* reading'. This will be followed by an analysis of an African (Northern Sotho) and Israelite worldviews regarding procreation and the value placed on children. I prefer to focus on the Northern Sotho context (based in the northernmost part of South Africa) because that is my own context. I will use Ps. 132.3-5 together with some Northern Sotho proverbs as a framework for this analysis. This analysis is done from an eco*bosadi* perspective, taking into account certain ecojustice principles that form the basis for the Earth Bible Project.

A Bosadi *Approach*

In my thesis (1996) I have proposed a *bosadi* (womanhood) approach as one of the appropriate ways of reading the Bible, informed by my experiences as an African-South African woman. A few aspects of this approach are relevant to the discussion that follows. The Northern Sotho word *bosadi* (womanhood) comes from the word *mosadi*, which means a woman, and or a wife (Ziervogel & Mokgokong 1975: 217). The word *mosadi* comes from the root -*sadi*, which has to do with womanhood; the word *bosadi* may be translated as womanhood or the private parts of a woman.

What prompted me to coin a *bosadi* women's liberationist approach was my perception that an African-South African woman's context cannot be successfully described by other frameworks such as feminism and womanism. In my view, most forms of feminism and womanism reflect Western (American) frameworks which cannot *fully* address a different context like mine. Though the *bosadi* framework, like these other frameworks, makes woman the main hermeneutical focus, what makes this approach distinctive is that it addresses a unique context and is committed to an African-South African woman as the 'other' in her unique context. The naming of this approach was also prompted by my concern that for so long Africa and Africans have been defined by others outside our boundaries.

Some Aspects of the (Eco)bosadi Approach

1. The *bosadi* approach acknowledges the uniqueness of the context of African-South African women. This context is characterized by sexism in society and, in African culture, post-apartheid racism and classism. This is also a context characterized by hierarchies. Such a context will shape the way African women interact with the Bible. As a *mosadi* reader reads the biblical text from an eco*bosadi* perspective, she will not only discern the androcentric elements in the text but also the class, race and Earth-demeaning elements. Such elements are critiqued in a liberating way for the marginalized— women and Earth in this instance. The eco*bosadi* approach then acknowledges that women and Earth, unlike the male members of the Earth community, have been traditionally relegated to the realm of the inferior. The approach therefore critiques elements in the Bible that devalue Earth and women and embraces the liberatory traditions.

2. The approach acknowledges the points common to the Israelite and African worldviews. If we acknowledge that both the Israelite and Northern Sotho African worldviews are holistic, we will agree that such an outlook, if taken seriously in our hermeneutical endeavours, can save us from the dualistic Western mentality which has contributed immensely to the historical marginalization of Earth and women.

3. In its analysis of the context of the reader, the *bosadi* approach highlights the significance of the element of faith in the life of an African woman in her encounter with the Bible. Such an analysis is necessary because for many African-South African women, the Bible is not an ordinary book — it is a spiritual resource. An approach to the Bible that combines an element of faith with an element of critique will help readers to be wary of anthropocentric readings of the Bible, readings that have through the years served to cause harm to Earth, the non-male and the non-human members of the Earth community. As the *mosadi* Bible reader interacts with Earth and all its mysteries, an interaction that for her is natural, her faith in God the creator is likely to be deepened.

4. The *bosadi* approach is not only critical of the biblical text, it also criticizes the African culture. The oppressive elements of this culture for Earth and women (such as the worldview that perpetuates large families at all costs) are challenged and resisted, while the positive elements are embraced.

5. For the *mosadi* reader, both the contexts of the biblical text and that of a modern (woman) reader are significant. As part of her context, an African-South African woman cannot exist apart from Earth. She is a woman who has through the years been taught to listen and hear Earth's voice(s). The principle of voice espoused by the Earth Bible is fundamental to her culture. She is a woman who has been taught to understand times and seasons, not through a calendar but through a mastery of the movements of heavenly bodies — stars, sun and moon. She is taught to have a close interaction with the moon as the latter (its shape, direction and distance in relation to the ground) is still believed to have serious connections with her femininity (in the monthly cycle and in birthing).

The following example will suffice to demonstrate women's close links with the moon. The Northern Sotho word for moon, *kgwedi*, is also the word for month. A woman can simply point to the sky and that will be sufficient information to fellow women that she has 'seen the moon', which means that she is menstruating. An expectant woman will know when the pregnancy started, not from the days on the calendar, but in relation to the moon's distance to the ground, its direction and its shape. In the same way, by interpreting the moon's movements, she will know when the baby is due. The traditional Northern Sotho woman, therefore, has a bond with Earth and can actually hear Earth's voices more clearly that her male counterpart. She knows that there are certain taboos to be observed by human beings even as they co-operate with Earth; for example, it is against traditional belief for people to commit 'abominations' on the land (such as throwing a foetus and leaving it to die on the land) or killing certain animals (such as totemic species) that are not supposed to be killed. Such actions, it is believed, cannot be left unpunished. Sometimes if drought is experienced after the violation of such taboos, Earth is seen as acting in retaliation. In the same way, traditionally, only dead trees, not green ones, could be used as wood. In certain instances, if people transgressed against these expectations and chopped green trees, the latter could at times 'retaliate' by releasing poisonous substances! This aspect of African life is consistent with the principle of resistance enunciated in the Earth Bible. The Earth Bible Team (2000: 52) argues that Earth and its components do not suffer passively from the injustices done to them by people 'but actively resist them in the struggle for justice'. A *mosadi* understands that she cannot live apart from Earth and that the other side of the coin also holds true. She participates in the struggle of Earth for justice.

With the above aspects of the *bosadi* perspective in mind, the eco*bosadi* approach can be defined as a perspective for reading the Bible that takes seriously, not only the experiences of the African-South African woman, but also of Earth which, like women, has long been marginalized and oppressed. This approach reads the Bible having taken sides with the oppressed Earth and aiming at its liberation.

The African Worldview on Procreation and the Value Placed on Children

In my Masters dissertation (1989), my analysis of parent–child relationships as portrayed in some proverbs in the Hebrew Bible and the Northern Sotho proverbs, revealed significant similarities between the Israelite and African worldviews, including the value placed on children by both cultures. Children in the Northern Sotho culture are valued as a continuity of the line and for their capacity to take care of their parents when they grow old. An outsider to these cultures may quickly castigate their adherents for not reducing their families, as illustrated in the following quotation from Oduyoye:

> Westerners often see the African woman as a beast of burden walking behind her husband, carrying his children, one inside, one on her back, and many more following in a long procession of children whom she brings forth from puberty to menopause. She is clearly an inferior creature to the Western woman, a person at the bottom of the human pecking ladder (1995: 78).

Before we criticize these cultures from outside, however, we will do well to note with Mbiti (1989) and Oduyoye (1994) that childbearing is one of the sacred activities in African culture. According to Oduyoye (1995: 63-64), in the matrilineal Asante culture, if a woman is childless, the community assumes that the fault is the husband's (in the patrilineal Northern Sotho culture, the first—if not only—suspect is the woman), and they will not allow their daughter to serve a man who cannot enable her to fulfil her role as the channel by means of which the ancestors in the spirit-realm return to join the clan in this realm. Elsewhere, Oduyoye argues:

> For Africans, every new born is an ancestor returned. This belief in reincarnating one's forbears is seen in the principles underlying the naming of new borns (1995: 45).

The belief that parents will be remembered by children after their death is also instrumental in the great value placed on children in African cultures. Hence the high value placed on women as mothers in these cultures.

Women as Mothers in an African-South African Context

In the Northern Sotho culture—as in many societies, both matrilineal and patrilineal—a woman is basically valued as a mother. Though there are very few proverbs which deal with women as mothers, this role is implied in the many proverbs that deal with the care parents (*batswadi*) should give to their children, the discipline (teaching) they must impart to them, and the significance of the parents' influence in the lives of the children (Masenya 1989).

In everyday Northern Sotho culture, a barren woman causes great concern. Measures are taken to address her barrenness (as in the narratives on the barrenness of the matriarchs in the biblical book of Genesis). The following proverb brings this to light: *Teng ga kgomo ga go hlobogwe* (literally: Do not give up on the stomach of a cow). This proverb means that if a woman does not bear a child, she must not be designated as barren; she must be taken to traditional doctors to be attended to so that she will be able to have children like other women (Rakoma 1971: 219).

In some other African tribes, marriage cannot be considered complete unless there are children (Mbiti 1989: 107). Krige (1956: 62) notes that among the Zulus, marriage is considered complete only after the birth of a child. The first child, particularly if it is a boy, is very important to this group. The last point also holds true for Northern Sotho patrilineal family groups.

Commenting on the conceptions of the role of women in Ghanaian proverbs, Amoah (1995: 5-6) observes that women are basically conceived as life-givers and their motherhood role is emphasized. The following proverb throws light on the preceding fact: *a yie* (literally: motherhood is supreme).

Oduyoye (1995: 45) makes an interesting observation about the obsession of the Yoruba people with childbearing: 'Yoruba culture, a patrilineal group, is so obsessed with having children that tales even tell of men becoming pregnant'. The preceding information reveals that Northern Sothos, like their fellow Africans elsewhere, value children highly, as the following proverbs demonstrate:

Go tswala ke go feka maano (literally: to give birth is to devise plans). This proverb asserts that it is a blessing to have one's own children as they will take care of one in old age and in other times of need (Rakoma 1971: 133).

O kgalemetše Morwa' Ngwato-a-šiko, mpheng wa robega selepe se tlo šala (literally: congratulations son of Ngwato-a-šiko! If the handle [of the axe] breaks, the axe will remain). This proverb asserts that children carry on the line and take care of parents in old age, hence it is a blessing to have them.

Northern Sotho women also feel the satisfaction of fulfilling the motherhood role, as the following proverb reveals: *Mosadi a hlaletša ngwana bolwetši bo a fola* (literally: once a woman rocks a child, her illness gets healed). Again, the tenor of this proverb is that once a woman delivers a child, she becomes excited to the extent of forgetting about her troubles and problems. Even if she still has problems, she will be able to cope with them for she will be so satisfied with the gift of a child.

A reaction such as this is understandable in a cultural setting where a woman's status is defined primarily by her ability to be a mother. No room is provided for women who may choose to lead a childless life, nor is room given for women or men who cannot bear or begat children naturally. A marriage in a typical Northern Sotho context would not be allowed to continue without children. One would scarcely find a couple who have reached old age without having children: either the man would opt for polygamy (Oduyoye 1994: 169; Mbiti 1989: 139), or if it was discovered that a man was infertile, a woman would be encouraged to have sexual relations with somebody outside the marriage, preferably her husband's next of kin. Even in cases of the death of a husband, someone from the husband's lineage would be expected to carry on the line of the husband in this culture.

Population, Family Size and the Environment

That the unbridled population explosion is hazardous to Earth and the non-human members of the Earth community now seems self-evident. South Africa provides a sobering example. South Africa is not a big country: 1,221,037 square kilometres in area. The total population of this small country, according to the 1996 census, was 37,859,000. The projected estimate for the year 2001 was 48,904,000 which implies a population growth of more than 10 million in 11 years (World Book Encyclopedia 2000: 609). A racial breakdown of the South African population in 1996 demonstrates the complex nature of the problem: 76% Blacks, 13% Whites, 9% Coloured and 2% Asiatic.

The greater the population explosion, the greater the need for a growing economy. In order to attain the latter, South Africa would have to concentrate on industrial development. The more the population, the more the exploitation of natural resources. The resources and arable land of Earth are both fixed. As the population increases, the resources and arable land do not; as a result Earth is under stress. Industrial development means urbanization. According to World Book Encyclopaedia, it is projected that by the year 2000, 35.7 million people would live in South African cities (compared to the 16.2 million in 1985), meaning that some 750,000 South African Blacks would move to cities every year. In the year 2000, 57 per cent of the Black population lives in cities while 43 per cent of the Black population lives in rural areas (World Book Encyclopedia 2000: 610).

Apart from the fact that 'urban' Earth would be pressured by such a move, industrialization brings other problems, such as environmental and air pollution, which leave Earth sick and depleted. The beauty of nature becomes history as humans, Earth and other non-human members of the Earth community are affected negatively by this state of affairs. The lives of some South African Blacks (in the Northern Cape Province and in the Northern Province) have been destroyed by the pollution from the mining plants which operated in their neighbourhood without any concern for the environmental repercussions. The Western secularist and consumerist worldview, given its individualistic inclinations, brings its own problems. Those with such a worldview (Whites in apartheid South Africa) had no qualms with arrangements such as these, particularly when those (Blacks) who were to suffer were not of their own and not even viewed as being as human as themselves.

Because of the tendency of many human beings to satisfy their desires at all costs, and because of our preparedness to ever ignore the word of the ancestor—*lešaka la pelo ga le tlale* (literally: the kraal of the heart is never satisfied)—we have participated in all these atrocities to Earth, even without noticing them at times! We have failed to realize that we are part of the interconnected systems of the Earth community and that we need to take care of Earth even as it takes care of us, as the Earth Bible principle of mutual custodianship affirms. We have opted to listen to the call of our culture to have as many descendants as we possibly can, forgetting that being responsible parents also means being responsible members of the Earth community and pre-serving its future. Even the move by modern African-South African families to reduce their family sizes is not motivated by our concern to take Earth seriously, but basically by self-centered motives which are influenced by the globalised context.

We need, however, to be reminded that the big family sizes typical of traditional Africa did not have a negative impact on Earth and the non-human members of the Earth community in a pre-colonial Afri-can-South African setting. This was the case because there was ample land for our forefathers and foremothers—lands were allocated to indi-vidual men by idikgashi (chiefs) who were the traditional custodians of the land—for the limited flocks of sheep, cattle, goats and other domestic animals which they needed to live their lives. With the colonial invasions, however, the situation became undesirable for Afri-cans in South Africa because of forced removals and land redistribu-tion. The indigenous peoples of the land were squeezed into infertile areas, some of which were not even good for habitation, while the powerful White minority kept all the good land to themselves. This situation was exacerbated by the fact that in South Africa the distribu-tion of resources in the new capitalist Western economy, with its demanding lifestyle, was based on one's 'race'. One needed to be white in order to benefit from the system. As a result, African values of family and corporeality were undermined by this unfortunate new arrangement and the ecological crisis was heightened.

Psalm 127.3-5 in Context

Scholars are divided regarding the relationship between the two units constituting this psalm: Ps. 127.1-2 and Ps. 127.3-5. Some scholars view these pieces as two independent units while others view them as a unity. Arguing for the unity of the two units, A.A. Anderson (1983: 866) alludes to a Sumerian song dedicated to the goddess Nisaba. The latter is praised as the one without whom no house and no city is built and as the one responsible for growing children. The collocation of these themes reveals that there is no reason to doubt the unity of the two sections (A.A. Anderson 1983: 866). I am also of the opinion that the subject matter of the two sections is related: the word 'house' used in Ps. 127.1 is linked with the core family imagery of Ps. 127.3-5. 'Building a house' can refer to founding a family (Gen. 16.12; 30.3); and raising up a family can be described as building a house (Exod. 1.21; Ruth 4.11; 1 Sam. 2.35; see A.A. Anderson 1983: 866). Even if the word 'house' is understood to refer to an ordinary building in Ps. 127.1, the sons/children mentioned in Ps. 127.3-5 are members of this house, whether within Jerusalem or some other city of ancient Israel.

In my opinion, however, the building of the house in Ps. 127.1, in view of the contents of Ps. 127.3-5, refers to the founding of the family, or more specifically, the father's house (*bet'ab*). Apart from the emphasis on the man/father in Ps. 127.3-5, the father's house in ancient Israel was the fundamental unit of society. According to Ps. 127.1, it is not the father who builds the house, but YHWH. This expression, in my view, implies that the man who builds the house is a righteous one and hence is blessed with sons. Such an argument also makes sense if we classify this psalm as a Wisdom psalm that reflects the optimistic worldview shared by both Israel and Africa (Masenya 1989): good actions are rewarded and bad ones are punished.

A man who trusts in YHWH to found his family will be blessed with *naḥᵃlā*, a term which also carries connotations of land/Earth. If we note with Wright (1979: 102-105) that the family was understood by the Israelites as the mediator of the covenant between God and the people, and that all the other blessings followed pending on a good relationship between the family and God, we may also assume here that the man who is being blessed is a righteous man; he is not only blessed with the sons, but probably also with the land. Since the word *naḥᵃlā* is mostly used for land as an inheritance or entitlement from YHWH, the use of this term for 'sons' may also connote keeping land/Earth in the family.

Camp (1985) argues for the resurgence of the family as the locus of authority in the post-exilic period. A close reading of the passages about Woman Stranger in Proverbs 1–9 reveals a concern that the 'right' or rather 'pure' Israelite female marriage partner was linked with the inheritance of the land/Earth (Blenkinsopp 1991; Washington 1994; Camp 1991).

Just as this text implies—as we try to retrieve its suppressed voices —that the land/Earth played an important role in the life of the post-exilic community, it may also imply the role of woman as house builder. The Woman of Worth in Proverbs 31 highlights not that the father built the house, but that the God-fearing mother played an even more significant role through procreation, nurturing and managing the household activities and commerce. I therefore agree with Meyers that because

> the public record of ancient Israel, like that of traditional societies, is so androcentric, aspects of female power within the Israelite household can rarely be seen. Yet the relative invisibility of female power does not mean it did not exist, and occasionally it can be glimpsed even in the male-oriented canon (1991: 42).

In the Northern Sotho culture, building a house or founding a family also entails being allocated a land of one's own. As in ancient Israel, a newly married son is usually given land within the land occupied by the extended family — the land is so valuable that the two are inseparable. Take land away from Africans and you have taken away their very essence. People in both the Israelite and African cultures understood that if you tampered with their land, you also tampered with their ancestors, as the land is viewed as an ancestral heritage.

The Ecobosadi Debate and Psalm 127.1-3

An important question that we need to ask for the present debate is: how helpful is this obsession with children in the current ecological crisis? Whose interests are being served by such a worldview? How may Bible readers, particularly traditional African readers, under-stand the worldview underlying the contents of Ps. 127.3-5? With regard to the last question, it is obvious that many Africans would identify with the testimony of the psalmist that children, especially sons, are a blessing from God (and the ancestors). The male orien-tation of the psalm is especially evident from the fact that the children whom the psalmist anticipates are specifically male (Ps. 127.3).

Though the Hebrew word *ben* can also be used in an inclusive way as in *bene yisra'el* 'children of Israel', the plural form (*banim* [Holladay 1971: 241; cf. 127.4b] can include both sexes [Ruth 2.21; Job 1.19]), and though the *peri habbeten*, 'the fruit of the womb', which forms a paral-lel pair with *bānîm* (sons) in the first stichos, can possibly be inter-preted to mean children, in my view, the tone and contents of Psalm 127 are heavily, if not exclusively, masculine. Though woman as 'invisible other' can be implied only indirectly through the role she played as mother in ancient Israel and in post-exilic Yehud, she is conspicuous by her invisibility in this psalm. I therefore do not agree with Efthimiadis (1999: 35) that 'Psalm 127.3 celebrates the joy of motherhood by affirming that "children are a heritage of the Lord"'. She also notes that such an affirmation may be negative towards women as the psalm may conjure up the converse: that a woman without children is cursed through some fault of her own. In my view, though the psalm implicitly reflects on the important role women played as mothers in the society of the time, what is celebrated is the joy of fatherhood! Though it is acknowledged that the 'sons' are the fruit of the womb (*peri habbeten*), that this expression can also be translated as the 'fruit of the body' — an inclusive expression — demonstrates that the one who benefits from these fruits is the father.

Even the reasons for viewing the children as blessings serve the interests of the man/father involved: such a man would not be ashamed when confronting his enemies 'in the gate'. These sons, particularly the sons of his youth, will fight for him in the gate when he is old (Briggs and Briggs [eds.] 1969: 458; Buttrick 1955: 670-71). The gate of the city was a public sphere of men. This is the place where the Israelite elders gathered to settle disputes and other matters pertaining to the welfare of the city dwellers. It is interesting to note that though women in public Scriptures such as the Hebrew Bible are not always in the foreground, it is through their influence in the private sphere of the home that their husbands are praised in the city gates. The sons, who were born and nurtured by the mother in the home, are the ones who will support their father in the gates of the city. In Prov. 31.23, the influence of the Woman of Worth in running the household of her husband is ultimately felt in the gates of the city where her husband, not she, is praised. It can therefore be argued that the women subvert the patriarchal status quo by becoming its *necessary* component. The military language used in this text, whether or not the fight to be waged against the enemies was a physical battle, also highlights the male orientation of this pericope.

Another indication of the male orientation of Psalm 127, which corresponds to the worldview of Northern Sotho culture, is the way in which the family line is perpetuated through the male. In such a worldview, little consideration is given to the possibility that the many children who are born are likely to suffer a poor quality of life due to the poor planning on the part of their parents. This is understandable within a worldview in which it is assumed that an older member of the community, such as a parent, cannot offend a younger member, such as a child. Deist's comments in this regard are helpful:

> The traditional moral codes of Africa are transgressed only when someone with a lower social status offends against someone with a higher status, it is not really possible for parents to offend against children.

Therefore the idea that the African idea of an ancestral immortality is
harmful to descendants is not readily acceptable (1990: 45-46).

Such a worldview can also be detrimental to a human being's relationship with Earth. Motivated by their self-centred desire to be
remembered in their offspring, many have chosen to have as many
children as possible irrespective of the negative effects which this
remembrance could have on Earth and the other non-human members
of the Earth community. It should also be borne in mind that in these
cultures—such as the Northern Sotho culture—those ancestors who
are remembered are mostly, if not exclusively, men. Women's marginalization and segregation reach even beyond the grave!

Such a worldview tends to value a woman not basically for who she
is—as a complete human being without a man and children—but
mainly for being instrumental in bearing children, particularly sons,
as a married woman. In ancient Israel barren women, in line with the
expectation of the time, had to provide their husbands with maids for
procreation, a situation reminding us of the Northern Sotho custom
outlined earlier.

Psalm 127.3-5: Procreation and the Value Placed on Children

Though the unity of the two pericopes of the psalm is acknowledged, I
have chosen in this paper to focus on Ps. 127.3-5 due to its similarity in
worldview with the Northern Sotho—one which lends itself to critique
if read from an eco*bosadi* perspective. The whole psalm reminds us
that in all their endeavours, human beings, one of the species in the
Earth community, cannot hope for any success if the creator is left out.

As I noted earlier on, the contents of Ps. 127.3-5 assume an Israelite
worldview supporting the significance of a big family. Such a worldview understandably values women first and foremost as mothers. In
the present psalm, the blessing of children as a heritage from YHWH
is set in the context of the house that is built by God—meaning a
household that trusts God—and the city that is guarded by God.

The value placed on sons as blessings from YHWH is expressed by
the Hebrew word *nachalah* (inheritance/entitlement), which is regularly used to denote the land of Israel as the gift of YHWH (Ps. 105.11;
2 Sam. 20.19; 21.3). As I noted previously, children as a heritage imply
continuity and connectedness with land/Earth. Similarly children,
who are a gift of God, are a strength of the family (A.A. Anderson
1983: 868). Though we cannot deny the importance of sons in families
and in patriarchal cultures in particular, the emphasis on one gender
over and above the other is problematic. Through the years, texts like

these, and many other androcentric texts in the Hebrew Bible — together with the androcentric interpretations of these texts — have been
detrimental to the welfare of the female human members of the Earth
community. From an eco*bosadi* perspective, sons and daughters should
be valued equally as gifts, a heritage (*nachalah*) from YHWH.

The importance of the role of the woman and the need to develop a
large family are illustrated by the following situations. In the period of
the settlement of Canaan, given the precariousness of the situation,
the fact that Israel's population as foreigners in Canaan was far
smaller than that of the indigenous inhabitants of the land, and the
fact that many of their men may have died in battle, make plausible
the claim of Otwell (1977: 40) that the role of woman as mother would
occupy a central position.

In the post-exilic setting, which is the most likely setting in which
the present psalm arose, the elevation in the status of the family — and
a big family at that — would also make sense if we consider again the
precarious conditions of post-exilic Yehud. According to Camp (1985),
in the absence of the monarchy, the family regained power as the
locus of authority in this period. It is no wonder that a book such as
Proverbs — probably originating in the same period — is replete with
female imagery. It is also understandable that in a period such as this,
the role of woman as mother of many children — particularly sons — to
perpetuate the family line would move into the foreground.

It should also be noted that, just as in Africa, early Israelite parents
also desired to be remembered by their descendants. The people
depicted in the Hebrew Scriptures also attached great significance to
the family grave (cf. Gen. 23.19; 25.9; 50.13) and wanted their graves to
be close to their family lands. Joseph insisted that his bones accompany his descendants when the children of Israel left Egypt (Gen.
50.25). The worst fate that could befall the dead was that those who
were still living would forget their names (Job 18.17; Ps. 9.6; 34.17).
According to Deist (1990: 44) this partly explains why the number of
children was a measure of God's favour (Ps. 127.3), why a childless
person was considered already dead (Gen. 30.1), why polygamy (e.g.
Gen. 4.19-24; 16.1; 22.24; 26.34; 28.9; 2 Sam. 3.2-5; 1 Kgs 11.3) was
common, and why anyone who refused to raise progeny for someone
who died childless was considered despicable (Gen. 38). In the light of
all these factors, I agree with Camp (1985: 40) that motherhood played
a crucial role in Israel. Questions worth asking as we conclude are as
follows.

Conclusion

How helpful is a focus on large families for the future of Earth and the non-human members of the Earth community? How did the large families in Israel affect Israel's care for Earth? The mandate of Gen. 1.28 to 'fill' Earth has long been associated with having sufficient children to have dominion over and subdue Earth. We thought we were honouring God by multiplying humans in the image of God (Gen. 1.26-28). Africans, too, have come to embrace this belief. The result is that humans — especially Christians — have abused Earth for centuries. Many African Bible readers are motivated to embrace these potentially destructive traditions because they appear in the Bible, a book that is highly esteemed as a spiritual resource. If, however, we read Psalm 127 from an eco*bosadi* perspective, recognizing the mutual interdependence of woman, children and land, the focus moves from 'filling' Earth to preserving Earth as part of who we are — including recognizing the human family as a heritage of God.

Both the Israelites and Africans place a high value on children: children are a blessing from God. A woman is to be honoured as a co-creator with God in bringing forth children. From an eco*bosadi* point of view, however, the goal of motherhood should not be pursued at all costs. Motherhood should not be viewed primarily in terms of the man involved, but in terms of the descendants, the woman involved and Earth itself which has for so long been oppressed. Mothers and Mother Earth suffer a common abuse from the male drive to multiply children. They are not only interconnected as parts of the web of co-creation, but also as abused creatures in the cycle of misguided procreation.

An eco*bosadi* orientation will enable even a patriarchal society to appreciate that marriage can be successful even if no blood children have been born. Even if there are no children in marriage, it is not necessarily an indication that God has not blessed the marriage or that this is a sign of the ancestors' wrath. It also pleases God when a family devotes full attention to those 'outside' members of the Earth community as an extended family.

The androcentric nature of the Psalm 127 pericope, with the consequent suppression of the voices of Earth and women, can only serve to perpetuate the received belief that some members of the Earth community are more important than others. Such hierarchies have, through the years, contributed significantly to the devaluing of Earth and the marginalization of women, and continue to do so today. The reading of Ps. 127.3-5 from an eco*bosadi* perspective will hopefully bring healing to those who have been trampled upon for so long.

A Prophetic (Fore)Word:
'A Curse Is Devouring Earth' (Isaiah 24.6)

Norman J. Charles

> Earth dries up and withers,
> the world languishes and withers;
> the heavens languish together
> with Earth.
> Earth lies polluted
> under its inhabitants;
> for they have transgressed laws,
> violated the statutes,
> broken the everlasting covenant.
> Therefore a curse devours Earth,
> and its inhabitants suffer for their guilt;
> therefore the inhabitants of Earth dwindle,
> and few people are left (Isa. 24.4-6; NRSV).

With strains of 'Auld Lang Syne' echoing around the world on 31 December 1999, people awaited the dawning of a new millennium with bated breath. Amid stockpiles of non-perishable food items, supplies, batteries and flashlights they waited for the big crash.

From time zone to time zone around the world, the countdown began...3...2...1...and...nothing. No planes fell from the sky; no mass power cuts occurred; no computers self-destructed. Life continued. New Year's Eve had come and gone. The Y2K bug had died at birth. Technology had survived—but at what cost?

Air, water and noise pollution; acid rain; deforestation; clear-cutting;[1] the greenhouse effect; nuclear waste; toxins in the soil, air and water; lead poisoning; mercury-laden fish; holes in the ozone layer; smog in the cities; styrofoam and plastics in the landfills; beer cans at the bottoms of the oceans...the litany continues ad infinitum. In the words of the prophet Isaiah, 'a curse is devouring Earth' (Isa. 24.6).

---

1. In some areas, clear-cutting is better known as clear-felling.

Where now the pristine forests of mighty trees, boles marching on and on? Where now the clear waters of rivers and lakes and brooks and streams? Where now the species of bird and beast and fish and field? Where now the remnants of conquered civilizations, once proud and free First Nations, once prosperous Indigenes in the great circle of life, now languishing beneath the feet of the conqueror? Where now the wise men and wise women, the medicine gatherers and healers, the elders and the warriors, the mothers and the fathers and all my relations? Where now the lovers of Mother Earth, the respecters of creation in whom they lived and moved and had their being? Where now indeed? The juggernaut of progress continues to march across Earth and her orphaned children still pay the price.

Capitalism and communism, commercialism and consumerism—do they not see? What happens to the colonized and marginalized is a harbinger of what will happen to them. The microcosm portends the macrocosm. The fate of the oppressed becomes the fate of the oppressor. What goes around comes around; for 'what ye have sowed, that shall ye reap'.

The tide is not spent; mayhap it can be turned; perhaps it can be stopped. In the Creator's prophetic pronouncements there is always a ray of hope, an opportunity to change the direction of the tide. Will we listen? Will we hear what the Aboriginal peoples have to say? Take heed of Indigenous wisdom? Allow First Nations to speak? There is yet time. There are still some forests standing, there is still some water to drink and some food to eat. Mother Earth may still be healed; if not, she will strike back. The Creator has warned. Prophets have spoken. 'Verily, verily they say unto thee, academics, authors, biblical scholars, ecotheologians: Mother Earth has been cursed. Time to do more than talk about her pain!'

A Spiritual Connection to Earth

Dennis White Bird tells the story that when Turtle Island (North America) was created there was a clay model of a human into which the Creator blew four times. When the figurine came to life, the *Anishinaabe* (people of the land) were given the responsibility of looking after Turtle Island. Each of the nations was given its own territories to care for and to love.

The *Anishinaabe* people were taught to live in harmony with nature and in relationship with Earth. They were taught to respect each other and all things. They not only lived off the land—they lived with the land. They were told to look ahead seven generations. With a notion of circular rather than linear time, they still look ahead to those not yet born.

There are a few interesting points to be made about this Creation legend:

1. The figure was made of clay. Clay is formed by a specific process in which soil and water are blended. A literal translation of *'adam* in the Genesis story of creation is 'red clay'. Human beings come from Earth.
2. The Creator blew into the figure four times. Four is a sacred number in aboriginal cosmology: four directions, four winds, four ribbons, four times offered… Four signifies balance and harmony to North American First Nations.
3. The Creator blew into the figure to give it life. In the Hebrew Old Testament, the Greek New Testament and in many North American Native languages, the word that is translated 'spirit' is also used of wind or breath.

Language is also important to the relationship an Aboriginal person has with the land. In its essence, language is what the land and sky are all about. It is the essence of the *Anishinaabe* individual. 'Our language relates the landscape, both in our spirit and in the land' (Kinew 1996: 36). Expanding on Lakota-woman Elaine Jahner's words about a spiritual landscape existing within the physical landscape, Lopez (1987: 273) writes:

> To put it another way, occasionally one sees something fleeting in the land, a moment when line, color, and movement intensify and something sacred is revealed, leading one to believe that there is another realm of reality corresponding to the physical, but different.

Among aboriginal peoples there is a spiritual connection to the land. It is in the blood; it is in the bones; it is the very source of life. This sacred connection to Mother Earth still underlies the heart of Indigenous wisdom and spirituality.

Who does not appreciate the natural beauty of a sunset reflected in a lake or the sea or the ocean? It does not matter what colour one is or with what race one identifies. With just a nodding acquaintance with the Creator one can appreciate the beauty of creation—it is intrinsic in itself, and it is intrinsic to the people who come from the clay.

A Physical Connection to Earth

Regarding the James Bay Cree, Margaret Sam-Cromarty echoes the words attributed to Chief Seattle when she says that the wisdom of her people teaches that the people belong to Earth, not Earth to the people. Earth is to be cared for, not 'subdued and ravaged for its wealth' (Sam-Cromarty 1996: 104). A practical example of reliance on Earth is provided by Martin and Violet Tuesday when they report that the aboriginal peoples of Lac Seul and Lake St Joseph looked to the land and lakes for their sustenance. They knew the ways of the animal life on Earth and in water. In their hunting, trapping and fishing, the people developed diversification and conservation techniques. Donald Fixico states that the Aboriginal peoples depended on the natural environment and utilized all that Earth provided. From lodges to food to medicines, Native Americans relied on Mother Earth. Their stories, legends and teachings all show that they valued and respected life and its creator.

Reciprocity was an important aspect of this connection to Mother Earth. The Aboriginal peoples thanked the animals they killed for food. They asked permission from the Creator to hunt on land and lake and sea. They offered medicines in exchange for medicines. They did not take more than they could use and they did not waste what they took. They followed game and experienced feast and famine. Even the buffalo harvested in the 'runs' were completely utilized. Extra meat could be used for pemmican which could sustain them for days. Not only did they live off the land, they lived with the land.

The Aboriginal peoples did not have a concept of owning land. They had a notion of communal sharing and caring for the land. They practiced 'commonism' — everything in common. This worldview holds that the land is to be utilized by the community — past, present and future; thus there is an injunction to watch out for future genera-tions. The land also belonged to other living things: the four-legged, many-legged, non-legged, those that stood and those that moved, those that swam and those that flew. Earth was provided by the Creator with everything needed for the sustenance of all life. This is in direct contrast to the Western colonial mentality that has brought the planet to the very eve of destruction. The dawn is now faded, the dusk is at hand.

A Prophetic Connection with Earth

As an example of the way Aboriginal peoples made predictions based on a cyclical, spatial way of thinking, we find the Lakota peoples utilizing powers of observation in the naming of their months: Moon of Frost in the Tepee; Moon of the Dark Red Calf; Moon of the Snow-blind; Moon of the Grass Appearing; Moon when the Ponies Shed;

Moon of Fatness; Moon when the Cherries are Ripe; Moon of Black Cherries; Moon when the Plums are Scarlet; Moon of the Changing Season; Moon of the Falling Leaves; and Moon of the Popping Trees.

By observing their environment, the Lakota could make informed decisions regarding outcomes. All human beings are born with this ability. Prophetic vision is available to all who are willing to observe, to listen, and to learn.

The evidence is all around us. Earth herself cries out for redemption. Earth cannot sustain humanity for more than a century or two. If the rape of Earth for her resources continues at the present rate, the end is much closer than we think.

Norma Kassi notes that the elders say Earth has tilted recently. They noticed that the birds and fish are acting strangely. The salmon have gone up the river to spawn and have turned back. Are they suicidal? Salmon never turn back. The elders have also said that in the wake of the great cleansing that is to come, those who survive will be the ones who are living closest to the land. 'Perhaps, then, we will have learned our lesson' (Kassi 1996: 83).

This is also a prophetic utterance: continue the way we're going and we will either self-destruct or Earth will avenge herself. Either that or we can 'raise awareness, resolve conflicts, and begin the healing process for Mother Earth' (Oakes *et al.* 1998: ix). The choice is ours.

Conclusion

In the beginning, whether in Adamic or aboriginal or another creation story, the Creator gave humanity responsibilities to care for their respective lands. Somewhere along the line, the original attitude of custodianship was replaced by the will to dominate, command and conquer. This led to the holocausts experienced by people around the world, from the Canaanites of old to the aboriginals of the 'New World'. This will to power induced by patriarchal colonial notions of conquest and greed led to genocide for peoples throughout history who had connections to Earth. This conquering mentality and the concept of extraction of resources from Earth for personal and corporate gain has resulted in the environmental problems experienced today around the world.

Noted Aboriginal theologian George Tinker argues that a definition of theological analysis that accommodates people of different languages and cultures is required. He calls for a reversal of the Christian missionary approach that sought to stamp out other peoples' cultures and to assimilate them into the 'mainstream of society'. A more cooperative approach should be utilized. 'Otherwise, the Christian enterprise is forever condemned to perpetrate imperialist acts of colonization and conquest' (Tinker 1996: 155). It is not yet too late. Now is the acceptable time and here is the acceptable place to recreate an environment more favourable to the dawn of yet another millennium, rather than to create an environment favourable to the death of this postmodern age. *Miigwetch!* Thank you!

The Vision of Land in Jeremiah 32

Gunther H. Wittenberg

Introduction

In their book *For the Common Good* Daly and Cobb (1994) investigate and critique the discipline of economics as currently practiced in universities. They deal with, among other things, the role of land in economic theory. They note that there is a widespread lack of attention to land, except in 'land economics', but that 'land economics' subsumes land under property relations—it is one commodity among others (1994: 98-9). They trace the role of land in the history of economic thinking and find that in the writings of eighteenth-century economists land is already considered only an inert and passive factor, not in itself productive (1994: 109). This passivity of land was followed by its exclusion in the nineteenth century from rendering any contribution of value (1994: 110). The final point is reached in Henry C. Carey, who 'argued that the earth is only the material for machines. It represents the farmer's capital' (1994: 110). Daly and Cobb conclude that

> the discipline of economics has come to treat land as a mixture of space and expendable, or easily substitutable, capital. Both are treated as commodities, that is, as subject to exchange in the marketplace and as having their value determined exclusively in this exchange (1994: 111).

In view of the environmental crisis Daly and Cobb demand a paradigm shift in economics (1994: 5) that moves away from the 'widespread modern view that capital can substitute for land, and that consequently the goal of increasing capital can proceed without attention to what is physically happening to the land' (1994: 110). Daly and Cobb believe that there are richer alternatives available for thinking of land in economics and they refer specifically to the 'primal vision of land' as transmitted through the Hebrew Scriptures (1994: 100).

The first element in this vision is the conception that the land was given to the people of Israel by YHWH, and could again be taken away from them if they did not live rightly in the land. Separation from the land was the supreme threat, and being able to dwell in the land forever was the supreme promise. Thus their dwelling in the land, the fulfilment of their hopes, was contingent on their relations both to the land and to their God (1994: 102).

The second element of the vision focuses on the land itself:

> The land was not an inert member of the triad. It bore fruits and gave good gifts. It was to be treated with respect and allowed to cease from work on the Sabbath. It could be described as mourning, or rejoicing, and even as vomiting the people as a result of their numerous sins. The land could be polluted by human sin and require cleansing (1994: 102).

The third element of the vision had to do with Israel's self-understanding. The people understood themselves as 'planted' in the land. Above all they 'dwelt' there. They belonged to, or at least with, the land. They were the people of the land (see Wittenberg 1991). It was home, beloved when they were there, longed for when they were away. Existence separated from the land was incomplete. To dwell in their inheritance forever, faithful to the covenant with YHWH, was for them salvation (Daly and Cobb 1994: 103).

A further important element in this vision was that land was seen as the 'inheritance' of Israel. This did not mean property in the modern sense. The land was entrusted to Israel as long as Israel kept the covenant with YHWH and with the land. Further, the inheritance was personalized. Each family received its inheritance, and was responsible for keeping this inheritance; YHWH held the community as a whole responsible for maintaining an order in which each family preserved and transmitted its inheritance. Stewardship comes closer than ownership to express this relation (1994: 102).

This widely distributed system of land rights had its origin in Israel's early pre-monarchic history, but due to the political and socio-economic developments during the period of the monarchy, especially during the eighth and seventh centuries, it proved more and more difficult to maintain. In this essay I wish to investigate Jeremiah 32, and to explore what effect the greatest disaster in Israel's history, the destruction of Jerusalem and the exile, had on Israel's 'primal vision of land'. I want to see whether in the triad of YHWH, Israel and the land, the land retained its intrinsic worth (second ecojustice principle), and whether the principle of mutual custodianship (fifth ecojustice principle), so central in Israel's primal vision of the land, could be upheld. In the essay I will first of all deal with the structure and literary problems of Jeremiah 32 and then focus on the vision of land in Jeremiah's autobiographical account of his acquisition of his cousin's field at

Anathoth. In the third section I will show how this vision of land has been modified by the Deuteronomistic redaction in the latter part of the chapter. In my concluding remarks I wish to draw out some implications for our own view of land, especially with regard to the ecojustice principles affirmed by the Earth Bible Project.

Structure and Literary Problems in Jeremiah 32

Jeremiah 32 can be roughly subdivided into three sections (Kilpp 1990: 68-70). A fairly detailed introduction (Jer. 32.1-6a) places Jeremiah's purchase of the family plot in the context of an account of Zedekiah's arrest and imprisonment of Jeremiah during the siege of Jerusalem in 588–587 BCE (Carroll 1986: 620). The heading in Jer. 32.1, when cross-referenced with other sections of the tradition (Jer. 34.2-7; 37.5-21; 38.3), reflects a certain inconsistency in the reason given for Jeremiah's arrest (Jer. 32.3; cf. 37.12-16 with 37.21). The narrative style suggests that this section was added later to the autobiographical account in Jer. 32.6b-15. Thiel (1981: 30) sees in it a post-Deuteronomistic addition.

The second section, Jer. 32.6b-15, is generally taken as the oldest part of the tradition. Carroll (1986: 620-22) disagrees. He denies any authenticity to the tradition in Jer. 32.6-15. He takes it as 'a paradigmatic account of how the future was secured by Jeremiah *the prophet'* (1986: 621). But his arguments do not seem to be convincing. The view of Kilpp (1990: 68-70) that an autobiographical account going back to Jeremiah was successively expanded by redactors seems to give the most plausible account of the heavily edited chapter. Verses 6b-15 are, then, probably the kernel of Jeremiah 32. At the same time they are also the most significant because they contain Jeremiah's vision of land, which I want to investigate in greater detail.

The third section of the chapter, Jer. 32.16-44, has long been recognized as belonging to the Deuteronomistic redaction of the book of Jeremiah. Terminology and theological intention show that these verses are an expansion of the autobiographical report in Jer. 32.6-15 (Thiel 1981: 37). Jer. 32.16-25, in the form of a prayer, is really a comment on the oddity that in view of the impending disaster of the city, YHWH can promise a new future. Jer. 32.26-44 contains the answer of YHWH. This passage is a theological reflection on the symbolic action by the prophet reported in Jer. 32.6-15. The last three verses round off the discourse by taking up the promise of Jer. 32.15 again with a characteristic expansion, the significance of which I will analyse below.

Jeremiah's Vision of Land in Jeremiah 32.6b-15

Jeremiah 32.6-7

The introduction to the story in Jer. 32.6a is a rather awkward attempt by the redactor to provide a plausible transition from the third-person account in Jer. 32.1-5 to the autobiographical account by Jeremiah in the first person starting in Jer. 32.6b. Here Jeremiah tells how he received a word from YHWH that his cousin Hanamel would come to offer him family property, because the *mishpaṭ hagge'ullah*, 'the right of redemption', was his. And indeed, this is what happened. His cousin arrived and urged him to 'buy my field', just as he had been forewarned by YHWH. We are not told why Hanamel wanted to sell his field, but he supports his plea by again claiming 'for the right of possession(*mishpat hayerushshah*) and redemption (*ge'ulla*]) is yours' (Jer. 32.8).

Jeremiah is Hanamel's *go'el*. He should become involved on his behalf and help him out of his financial difficulties. The term derives from the realm of Israelite family law. It describes a close relative, a 'kinsman-redeemer', who takes upon himself the duties of *ge'ulla* — 'redemption' or 'recovery'—on behalf of a needy family member (Hubbard 1991: 4). Originally the duty of the *go'el* was to avenge the death of a relative— the so-called 'redeemer or avenger of blood', *go'el haddam* (cf. 2 Sam. 14.11). The stipulations in Num. 35.9-34, Deut. 19.1-13 and Josh. 20.1-9, dealing with asylum, regulate the practice of blood revenge and the institution of the *go'el haddām* is presupposed (Kessler 1992: 141). The concept of *go'el* therefore implies custodianship among blood relations. But it is an indication of the close bond between the Israelite farming community and the land that the institution of *ge'ullah* was extended to the family property as well.[1] Just as there was mutuality in blood relations, there was also mutuality between family and the land because the land itself had intrinsic worth. It nurtured and sustained the family, but the family in turn had to care for the land and to maintain its fertility. The *go'el* was the custodian of the

---

1. Earlier scholars, such as Martin Noth (1962: 110) believed that the institution of 'redemption of family property' was very old and may have gone back to the early post-settlement period, but recent investigations into the background of Hebrew Bible law (cf. esp. Crüsemann 1996) have shown that the stipulations dealing with redemption in Lev. 25 presuppose the social crisis during the latter part of the monarchy in both Israel and Judah (Kessler 1992: 144). See also Hubbard (1991: 6), who believes that these concepts and practices were observed during the monarchy if not earlier.

family, and he was the custodian of the land (fifth ecojustice principle). If a certain family member, due to economic misfortune, was not able to live up to this expectation, the *go'el* had the responsibility to redeem the land in order to maintain the bond between family and land.

I have shown that, according to Daly and Cobb, the concept of 'inheritance' played a central role in the 'primal vision of land' in ancient Israel. A deep religious significance was attached to the family property, its 'inheritance', *nachalah*, or 'possession', *yerushshah*, a term with which it is often linked (cf. Schmid 1971: 778-81). *Nachalah* is the land of the family, the ancestral estate, which in a strict law of inheritance is handed to the descendants and is defined by boundaries which may not be removed.[2] We therefore often find the phrase 'inheritance of the fathers'.[3] The most tangible sign of the close bond that existed between the *nachalah* and the family was the family tomb which linked the present generation with the ancestors.[4] Pedersen (1976: 82) points to the Naboth incident in 1 Kings 21 which highlights the close bond between the Israelite peasant and the land. When King Ahab wanted to buy his vineyard and offered him full compensation in money or an even better vineyard elsewhere, Naboth reacted in great fright: 'Yahweh forbid that I should give you my ancestral inheritance' (1 Kgs 21.3). Naboth cannot part with the property which he has inherited from his fathers without committing sacrilege against himself and his kindred, so closely do kindred and property belong together (Pedersen 1926: 82-83).

The ideal of the social order of Israelite families rooted and attached to the land is clearly enunciated by the prophet Micah: 'a man and his house, a fellow-man and his inheritance' (Mic. 2.2b). Every man of the agricultural community should have enough land to live 'under his vine and under his fig-tree' (1 Kgs 5.5; Mic. 4.4) in order to be able to tend for himself and for his family (Alt 1968: 349).[5]

Due to socio-economic developments during the monarchy, more and more of the Israelite farming community lost their land. The great eighth-century prophets Amos, Micah and Isaiah highlighted the

2.   Deut. 19.14; 27.17; Prov. 22.28; 23.10; cf. De Vaux 1968: 166. The tenth commandment protects the right of the family property; cf. Wittenberg 1978: 3-17.

3.   E.g. Num. 27.7; 36.8; 1 Kgs 21.3-4; Prov. 19.14; Ruth 4.5-10.

4.   Josh. 24.10-32; 1 Sam. 25.1; 1 Kgs 2.34. The deep bond between African tribes and the land that contained their ancestral tombs was demonstrated again and again during the forced removals by the South African apartheid government.

5.   Under the patriarchal system in ancient Israel, in most circumstances only males inherited land.

mechanisms of oppression and exploitation which led to the accumulation of land in the hands of a few landowners, rich grain-merchants and moneylenders residing in the cities. Ancient Israel became more and more part of an exploitative socio-economic system that emanated from the urban centres.[6]

Particularly telling is the Woe Oracle in Isa. 5.8:

> Woe to those who add house to house who join field to field till no space is left and you live alone in the land.

The urban elite controlled the use of the land but did not work the land themselves. This was done by a large labour force of dependent peasants, serfs and slaves. There was no personal attachment to the soil on the part of the landowners, who obtained their wealth through rents and dues extorted from the dependent peasant population, and who 'turned agriculture from village subsistence to mono-cropping for export, forcing peasants to become day laborers on large estates instead of independent farmers' (Daly and Cobb 1994: 102-103). Land had become a saleable commodity, an asset for an early form of capitalism.[7]

In this situation the ancient institution of *ge'ullah* was invoked in order to counter these baneful consequences for the Israelite social order. This is shown by the law on Jubilee in Leviticus 25 in which the root *g'l* occurs altogether seventeen times (Kessler 1992: 143). Two forms of redemption are mentioned: the redemption of family property and the redemption of people who had to sell themselves into slavery on account of debt. Both issues were of course very closely linked in reality. But in Jeremiah 32 Hanamel approaches his cousin only with regard to the redemption of property. He was obviously in great financial difficulties and needed his kinsman-redeemer to avert foreclosure and possibly slavery for debt. The stipulation in Lev. 25.25 can highlight the issue: 'If anyone of your kin falls into difficulty and sells a piece of property, then the next of kin shall come and redeem what the relative has sold'.

There is a certain ambiguity in the understanding of the process of redemption here. Did Hanamel hope that Jeremiah would redeem his property in order to return it to him as the original owner, and not to keep it for himself? This is what Noth assumed (1962: 165-66, cf. also Hubbard 1991: 6-7), but the law is not specific on this issue. Indeed,

---

6.   See Gottwald (1980: 468-70) for the fundamental contrast between the ancient Israelite tribal system based on the countryside and the exploitative political system of Canaanite city states and empires.

7.   The system has been called 'rent capitalism' (Coote 1981: 29).

Pedersen (1976: 84, cf. also Kessler 1992: 145) makes the point that the purpose of the law was not 'that the kinsman should assist the needy by keeping the property *for his person*', but that the property should not pass out of the hand of the family. The regulation reinforces the close bond between the land and the family in the face of mounting pressures on the peasant population leading to alienation of family property and its acquisition by the rich landowning class residing in the cities.

Jeremiah 32.8-14
There is a certain irony in Hanamel's appeal to Jeremiah. In Jer. 11.21-23 the men of Anathoth are represented as seeking Jeremiah's life. His own relatives therefore saw in his prophecy treachery against the nation of Judah. Could Hanamel really expect that Jeremiah now would help him, that family bonds would be stronger than the bitterness engendered by the family quarrel? There were other difficulties in the way of Hanamel's even considering Jeremiah as his kinsman-redeemer. Would he contemplate paying for a piece of property that in all probability he would not be able to care for himself? Jeremiah's imprisonment was also a factor. Would he be able to help even if he had the means? And finally, for whom would he redeem the property? He was not married and had no children—who would in future be custodians of the family land?

We do not know whether these thoughts even crossed Hanamel's mind. He was desperate and needed a redeemer and he turned to his nearest relative. Jeremiah, a prisoner in need of a redeemer himself, agreed to become the redeemer of his relative's land, because in Hanamel's request he heard YHWH speaking to him: 'Then I knew that this was the word of YHWH' (Jer. 32.8). Because YHWH wanted him to redeem the family property, the redemption of land now assumes a far greater significance than the mere financial transaction between two relatives, it becomes a symbol for what God had planned for the people of Israel.

The legal transaction of redemption is described in great detail. In contrast to the terse and concise 'buy!', nine verbs are used to describe how the deal was implemented: 'I bought, I weighed out the money, I signed the deed, sealed it, got witnesses, weighed on scales, took, gave, charged' (Kilpp 1990: 73). The whole transaction is scrupulously observed, a written deed of sale is drawn up with the appropriate witnesses. Jeremiah instructs Baruch ben Neriah, appearing in the tradition for the first time (Carroll 1986: 623), to take care of the deeds, which are placed into a jar to insure their preservation for a long time.

And then in the presence of all the witnesses Jeremiah proclaims the meaning of his action: 'Thus says YHWH of hosts, the God of Israel: Houses and fields and vineyards shall again be bought in this land' (Jer. 32.15).

Jeremiah 32.15
What is the significance of this short proclamation for the future of Israel, and what is the vision of land which emerges in this verse?

1. For Jeremiah there is no future for Israel apart from the land (Diepold 1972: 134). Houses, fields and vineyards belong together. Jeremiah reaffirms the vision already enunciated by Micah that the family belongs together with the land. New life beyond the disaster is only possible on the nourishing and sustaining Earth. This same view is also expressed by Jeremiah in his letter to the exiles in Babylon: 'Build houses and live in them; plant gardens and eat what they produce' (Jer. 29.5).

We find a sequence of building and planting that is characteristic for Jeremiah (cf. Bach 1961) with a significant addition: 'Take wives and have sons and daughters'. Jeremiah gives concrete instructions about actions which directly affect the welfare of the people. It is when people build houses, plant gardens and establish families that the basis is laid for a new hope in YHWH's saving activity in the future. In these very concrete and down-to-earth activities YHWH shows that he has different plans for them, 'plans for welfare and not for harm' (Jer. 29.11).

Jeremiah's vision of new life on the land in Jer. 32.15 is basically the same. Only in the harmony of houses, fields and vineyards, in mutual interdependence is new life assured. The house is the dwelling of the family, the place for rest, work and play. But it cannot be without the field guaranteeing sustenance, and the vineyard that assumes symbolic significance for a full and satisfying life. Fields and vineyards, in short the land, have their intrinsic worth. The land gives new life to wholeness and healing. But just as the land becomes the custodian of the new life, the families need to be the custodians of the land. A central element of this vision is mutual custodianship.

2. The short promise in Jer. 32.15 speaks mainly of the buying of houses, fields and vineyards as the basis of new life on the land in future. One could argue that this promise does not emphasize the intrinsic worth of the land, nor the principle of mutual custodianship. Does the emphasis on the financial transactions not contribute to the commodification of the land? Does the land here not become an object, instead of remaining an independent subject?

In the Deuteronomistic expansion in the remainder of Jeremiah 32, as I shall demonstrate presently, there is a shift that seems to support such an interpretation of Jeremiah's promise. But the promise of the prophet has to be interpreted strictly within the context of the ancient institution of *ge'ullah*. Buying and selling within this context meant restitution. It was the legal means of restoring life on the land to those who were in danger of losing it or who had already lost it. Buying and selling for the sake of restitution are completely different from buying and selling for the sake of the accumulation of land by rich land-owners in the early ancient Near Eastern form of capitalism that made the institution of *ge'ullah* necessary in the first place. Jeremiah's promise deals with restitution, with the restitution of land to individual families and to Israel as a whole.[8] Land in the vision of Jeremiah is not commodity, 'expendable, or easily substitutable, capital' (Daly and Cobb 1994: 111), but it is the nurturing and life-giving ground of all new life for the community in future. Buying and selling are only the enabling agents to make this happen, just as Jeremiah's own payment of money is only a symbol of it, especially as he himself derives no financial benefit from it.

3. Remarkable in this future vision is the complete lack of any reference to the city of Jerusalem. The houses mentioned in the prophecy are not city houses, but are the houses of peasants living on the land and working in their fields and vineyards. Mutual custodianship is implied, not exploitation by an urban elite for profit. The harsh prophecy of judgment against Jerusalem is not annulled. Jeremiah knows that the city will be destroyed. The prophecy for the new future on the land does not necessarily imply a new future for the city. Indeed, the conspicuous absence of any message of hope for the city at the time when the city of Jerusalem was already being besieged by the Babylonians and its capture was imminent makes it probable that Jeremiah did not expect a new future for Jerusalem. Jeremiah's vision was a vision for new life on the land; it was not a vision for the new city. This decidedly rural hope for a new future could not be accepted by the Deuteronomists who appropriated Jeremiah's message during the exilic period. They had to expand and reinterpret it so as to include a

---

8.   The fact that Abraham bought the field of Ephron in Machpelah in order to have a place for the tomb of his wife Sarah (Gen. 23) plays a very significant role in the Priestly narrative. It serves as a powerful symbol in the Priestly message that the exilic community would be restored to the land. Buying the land is simply a means of establishing the bond between Abraham, his descendants and their 'inheritance'.

message of hope for the city of Jerusalem. This is the purpose of the Deuteronomistic expansion in Jer. 32.16-44.

New Hope for the City: Jeremiah 32.16-44

The Deuteronomistic addition in Jer. 32.16-44 can be subdivided into three sections. In the first section (Jer. 32.16-25) the problem is raised which is expressed in Jer. 32.24-25: How can YHWH promise salvation in view of the imminent disaster befalling the city? The answer is given in Jer. 32.26-44: Nothing is too hard for YHWH. This is shown first of all with regard to the judgment which YHWH has brought on the city on account of all the transgressions of the people. But it further leads to the new statement ('now therefore', Jer. 32.36) that states that YHWH will also bring a new future and in which the promise in Jer. 32.15 is taken up and applied to Jerusalem and all its surroundings (Kilpp 1990: 70). The whole passage contains a detailed summary of the Deuteronomistic theology of history. In the following I will only highlight those statements which are of particular significance for the Deuteronomistic view of the land and of the city.

Jeremiah 32.16-25
In Jer. 32.16-25 Jeremiah explains why YHWH should expect him to buy land when the city of Jerusalem is being besieged and about to be taken. But Jeremiah does not answer this question immediately. A great doxology is placed into his mouth dealing with YHWH's long miraculous history with Israel. YHWH, the creator of heaven and Earth, had saved Israel from its bondage in Egypt with great signs and wonders and had given them the land. For the Deuteronomistic editors of Jeremiah (Deuteronomic Jeremiah), the land given to Israel is not an ordinary land, but is the land that has been promised by an oath to the fathers. It is theologically qualified. In contrast to Deuteronomy, the fathers in Deuteronomic Jeremiah are not the patriarchs Abraham, Isaac and Jacob. They do not distinguish between the recipients of the promise and its fulfilment as in Deuteronomy, because the fathers received the oath and they also entered and took possession of the land (Diepold 1972: 158-59). The present generation are identified with the fathers as well. They are partakers of promise, just as they are under the same guilt and judgment. Both are seen together in the formula 'the earth ['*adamah*] that I gave *to them and their ancestors*' (emphasis mine; Jer. 24.10; 25.5; 35.15). The promise is relevant not only for the original generation but also for the present one (Diepold 1972: 159).

Although Deuteronomic Jeremiah seems to have a positive view of the *'adamah*, land has really no value in itself. There is also no recognition of the close bond between the family and the land. In characterizing the land Deuteronomic Jeremiah uses conventional, typically Deuteronomistic formulas. The oath to the fathers is linked with the formula of giving the land 'flowing with milk and honey' (Deut. 11.9; 26.15: Josh. 5.6; Jer. 11.5) (Diepold 1972: 158). The giving of the land is conditional. It is dependent on Israel keeping the commandments. But Israel did not obey YHWH's voice; of all he commanded them to do, they did nothing. Therefore YHWH's punishment had come upon them (Jer. 32.23).

In Jer. 32.24 there is a shift away from the land to the city. 'You, O Lord YHWH, have said to me: "Buy the field for money and get witnesses" — though the city has been given into the hands of the Chaldeans'. This shift seems natural given the situation of the siege of the city, but it is nevertheless significant. From now on the focus is on the fate of the city, no longer on the land.

Jeremiah 32.26-35
In Jer. 32.26-35 YHWH answers Jeremiah's prayer in a lawsuit speech, containing indictment and sentence typical of Deuteronomistic theology. The opening words are set in juxtaposition to the opening words of Jeremiah's prayer (Brueggemann 1977: 128). Jeremiah praised YHWH for his mighty acts in the history of his people with these words:

> Ah Lord Yahweh! It is you who made the heavens and the earth by your great power and by your outstretched arm! *Nothing is too hard for you*... You showed signs and wonders in the land of Egypt... You brought your people Israel out of the land of Egypt...and you gave them this land (Jer. 32.16-22).

YHWH showed that nothing was too hard for him by starting his history with the people. But now he was bringing it to an end. In Jer. 32.27-28 YHWH echoes these words:

> See, I am YHWH, the God of all flesh; *is anything too hard for me?* Therefore, thus says Yahweh, I am going to give the city into the hands of the Chaldeans (emphasis mine).

Brueggemann (1977: 128) understands the beginning and the end of Israel's history in terms of the giving and the taking away of the land:

> Israel does not deal with a safe, predictable, conventional God but with one free to work his purpose. And so this terrifying word *pela'*, 'impossible' is used to assert his freedom against anything taken for granted.

> He does the thing that is too hard. He gives the land to Babylon which
> for so long seemed to belong to Israel.

Although the loss of land may also be implied, the focus of the text is
not the land but the fate of the city. YHWH can not only establish the
city, he can also have it destroyed. 'This city' is mentioned in the text
four times. Its burning by the Chaldeans is accounted for by the long
history of idolatry in Israel and Judah (Carrol 1986: 627) and the disobedience of the kings, princes, priests and prophets to YHWH's commands. Because the city aroused YHWH's anger, he had to destroy it.

Jeremiah 32.36-44

The impossible and unthinkable happened. Jerusalem had been given
into the hands of the Babylonians (Jer. 32.36). The Deuteronomistic
theology of history was an attempt to explain the disaster, and to
show that YHWH's punishment was just (cf. Perlitt 1972). But the burning question for the present was: Was there still hope for the future?
Jer. 32.36-44 seeks to give an answer to this question. Just as bringing
judgment was not impossible for God, so the new future, a new beginning also for the city, was not impossible for God to accomplish.

> See,
> I will gather them…
> I will bring them back to this place…
> I will settle them in safety…
> I will give them one heart…
> I will make an everlasting covenant with them…
> I will put the fear of me in their hearts…
> I will rejoice in doing good to them…
> I will plant them in this land (Jer. 32.37-41).

The new hope for the city consists ultimately in YHWH planting them
again in the land. At this point the editors come back to the motif of
the buying of the field which set their theological reflection in motion
in the first place. The promise in Jer. 32.15 is now repeated but with
characteristic additions:

> Fields shall be bought for money, and deeds shall be signed and sealed
> and witnessed, in the land of Benjamin, in the places around Jerusalem,
> and in the cities of Judah, of the hill country, of the Shephelah, and of
> the Negeb (Jer. 32.44).

It is not a grandiose utopian hope for the future—only a hope for a
return of normal conditions in which the buying of fields, the building
of houses and the planting of vineyards will again be possible (Kilpp
1990: 81). But whereas Jer. 32.15 focuses directly on the land without
any reference to the city, the Deuteronomists see the return to

normality with the city of Jerusalem and the cities of Judah as the focal point. Land is arranged around the cities. It does not seem to have intrinsic worth. We could possibly add: land is the source of life and nourishment for the cities. There is therefore a shift away from the principle of mutual custodianship that was such a central element of Israel's primal vision of land. Is it possible that the city in this vision again becomes the source of the exploitation of the countryside? Could the mechanisms for enslaving the rural population again emanate from the city? We do not know whether the Deuteronomists even contemplated this possibility. But the grievances voiced by the needy Jews (Neh. 5.1-5) complaining to Nehemiah that they had to pledge their fields, vineyards and houses to unscrupulous fellow Jewish citizens show that this danger was a very real one in the early post-exilic period.

Concluding Remarks

Two alternative views of land have emerged from my treatment of Jeremiah 32. The first is urban-based. Rich landowners residing in cities saw land mainly as a means for obtaining rent, that is as a form of capital that could be sold and traded at will. We saw that this view formed the basis of the social crisis in pre-exilic times that necessitated counter-measures such as the Israelite institution of *ge'ullah*, the redemption of family property. The Deuteronomistic hope for the replanting of Israel in the land is also urban-based. Although the land is the land of promise, it has no intrinsic worth, but is there to serve the needs of the city, and the danger that land would again be used for exploitation was very real indeed.

The other vision of land is the 'primal vision of Israel'. In the face of the coming disaster, this view is also maintained and reaffirmed by the prophet Jeremiah. According to this view land and family belong together. Families need the land to sustain them, but the land also needs the toil and labour of the peasant community to care for it and preserve its fertility in mutual custodianship. Land, in this view, has intrinsic worth. It has to be kept in the possession of the family, and to be redeemed from unscrupulous speculators, even if this redemption does not bring direct financial benefits.

It is obvious that for the rethinking of the role of land in economics that Daly and Cobb have demanded, only the second vision of land can make a contribution. The commodification of land, the mechanization of agriculture, the widespread use of fertilizers and chemical pesticides — in short the treatment of land as but an expendable and easily substitutable form of capital—has proceeded from the cities. It is urban-based. Only through a new vision of land, which rediscovers its intrinsic worth, so central in the ancient Israelite view that we also find in Jeremiah, and the close bond between people and land, can a new sense of custodianship be developed, which treats the land not as dead material for personal gain, but as the living Earth which needs to be nurtured and preserved for future generations.

Ezekiel's Formula of Desolation:
Harsh Justice for the Land/Earth

Keith Carley

Introduction

This article calls attention to some difficult concepts in the book of Ezekiel. It has been written not for the sake of provoking controversy but in order to state clearly the danger those concepts represent if they are assumed to convey God's attitude toward Earth correctly or taken as examples of how Earth should be treated on account of human misdeeds.

In an article entitled 'Christianity and the Need for New Vision', McDaniel writes:

> In some instances, of course, biblical literature must itself be transcended. Yet, even a transcendence of biblical thinking is not necessarily unbiblical, for the prophetic strand of biblical thinking points beyond itself... To move beyond biblical modes of thinking...can itself be biblical, if such movements occur in fidelity to the God of love and justice to whom the Bible most persistently points (1986: 204).

Considered in the light of the guiding principles of an ecojustice hermeneutic, there is urgent need to transcend the mode of thinking about Earth in the book of the prophet Ezekiel. For the most part, Earth is the passive object of horrifying maltreatment. The maltreatment is largely meted out by God in the process of punishing human misdeeds. However, Earth is not always portrayed as a passive object in the Ezekiel traditions. At one point God decides to restrain Earth from devouring its inhabitants! But while Earth is sometimes animated, it never speaks up for itself.

As the subtitle of this article suggests, in the book of Ezekiel 'Earth' is often referred to simply as '(the) land', whether it is the land of ancient Israel or Judah,[1] or one of their neighbouring states. Three

---

1. In the book of Ezekiel the phrase 'land of Israel' often refers to the political entity of Judah rather than to the northern state of Israel which was overthrown in 722 BCE. The phrase implies Judah's inheritance of the traditions of all Israelites.

Hebrew words are used for land/Earth in the book of Ezekiel. The
first and most frequent is *'erets*, which most often designates a specific
geographical area, such as 'the land of the Chaldeans' (Ezek. 1.3) or
'the land of merchants' (Ezek. 16.29). *'erets* is also used metaphorically
to designate the inhabitants of a land, as in 'when a land sins' (Ezek.
14.13). Examples of its use to designate Earth in general include 'earth's
most evil nations' (Ezek. 7.21); 'the spirit lifted me up between earth
and heaven' (Ezek. 8.3); 'the kings of the earth' (Ezek. 27.33); and
'sheep scattered over the whole earth' (Ezek. 34.6). However, 'it is not
always easy to determine whether *'erets* means "earth" or "land" in a
given instance' (Ottosson 1974: 393). As Janzen says, the Hebrew
Scriptures 'perceive as continuous what English distinguishes with
the words "earth" or "land, country"' (1992: 245). The second word,
'adamah, often translated 'ground', is nearly always used in Ezekiel in
connection with 'the land of Israel', but the text also uses the phrase
'the face of the earth' (Ezek. 38.20 NRSV). Finally, the word *ya'ar* may
be construed as 'forest land'[2] in Ezek. 20.46-7 (Heb. 21.2-3).

Desolated Land

It is only to be expected that a book as long and complex as that of
Ezekiel should contain diverse conceptions of land. One of the most
prominent, and one that impinges acutely on the issue of the maltreat-
ment of Earth in our own age, is the prophecy that God will make
Earth, or at least significant parts of it, a desolation in order to prove
God's presence and power.

The prophecy is repeated three times in relation to the land of
Israel, twice with respect to the land of Egypt, and again three times in
relation to Edom. Found at the end of accusations against the inhabitants' unjust deeds, God's intention to stretch out a hand may be
reported. Then, in a formulaic expression, it is said: 'I will make the
land a desolation, and they will know that I am the LORD'.

The first occurrence of the formula is in Ezek. 6.14:

> I will stretch out my hand against them, and make the land desolate
> and waste, throughout all their settlements, from the wilderness to
> Riblah. Then they shall know that I am the LORD.

'The land' referred to here is the so-called 'promised' land, to which
God had once led Judah's forebears from slavery in Egypt with an
outstretched arm (Exod. 6.6). The phrase 'desolate and waste' renders

---

2.   So the NRSV. The REB translates 'scrubland', but Zimmerli 'the forest (of
the south)' (1979: 420).

two words derived from the same Hebrew verbal root (*šmm*).[3] Together they seem intended to convey a scene of desolation so horrific as to make one shudder in despair.

Such an image can all too easily be conveyed in terms of our own experience. With the benefit of modern media, we are aware almost daily of scenes of appalling destruction and despair—scenes of widespread earthquake damage perhaps, or of ethnic cleansing that vents unforgiven feuds centuries old; images of forests defoliated by chemical weapons, or of eroding, uninhabited hills where—not long ago—rainforests were home to many species and to human communities.

The image Ezek. 6.14 conveys is that of the eroded desert, and the phrase 'from the desert to Riblah'[4] suggests the whole country was involved. 'The desert' probably marked the southern boundary of Judah in Ezekiel's day, while Riblah was north of the former state of Israel. It was at Riblah that Pharaoh Neco had deposed Judah's king Jehoahaz and appointed Jehoiakim his preferred successor (2 Kgs 23.33-4). It was also at Riblah that Nebuchadnezzar[5] of Babylon executed the leaders of Jerusalem in 587 BCE (2 Kgs 25.6-7, 20-21). So Ezekiel's words intimated the laying waste of all his people's history and hopes, from the desert wanderings after the Exodus through to the utter collapse of such independence as they had had under their judges and monarchs.

As if this was not enough, the prophet goes on to say that the scene of unmitigated disaster was intended to make his people and the surrounding nations know that the God of Israel was present and all-powerful: 'then they will know that I am the LORD'.[6] A similar message is conveyed in Ezek. 12.20: 'the land shall become a desolation; and you shall know that I am the LORD'. These words were addressed to the community of exiles in Babylon as part of the explanation of a symbolic act performed by Ezekiel. The prophet had previously mimed preparations for exile to demonstrate the fate awaiting those who had been left in Jerusalem after Ezekiel and others exiled with him in 597 BCE (Jer. 52.28) had been deported.[7]

---

3.   Technically the words are a hendiadys, which in R.E. Clements' translation of Zimmerli (1979: 182) are rendered 'a terrible waste' and by Richardson (1995: 649) 'horror and dread'.

4.   Reading the variant form 'Riblah' rather than the Hebrew 'Diblah' with numerous commentators; see e.g. Block 1997: 236 n. 91.

5.   Spelt 'Nebuchadrezzar' in the books of Jeremiah and Ezekiel.

6.   The phrase, termed 'the recognition formula', is examined in detail by Zimmerli (1979: 36-40; 1982: 29-98).

7.   On the current debate among scholars as to whether the exile was an

Only the first of the Hebrew words used in Ezek. 6.14 to convey horrifying devastation appears in Ezek. 12.20 and the act of devastation is described impersonally. The meaning is nonetheless clear and severe. And again, the punishment was to be positive proof of God's presence and power. Or, as Block says: 'when the inhabited cities lie in ruins and the land itself is wasted, then they [the exiles] will acknowledge the person and presence of Yahweh' (1997: 383).

The reasons given for these appalling manifestations of God's power are the idolatry and violence of the people. In Ezek. 6.13 allusions are made to the worship of alien gods at unauthorized sanctuaries. The Hebrew word for 'violence' (*chamas*) in Ezek. 12.19 ('their land shall be stripped of all it contains, on account of the violence of all those who live in it') can indicate both verbal and physical maltreatment of people, including minorities and other marginalized members of communities.[8] Weapons may be involved in such acts of violence.

A third example of God rendering the land a horrifying desolation appears in Ezek. 33.28-29:

> I will make the land a desolation and a waste, and its proud might shall come to an end; and the mountains of Israel shall be so desolate that no one will pass through. Then they will know that I am the LORD, when I have made the land a desolation and a waste because of all their abominations that they have committed.

The judgment of Ezek. 33.23-29 relates to those who, despite the forebodings previously conveyed by the prophet, survived the exile of 587 BCE and remained in the land. In Ezek. 33.28-29 the same two words used in Ezek. 6.14 to convey horrifying devastation—'a desolation and a waste'—appear again, twice. The abandonment of the land is prophesied, and once again the scene will be proof of God's presence and power.

The word rendered 'abominations' in Ezek. 33.29 implies that the people had been involved in acts which made them morally and cultically impure. The range of such activities was wide, from forbidden sexual behaviour (Lev. 18.19-30) to dishonest trading practices (Deut. 25.14-16); from consumption of meat from unclean animals, or sacrifice of imperfect animals (Deut. 14.3; 17.1), to offering false testimony in a legal suit (Prov. 6.19). Ezekiel includes idolatry, adultery, intercourse with women in their time of menstruation, robbery, neglect and oppression of the poor, and lending money in order to

historical event or a literary construct, see Grabbe (ed.) 1998.

8.   Cf. BDB 329, where Sarah's harsh treatment of Hagar (Gen. 16.5) is noted as an example.

gain interest, in his classic summaries of unrighteous behaviour (Ezek. 18.10-13; 33.15).

Similar behaviour is mentioned in other passages as reasons for God laying waste the land:

> When the house of Israel lived on their own soil, they defiled it with their ways and their deeds; their conduct in my sight was like the uncleanness of a woman in her menstrual period[9] (Ezek. 36.17).

> The land is full of bloody crimes; the city is full of violence (Ezek. 7.23; cf. 8.17; 9.9).

> 'I will make the land desolate, because they have acted faithlessly', says the Lord God (Ezek. 15.8).

Even the Righteous

Some of these misdeeds are reprehensible, divisive of community and requiring firm correction. But while they may not all seem to threaten devastation of the land and the environment, the punishment about to be meted out by God according to Ezekiel certainly does. There will be war (Ezek. 6.3; 21.8-27); famine, wild beasts and pestilence will ravage the land (Ezek. 7.15; 14.21); there will be drought (Ezek. 22.24), and all that contributes to making a desolated land, emptied of its people. This raises sharply the issue of justice for both the people and Earth in Ezekiel's portrayal of divine recompense.

The issue of justice is raised even more sharply in another passage. Even if the reader of Ezekiel at first assumes that the harsh divine punishment was deserved, in another passage the prophet declares to the land of Israel:

> Thus says the LORD, 'I am against you and I will draw my sword from its scabbard and hew down both righteous and wicked[10] within you' (Ezek. 21.3 [Heb. 21.8]).

It is not only the idolatrous and violent individuals who commit abominations who will suffer when God exacts recompense, but also those who have maintained righteous behaviour!

---

9.   Gottwald points out that 'the *stigmatization of menstruation* as a "blemish" strengthened the *marginalization of women* in cultic and public roles' (1985: 478).

10.   Both the Greek Septuagint and the Aramaic Targum adopt alternative readings at this point. The former renders the equivalent of 'unrighteous and lawless', the latter 'I will exile your righteous from you, in order to destroy your wicked' (Block 1997: 665 n. 41).

Ezek. 21.3 is a passage of Scripture that many people seem not to be consciously aware of, even though they may have read or heard it from time to time in the course of devotions or liturgy. It simply does not register with the force that Ezekiel seems to have intended. As Zimmerli says: 'Yahweh[11] strikes unmercifully... The formulation appears to be in flat contradiction to the statements of Ezek. 18 and also to know nothing of the preservation of a remnant, as Ezek. 9 leads us to expect' (1979: 424). Subconsciously the passage may register in the mind and reinforce the existential despair many people experience about themselves and life in general. It certainly appears to undermine any attempt to live a life consistent with the injunctions of divine teaching. It is also contrary to the broader perspective in the Hebrew Scriptures according to which righteousness was thought to be an attainable state or relationship.[12] Righteousness was no guarantee of protection from divine recompense as Ezekiel perceived things.

In another passage the prophet conveys a divine message apparently in response to a suggestion that the righteousness of a few might deliver the whole nation from judgment. Abraham is reputed to have once argued such a case with God (Gen. 18.22-33). But in Ezekiel the possibility is denied. Even the virtues of such ancient worthies as Noah, Daniel and Job would deliver them alone (Ezek. 14.12-20).

A final allusion to the desolation of Israelite land—so that the activity of God might be recognized—is found in Ezek. 20.45-49 (Heb. 21.1-5). In a passage concerning forest land in the south (the Negeb), Ezekiel prophesied that God would set fire to all the trees until the blazing flames were unquenchable. Then, in words familiar from the formula of devastation, 'all flesh will know [literally 'see'][13] that I am the LORD' (Ezek. 20.48 [Heb. 21.4]).

Such imagery reminds one of the unquenchable fires that have been lit in the forests of Indonesia in recent years, raising pollution to dangerous levels through much of South-East Asia. Rainforests have also been decimated by fire in the Amazon basin to make way for grazing and cash crops—much as happened in Aotearoa/New Zealand at the

---

11.   'YHWH' is the distinctive Israelite name for God, usually rendered in both Jewish and Christian literature as 'the LORD'. Washington outlines reasons for avoiding use of the vocalized Hebrew name out of respect for Jewish tradition (2000: 138-39).

12.   A different dynamic is involved in the perspective of the Apostle Paul: 'all have sinned' (Rom. 3.23), so grace is equally undeserved by all.

13.   *Ra'ah*, 'to see, perceive' is used loosely here for the usual *yada'*, 'to know' of the recognition formula (Zimmerli 1979: 420).

turn of the nineteenth century (Jones 1989: 190-95).[14] Such fires also
recall the scorched-earth policies in which napalm bombing was
employed to 'liberate' parts of Indo-China only a few decades ago.

Other Desolated Lands

It can have been little consolation to the Israelites that Ezekiel also
uttered prophecies of destruction and desolation against the lands of
other people. As in the book of Amos, neighbouring countries are
arraigned one by one — Ammon, Moab, Edom and Philistia in Ezekiel
25, Tyre in Ezekiel 26–28, and Edom again in Ezekiel 35–36. Egypt is
also condemned in Ezekiel 29–32 and among this collection of prophecies against Egypt we twice find the formula that has become familiar:
'the land of Egypt shall be a desolation and a waste. Then they shall
know that I am the LORD'. Thus Ezek. 29.9 prophesies that the land of
Egypt too will be utterly devastated,[15] so that the Egyptians might
also be aware of the presence and power of Israel's God.

Ezek. 32.15 interposes other images in the middle of the formula:
'When I make the land of Egypt desolate and when the land is
stripped of all that fills it, when I strike down all who live in it, then
they shall know that I am the LORD'. But the same Hebrew root we
have found elsewhere (*shmm*) underlies both of the words 'desolate'
and 'stripped'. Both passages relate to perceived Egyptian arrogance
and interference in Judean affairs.

In Ezekiel 35 the formula of desolation is used in relation to Edom
(Mt Seir) three times (Ezek. 35.3-4, 9, 15);[16] Ezek. 35.9 even prophesies
that the land will become a desolation 'forever'. Among the reasons
for the punishment of the Edomites is that they gloated over the desolation of their neighbour Israel:

> As you rejoiced over the inheritance of the house of Israel, because it
> was desolate, so I will deal with you; you shall be desolate, Mount Seir,
> and all Edom, all of it. Then they shall know that I am the LORD (Ezek.
> 35.15).

14. Jones documents 'the theme of the mutilated bush...in which stood the
burnt skeletons of the forest of the past' in the Late Colonial Period, 1890–1935 (my
thanks to a colleague, Dr Allan Davidson, for this reference). Swimme and Berry
report: 'We are extinguishing the rainforests, the most luxuriant life system of the
entire planet, at the rate of an acre each second of each day. Each year we are
destroying a rainforest the size of Oklahoma' (1994: 246).

15. Here nouns from the synonymous verbal roots *chrb* and *shmm* form the
hendiadys; compare n. 3 above.

16. Again words from the Hebrew roots *chrb* and *shmm* are used to signify
desolation.

This is somewhat surprising in view of the fact that God, in another passage, threatens to make Israel an object of derision among its neighbours: 'I will make you a desolation and an object of mocking among the nations round about you... You shall be a mockery and a taunt' (Ezek. 5.14). Moreover, in the verse which precedes that prophecy emphasis is placed on the overwhelming—one might even say disproportionate—recompense required to satisfy God's fury: 'I will satisfy my fury[17] against them, then I will be appeased' (Ezek. 5.13).[18] Again the now familiar chastisements of famine and warfare, plagues of wild beasts and pestilence are to be the weapons of punishment (Ezek. 5.16-17). Earth seems fated to suffer as much from the satisfaction of divine justice as from the jealousies and injustices perpetrated among its inhabitants.

Most readers of this article will be well aware that Ezekiel also received prophecies that—in the case of Israel—reverse these bleak scenarios.[19] But that does little to ameliorate the picture of the wholesale devastation of land and people that appears necessary to satisfy divine justice throughout significant sections of the book. The argument that the passages we have considered are simply examples of prophetic hyperbole[20] scarcely lessens their frightening implications. Whether or not the images of despoiled lands derive in some cases from secondary traditions of the prophecy,[21] and whether or not the prophecies were all fulfilled, a clear impression is given to readers of the book that God may be directly involved in bringing about the destruction of whole lands and their people.

Fear and Retribution

Passages such as we have just considered might well underlie the perception of God described by Nouwen, a highly respected priest and spiritual guide:

---

17. *chemah*, here translated 'fury', is also rendered 'rage, wrath', and found frequently in Ezekiel.

18. The translation here follows Block and the REB. Similar expressions are found in Ezek. 16.42; 21.17 (Heb. 21.22) and 24.13.

19. E.g. Ezek. 20.40-2; 34.25-31; 36.8-12, 22-38; 39.25-9; 40–48 and see below.

20. So Block with respect to Ezek. 21.3 (Heb. 21.8); 'Ezekiel's inclusion of the righteous with the wicked...[is] a deliberately offensive rhetorical device intended to shock' (1997: 669-70).

21. Perhaps from what Zimmerli calls Ezekiel's 'circle of disciples' (1979: 36, 70-74).

> Somehow, God's love for me was limited by my fear of God's power... I know that I share this experience with countless others. I have seen how the fear of becoming subject to God's revenge and punishment has paralysed the mental and emotional lives of many people, independently of their age, religion, or lifestyle. This paralysing fear of God is one of the great human tragedies (1992: 121).

From the point of view of Earth, the example of 'justified' retribution in Ezekiel is not helpful to the cause of ecological responsibility, let alone of peace for individuals or nations. While it might be argued that wholesale devastation of lands and people was not carried out as ruthlessly as Ezekiel envisaged until the twentieth century, we are aware that responsibility for such disasters lies with humankind, not with God. Yet still 'God's will' — or at least 'the demands of justice' — is invoked in local and international disputes.[22] Indeed, we must ask whether accounts of God's behaviour such as are found in Ezekiel do not set a precedent for punitive conflict, from Ireland and the Middle East to the bombings of Iraq and Serbia and Chechnya, with their concomitant 'collateral' damage to the infrastructure of those countries, not to mention the environmental damage done to their neighbours and the whole global ecosystem.

It is not difficult to find apologists for Ezekiel. Block, for instance, argues that Ezek. 6.13-14 offers vivid evidence of 'the impassioned side of God's character... the fury of his judgment arises out of the depths of his anger over covenantal treachery... [But God's] wrath is never so hot that it cancels out his grace' (1997: 239-40). However, such accounts of God's wrath certainly put awareness of God's grace in question, as Nouwen confirms, and they convey implicit approval of environmentally destructive behaviour.

Alternatively, it is often argued that the idea of vengeance in Scripture rarely means 'vindictiveness' or 'revenge' (Harrelson 1962; Pitard 1992). Harrelson comments that the only two uses of the adverb 'revengefully' are found in Ezek. 25.12 and 15, both in reference to the way enemies acted towards Israel. Thus vengeance was understood to be a means of redressing injustice, a 'just punishment meted out to a wrong-doer' (Pitard 1992: 786). However, in the second of the cases cited by Harrelson, the Philistines and Cherethites are charged with having acted vengefully. In response God threatens to execute not

---

22. International organizations based in Geneva report that currently 56 conflicts around the world are linked to religion (Roberts 2000: 12).

simply vengeance but 'great vengeance...with furious[23] rebukes', and to destroy the rest of the seacoast (Ezek. 25.16-17).[24]

Moreover, seen against a broader range of Scripture such a positive assessment of vengeance may be questioned. One of the clearest statements in the Hebrew Scriptures rejecting vengeful responses to human behaviour is found in Hos. 11.9:

> I will not execute my fierce anger; I will not again destroy Ephraim; for I am God and no mortal, the Holy One in your midst, and I will not come in wrath.

'This', Davies argues, 'may be understood to mean that Yahweh as God rises above the human responses of anger and vengeance, and shows mercy instead' (1992: 263). Similarly, Jesus teaches:

> Love your enemies and pray for those who persecute you, so that you may be children of your Father in heaven; for he makes his sun rise on the evil and on the good, and sends rain on the righteous and on the unrighteous (Mt. 5.44-45).

Thus the exercise of vengeance by God—however well intended it may have been in an earlier context—is set aside.[25] God's unconditional benevolence serves as an example for human behaviour towards wrongdoers. In contrast to Ezek. 21.3, both righteous and wicked are blessed!

Harder than Flint

Ezekiel himself began to glimpse something of the astonishing benefi-cence of God in his prophecies of the new heart and spirit (11.19-20; 36.26), in which God *enables* people to live rightly, although a shadow of shame clouds the gracious liberation of human will.

> A new heart I will give you, and a new spirit I will put within you; and I will remove from your body the heart of stone and give you a heart of flesh... [Yet] it is not for your sake that I will act, says the Lord God; let that be known to you. Be ashamed and dismayed for your ways, O house of Israel (Ezek. 36.26, 32).[26]

23. *chemah* is used again; see n. 17.

24. Referring to Ezek. 15.7, Zimmerli (1982: 93) comments on the 'merciless, continuing fury of God's wrath on the people, who had already gone through ravaging fire in 598 BCE'.

25. Lk. 4.18-19 does not include 'the day of vengeance of our God' (NRSV) when it quotes Isa. 61.1-2. The Greek version of Isa. 61.2, from which the quotation is taken, reads: 'the day of repayment/retribution'.

26. See also Ezek. 20.43: even after restoration to the land 'you shall loathe yourselves for all your evil deeds', and Ezek. 39.26, on which see n. 32 below.

The prophecies of restoration envisage cultivated fields where there had been desolation, a veritable Eden (Ezek. 36.34-35), with cities unwalled (Ezek. 38.11)[27] — a sign of confidence and security.

There is, however, no hint within the book of Ezekiel that the prophet himself was concerned about the impact on Earth of the judgments he delivered. His older contemporary, Jeremiah, of whose activity Ezekiel is likely to have known,[28] heard the mourning of the desolated land (Jer. 12.4, 11).[29] But Ezekiel appears to have had feeling only for his wife, and he claimed God told him to suppress every sign of grief even at her death (Ezek. 24.15-17). The prophet's forehead was indeed made 'harder than flint' (Ezek. 3.9).

It is of no little significance that the word most commonly used to designate 'love' in the Hebrew Scriptures[30] — including in such phrases as 'you shall love the LORD your God…[and God] will love you, bless you' (Deut. 6.5; 7.13) — is used in the book of Ezekiel only of sexual love and partners of seduction (e.g. Ezek. 16.37; 23.5). The Hebrew word commonly translated 'mercy, loving-kindness, loyalty' (*chesed*) does not appear at all in Ezekiel. One of the Hebrew words most frequently used to convey 'compassion'[31] is found only in Ezek. 39.25, and the following verse affirms that along with the restoration of God's compassion Israel will continue to bear the burden of shame for its past misdeeds.[32] Two other Hebrew words that are used to signify 'pity' or 'compassion' are each used once to confirm God's pity for the outcast child that Israel had formerly been (*chws*, Ezek. 20.17) and to express concern for the holiness of God's name (*chml*, Ezek. 36.21). But the words are used together in a number of passages to express God's determination neither to have pity nor to show compassion (e.g. Ezek. 5.11; 7.4, 9; 8.18).

The hard countenance of the prophet coheres with the portrayal of God in the book of Ezekiel and its depiction of God's attitude toward

27. Although Ezek. 36.34-35 envisages fortified cities when the desolated places are restored.

28. Carley 1975: 51-57; Zimmerli 1979: 44-46.

29. Cf. Earth Bible Team 2000: 48.

30. '*hb* and its derivatives.

31. *rhm* and its derivatives.

32. Contrary to the NRSV's preferred reading of Ezek. 39.26: 'They shall *forget* their shame', Zimmerli lists compelling evidence for not amending the Masoretic Text: 'They shall *bear* their shame', and observes: 'The thought of earlier sins being "forgotten" is quite unheard of in the book of Ezekiel' (1983: 295, 320).

Earth. Earth has no compassionate advocate in this prophetic tradition.[33]

Earth as a Living Entity

Earth is not extensively or vividly personified in the book of Ezekiel. The reference to 'the whole earth' rejoicing at Edom's demise (Ezek. 35.14) may be understood as a metaphor for the inhabitants of other lands.[34] However, there are some passages in which the land is explicitly distinguished from its inhabitants and Earth may be construed as a living entity. One such passage is found in the lament over the princes of Israel, who are described as young lions in Ezek. 19.1-10. Ezek. 19.7 may be rendered: 'the land was appalled,[35] and all in it, at the sound of his roaring'.

A more natural allusion to land as a living entity is found in Ezek. 34.27: 'the land shall yield her produce'. The context is an anticipated covenant of peace which God will establish for the restored Israelite community (Ezek. 34.25, cf. Hos. 2.18 [Heb. 2.20]). Such a bountiful response from the land was to be expected if the citizens obeyed God's statutes and commandments according to Lev. 26.3-4, which is part of a covenant tradition common to the book of Ezekiel and the so-called 'Holiness Code', Leviticus 17–26.[36] Under the covenant of peace, Ezekiel envisages God giving rain in its due seasons and the land subsequently producing what is needful for the sustenance and security of those who had been punished. That will be a sign of God's presence with the people (Ezek. 34.30).

The most remarkable example of Earth as a living entity is found in Ezek. 36.1-15. The land of Israel[37] is directly addressed. As in Ezek. 34.27, she is to yield produce for God's people as in former times. But the consoling speech goes on: 'they say to you, "You devour human

33. Cf. Habel's portrayal of Job as 'the voice for the wider Earth community' (2001: 65).

34. Cf. Ezek. 14.13: 'when a land sins'.

35. Thus the NRSV. BDB (445) and Clines ([ed.] 1998: 333) assume the word rendered 'appalled' derives from the verb *yshm*; Richardson ([ed.] 1999: 1564) assumes the word derives from the root *shmm*, which we have already found frequently. Brownlee translates: 'Earth and all in it were alarmed' (1986: 294).

36. David P. Wright describes Ezekiel as a 'literary cousin' of both the Holiness school (whose traditions include Lev. 17–26), and the Priestly Torah (1999: 358). Block illustrates the common elements derived from ancient covenant blessings in Lev. 26.4-13 and Ezek. 34.25-30 (1998: 301-307).

37. Specifically its mountains and arable land, Ezek. 36.9.

beings and leave your nation childless"' (Ezek. 36.13). This accusation is voiced by Israel's neighbours and the image is paralleled in Num. 13.32, when most of the spies sent to reconnoitre the promised land 'brought to the Israelites an unfavourable report of the land…[as]…"a land that devours its inhabitants"'.

This malign report of the land appears to Baruch Levine to be an element of the Priestly traditions of the Pentateuch, predicting that the Judeans would be devoured in their place of exile (1993: 358). The book of Ezekiel has numerous links with the Priestly traditions,[38] but in Ezek. 36.14-15 God acts to restore the exiles to the land of Israel and, as we have already seen in the case of Edom, to silence the taunts of other nations against it:

> no longer will you devour people or leave your nation childless… no longer will I let you hear the insults of the nations, no longer shall you bear the disgrace of the peoples…says the Lord GOD (Ezek. 36.14-15).

Suggestions as to what the image of land devouring people signifies include the following: 'that the land was infertile, or unstable, warlike, and unforgiving, or even comparable with Sheol [which could swallow people alive (Prov. 1.12)]' (Ashley 1993: 243).[39] Whatever the explanation, the impression conveyed is of the land acting aggressively against its occupants, and there appears to be, here at least, some evidence of Earth's resistance to injustice.

Is there perhaps also insight here into the natural reaction of Earth to its contemporary desolation—its inability to remain fertile and sustain life when over-cultivated, regularly sprayed with biocidal toxins, even mined and bombed in warfare? Whether this is the case or not, these brief glimpses of Earth as a living entity contrast sharply with the image that is dominant in the book of Ezekiel, of Earth as a passive stage on which the drama of divine retribution for human misdeeds is acted out.

Conclusion

Collins observes that the book of Ecclesiasticus (Sir. 49.9) 'remembers Ezekiel for his visions of the Glory of God, not for his severe condemnations' (1993: 98). But we should not let the condemnations go

---

38. See the works referred to in n. 36 above.

39. Block notes the impersonal nature of the expression 'your nation' in Ezek. 36.13 and suggests the land is portrayed as the owner of the nation that inhabits it. God's intervention (Ezek. 36.14-15) transforms the relationship between land and people and ends the land's appetite for human flesh (1998: 335-36).

unmarked, for they convey a shadow side of God almost as troubling as that conveyed by the enormities of the Holocaust. Dominated as the book of Ezekiel is by the radical dualism of old Israel's total rejection on the one hand[40] and hope centred on the exile community of new heart and spirit (Ezek. 11.19-20; 36.26) on the other, there is profound silence about the suffering Earth undergoes as God punishes its occupants, both righteous and unrighteous. Preoccupation with the vindication of God's honour, particularly the honour of God's holy name (Ezek. 36.20-22),[41] appears to render God oblivious to the fate of Earth—scarcely a positive example of custodianship. Only with the prospect of the newly cleansed and inspired Israel's return to the 'promised land' is the formula of desolation reversed:

> See now, I am for you [O mountains of Israel]; I will turn to you... the towns shall be inhabited and the waste places rebuilt... Then you shall know that I am the LORD.

> On the day that I cleanse you from all your iniquities [O house of Israel], I will cause the towns to be inhabited, and the waste places shall be rebuilt. The land that was desolate shall be tilled, instead of being the desolation that it was in the sight of all who passed by... Then the nations that are left all around you shall know that I, the LORD, have rebuilt the ruined places, and replanted that which was desolate (Ezek. 36.9-11, 33-36).

However unappealing a view of God the book of Ezekiel presents in places, we cannot rewrite the book. Nor should we try to. It stands as a classic portrayal of harsh justice,[42] though also of surprising—if not unqualified—grace. The book serves to remind us that, while justice is essential, it alone is not sufficient to heal Earth or to promote positive environmental values. Whatever the reason for Ezekiel's perception of divine retribution, his prophecies exemplify justice that endangers Earth, setting an unfortunate precedent for environmentally damaging behaviour under the guise of righting injustice. We currently have glaring examples of nations engaging in what they perceive as 'justified' retribution against their opponents, whether trade sanctions as in the case of Iraq and Cuba or outright war as in the case of Chechnya,

---

40. 'Yahweh puts a complete end to Old Israel... The fact that the book of Ezekiel speaks of Jerusalem's punishment in terms of a complete annihilation is thus an essential part of the argument of the book' (Renz 1999: 198-99).

41. 'It is not for your sake, O house of Israel, that I am about to act, but for the sake of my holy name, which you have profaned' (Ezek. 36.22).

42. Justice that fails to uphold the rights of the vulnerable. Support of the vulnerable is a fundamental characteristic of God's justice (Birch 1991: 121, 156).

which result in further oppression of already afflicted lands and people.

Among the glimpses of a living Earth that we find in Ezekiel we have another example of what might appear to be harsh justice, with Earth devouring its own inhabitants. Again, such justice is clearly not able to restore balance to the finely tuned, interdependent relationships that constitute healthy communities and ecosystems. We now know clearly that Earth is a living organism and we might expect from one so ravaged a longing for retribution as demanding and desolating as God's, as it is portrayed in the prophecy. But, while Earth may from time to time appear to 'devour' its inhabitants, now that we understand the principles of plate tectonics, weather patterns, tidal movements, and other such processes that underlie 'natural disasters', we can recognize that these are not 'punishments' exacted by either Earth or God in the manner envisaged by Ezekiel. Moreover, despite human abuse and contamination of the environment, Earth continues to display the generous beneficence of its creative source. Gratitude for this beneficence; a vision of the sacredness of the whole living creation; and faithfulness to the God of love as well as of justice (McDaniel 1986: 204, quoted above) are essential elements of an ecojustice perspective.

If we are to speak up for Earth in the light of its desolation—whether as portrayed by Ezekiel or as evident in the reports of environmental organizations in our own generation—we need to look beyond the book of Ezekiel to see that proof of God's presence and power is demonstrated best in Earth's continuing provision for animate creatures, irrespective of their deserts or status. And despite the continuing—escalating!—pressures exerted upon Earth by humankind (especially its more affluent members), Earth persists—thus far—in sustaining abundant life. May we learn from its example to live in a more sustainable and generous way, so that the whole creation might continue to share that life.

If Earth Could Speak:
The Case of the Mountains against YHWH in Ezekiel 6; 35–36

Kalinda Rose Stevenson

Introduction

Earth takes a beating in the book of Ezekiel; God is the one who does the beating. These intersecting realities plunge us head-first into the heart of a problem. When we read from the perspective of Earth, that vantage point reveals unquestioned assumptions about Earth and our relationship to it. An Earth-centered perspective also raises disconcerting theological questions. We cannot ask about the fate of Earth in Ezekiel[1] without looking at the face of Ezekiel's God.

In a Hans Christian Andersen fairy tale, con artists convince the emperor, his retainers and the citizens of the city that the emperor is wearing marvelous clothing visible only to the good and the wise. Only the small child who speaks the truth cuts through the collective delusion when he announces: 'The emperor has no clothes on'. When we speak the truth about Ezekiel's God, we can see with painful clarity that his God batters Earth.

Does this truth tell us anything about God? Or does it tell us only about the prophet Ezekiel? How can we know the difference? If this is only Ezekiel's God, what do we do with this book as Scripture? Such questions rise to the surface, uninvited, unwanted and unyielding. This short paper makes no effort to explain, justify or dismiss the violence of this book, or to distinguish between the 'real' God and 'Ezekiel's God'. My purpose here is to make the case that the God of Ezekiel fits the profile of a batterer, and that Earth is one of his battered victims.

If this claim seems outrageous, it fits the character of Ezekiel's book. Apparently, much of the book originated in performance art, exaggerated play-acting designed to elicit a response from an audience. Whether or not the prophet Ezekiel succeeded in getting the response

---

1. In this paper, 'Ezekiel' refers both to the book, and to the prophet to whom the book is ascribed.

he wanted—all indications are that he did not[2]—Ezekiel's words still have power to elicit a response from those who read them. For many readers, the response is offense. Anyone who can read Ezekiel without being offended by something is not reading carefully enough. Ezekiel's book brims over with graphic images and disturbing language. In Tarlin's incisive description, the book 'radiates violence' (Tarlin 1997: 175). Church lectionaries avoid the problem by selecting only a few passages for readings, extracting them from the battering, sex and violence that fill the book.

Another common response lays the blame on Ezekiel's own pathology. Scholars have written articles offering varied diagnoses of mental illness lying behind Ezekiel's behavior and words. As long as we can pigeon-hole Ezekiel as an irascible crank with a mental problem, we can dismiss his violent theology, and let God off the hook. In either case, whether we read only the few passages that promise restoration, or let God off the hook by blaming crazy Ezekiel, we miss the theology of violence that saturates the book.

The book not only radiates violence, it radiates urgency. The prophet play-acted impending destruction. Ezekiel dramatized danger for people who would not take seriously the fact that their lives were at stake. For Ezekiel, the impending crisis was military conquest and exile. For many Ezekiels in our own era, the impending crisis is ecological. The harm we have done to our Earth threatens our own lives. Ezekiel used highly exaggerated figurative speech to dramatize the dangers to come. My paper adopts a similar model, by using figurative speech to dramatize the plight of Earth in Ezekiel. Such a strategy also carries a similar hazard. It risks offending without persuading, allowing readers to dismiss the writer as another crank. Yet underneath the method lies a similar sense of urgency. We need to listen to Earth for the sake of our own lives.

Figurative Language

The Bible becomes problematic in contemporary life when readers mine its pages as a sourcebook for human behavior or doctrine, without paying sufficient attention to the differences between figurative and factual language. This problem is particularly acute with the book of Ezekiel. In the book of Ezekiel, both God and Earth lie hidden behind a tangle of metaphors.

---

2. Fisch (1990: 114-15) argues that Ezekiel has failed the expected contract with his audience. They gathered to hear an artistic performance. The prophet rejects this role.

Ezekiel's highly exaggerated figurative language constitutes the greatest obstacle to hearing Earth.[3] Much of Ezekiel's figurative speech comes from nature. Ezekiel makes metaphors of hills, valleys, watercourses, vines, lions, cedars and, especially, mountains. In the book of Ezekiel, 'the mountains' function as two distinct figures of speech, metonymy and synecdoche. In Ezekiel 6, and again in Ezekiel 35–36, prophetic speech addresses 'Mount Seir' and 'the Mountains of Israel'. As metonymy, 'the mountains' refer to the people who live in Edom and Israel, substituting the mountains for the people, the container for the contained. As synecdoche, 'the mountains' stand for the whole land, a figure of speech that substitutes a part for the whole. In the complicated figurative language of Ezekiel, 'the mountains' are both a metonymy for the people and a synecdoche for the whole land. This figurative language itself obscures Earth. From our anthropocentric bias, we cannot see the mountains for the metonymy.

Reading from the Perspective of Earth

In Ezekiel 35, YHWH makes a case against Edom by bringing charges against 'Mount Seir'. Scholars have used a variety of methods to analyse this material, including form criticism, historical criticism, textual criticism, literary criticism, redactional criticism and theological interpretation, without asking how Ezekiel's use of metonymy and synecdoche has affected Earth. These methods are both theocentric and anthropocentric: about God and people. None is geocentric and none gives voice to Earth. As a method for listening to Earth, I am going to imagine a courtroom scene in a movie in which Earth itself brings a case against YHWH for turning the mountains of Edom and Israel into a desolation and a waste.

Ezekiel, the Movie

At the heart of all drama, the protagonist and the antagonist share a common want. In Ezekiel, the common 'want' is the land. Ezekiel makes claims about ownership of the land, pollution of the land, loss of the land, exile from the land, abandonment of the land, and restoration to the land. The protagonist and antagonist struggle over control of the land.

---

3.   Preminger and Greenstein (1986: 379-86) have collected several comments about the literary quality of the book of Ezekiel that span three centuries. The collective assessment is that much of the language of Ezekiel is the poetry of highly exaggerated figurative speech.

If we imagine a movie scene in a courtroom, we need a script. In Ezekiel's version, no one has any lines except YHWH and YHWH's prophet. We have hearsay about the adversaries, but no direct speech. Although YHWH addresses the mountains, the mountains do not speak. Despite its central importance in the book, the land has no voice.

Except in kangaroo courts, inquisitions and prophetic lawsuits, the accused has the right to a defense. In the book of Ezekiel, YHWH is prosecutor, judge and executioner. YHWH brings charges against the mountains but the mountains have no opportunity to defend themselves. What would happen if the tables were turned? What charges would Earth bring against YHWH?

Earth Brings a Case against YHWH

For my imaginary courtroom drama, the mountains of Edom and the mountains of Israel are plaintiffs rather than defendants. The hills, the ravines, the valleys and the watercourses also sit in the courtroom, as friends of the plaintiffs. Earth itself is the prosecutor, while YHWH is the defendant and must listen to the prosecutor's charges against him. What is our role? We are the jurors, sworn to hear the charges and the evidence, and to decide the verdict.

Clearly, my courtroom scene is as figurative as anything else in the book of Ezekiel. It requires imagination of the impossible and a willingness to tweak the categories of both biblical scholarship and law. Although I am creating a genre and a set of specific charges that both biblical scholars and lawyers might find problematic, my goal is to see what we have not seen. The basic question remains: What would we see if we read these chapters from the perspective of Earth?

The Trial Begins

Prosecutor Earth speaks. 'YHWH, Earth brings three charges against you for your crimes against the mountains. Through synecdoche, you have made the mountains stand as the representative for my hills, my ravines, my valleys and my watercourses. What you have done to the mountains, you have done to the whole Earth. We charge you with assault and battery, transference of guilt, and discrimination. As evidence for these crimes, we submit your own words as quoted by your prophet, Ezekiel. Hear the charges against you and the testimony of expert witnesses about your crimes.'

The First Charge: Assault and Battery of the Mountains

'Earth first charges you with assault and battery of the mountains of
Edom and Israel. We define assault as an unlawful threat of harm and
battery as unlawful violence. You assaulted both plaintiffs with threats
of desolation and waste and your claims that you would fill the
mountains with the bodies and bones of the dead' (Ezek. 6.1-9; 35.1-9).

The Profile of a Batterer
Earth calls Pamela Cooper-White to the witness stand. She defines
battering as 'abusive behavior that intimidates and controls the battered partner, for the purpose of establishing and maintaining authority' (1995: 119-20). Although sociopathic batterers are irritable and violent in most situations, most batterers inflict their violence only upon
their intimate partners or their children. The outside world regards
such batterers as ordinary and decent men. At home, they display
explosive tempers, low self-esteem and possessiveness, with strict
ideas about sex roles, and extreme dependence upon their partners to
meet their needs. They blame others for their own actions (Cooper-
White 1995: 119-20).

   Prosecutor Earth addresses the jury. 'You have heard the words that
YHWH spoke to the mountains of Edom and Israel. If these were not
the words of YHWH, what would you think about anyone who speaks
this way? We believe that YHWH's own words demonstrate his explosive temper, his possessive jealousy, and his threats of violence. YHWH
fits the profile of a batterer.'

Then You Shall Know that I am the LORD
Consider YHWH's words: 'Then you shall know that I am the LORD'.
Ezekiel records this statement more than fifty times. Scholars use various names for this phrase, such as 'recognition formula' or 'acknowledgment formula'.[4] Such neutral labels allow scholars to study these
words at a safe distance, without paying attention to the effect of such
threats on the batterer's victims. Without such buffering, we can hear
the words of a batterer. He threatens violence and gloats over the
harm he has done to his victims to protect his name, his reputation,
his possessions and his pride.

---

4.   For a discussion of this formula, see Zimmerli 1979: 37-38; Eichrodt 1970:
15; Hals 1989: 31-33.

YHWH the Masculinist

Earth then calls James McBride to the witness stand. McBride identifies as 'masculinist' a psychology that affirms a man as male rather than female, or even worse, a feminized man (1995: 18-20). By connecting war, battering and American football, McBride testifies that a masculinist man uses violence to prove that he is a man. Generals and football coaches use the same strategy: they motivate their men by insulting them as 'girls' or 'ladies' before they send them out to castrate their opponents (McBride 1995: 18-20; 90-97).

Earth again faces the jury. 'Members of the jury, if you read the statements of YHWH recorded by Ezekiel, you will see over and over again the words of a masculinist batterer. He threatens war, degrades women, and uses violence and destruction to assert his own power. Sex and violence are part of the same package.[5] Masculinist psychology reveals why Ezekiel used the metaphors of Oholah and Oholobah to describe the male political leadership of Samaria and Jerusalem as female whores. As offensive as these metaphors are to women, Ezekiel meant them to be even more offensive to men. He launched the ultimate masculinist insult at the men of Jerusalem and Samaria: he called them women'.

YHWH's Jealousy

Earth admits the words of Ezek. 36.1-7 as evidence.

> 'Therefore, thus says the Lord GOD: I am speaking in my hot jealousy against the rest of the nations, and against all Edom, who, with wholehearted joy and utter contempt, took my land as their possession, because of its pasture, to plunder it' (Ezek. 36.5).

'Batterers are jealous and possessive, regarding their women as sexual property. Just as YHWH denounced Oholah and Oholobah as whores, batterers often fling the same accusations against their women. Consider how often YHWH says that he is jealous.[6] Consider also how he claims the hills, the watercourses and the valleys as his possession. He speaks about "my land" in his "hot jealousy" and "jealous wrath". We detect little concern for the well-being of the land in these speeches. We see only YHWH's jealousy for his "possessions" (Ezek. 36.2, 3, 5).'

---

5. In another memorable phrase, Tarlin (1997: 176) writes: 'the more deeply one becomes involved with this text, the harder it is to avoid the impression that its violence is deeply eroticized'.

6. See Ezek. 5.13; 16.38, 42; 23.25; 35.11; 36.5, 6; 38.19. In addition, see Ezek. 8.3, 5 where the text refers to 'the image of jealousy' in the Jerusalem Temple.

Women and the Mountains in Ezekiel
'Since we are bringing this case on behalf of the mountains, we will say little more about YHWH's violence toward women. We do want to make clear that women and the mountains share a similar status in this book. Both suffer violence and degradation for the sake of YHWH's male pride. As a result of YHWH's battering, the mountains share the status of a raped woman: used and abused as a spoil of war.'

The Cycle of Battering
Earth admits the text of Ezek. 36.8-11 into evidence. 'Although many of YHWH's followers claim that these are words of salvation and restoration for the benefit of the mountains of Israel, we hear them as further evidence that YHWH fits the profile of a batterer.'

Earth calls Lenore Walker to testify about the three-stage cycle of battering. Walker (Cooper-White 1995: 106-109) observes that in the first stage, tension builds; in the second stage, the batterer batters; in the third stage, the batterer expresses his remorse, and promises never to do it again. Despite this pledge, the third stage is a truce rather than a transformation. After an uneasy interlude, a new cycle begins, with escalating violence. This three-phase cycle continues until it reaches one of three possible outcomes: the batterer undergoes a profound change; the battered one finally escapes; someone dies.

Earth speaks again. 'This speech demonstrates the third stage of the cycle, when the batterer vows to make it better and never do it again. In the first stage, there are threats against the mountains; in the second stage, YHWH's violence turns the mountains into a desolation and a waste; when YHWH reaches the third stage of expansive promises, he says: "See, now I am for you: I will turn to you" (Ezek. 36.9). He vows: "I will do more good than ever before" (Ezek. 36.11). For those who hear only this part of the speech, without setting it in the context of all that has gone before, these words prove YHWH's beneficent character. Those who are wise to the ways of batterers know better.'

The Second Charge: Transferring Guilt to the Mountains

'We also use this speech as primary evidence for the second charge. YHWH has transferred his own guilt to the mountains. Just as batterers refuse to take responsibility for their own actions, YHWH blames others for what he has done. He made threats and did violence to the mountains of Edom and Israel in the first two stages of battering. Now that he has reached the third stage, he transfers responsibility for his actions to the nations.'

The Illogical Logic of Battering
'We admit into evidence Ezek. 36.1-15. These words also demonstrate
the illogical logic of battering. Although most scholars who read this
speech comment on the repetitiveness and disorder of the logic, they
do not hold YHWH responsible. Instead, they say that we have a
redactional dumping ground here, with fragments of speeches gathered by an incompetent editor. Perhaps an editor is to blame. Perhaps
not.

'Most batterers keep their battering at home. Domestic tyrants become public paragons. When victims speak the truth about domestic
bullies, most people who have seen only the public face of these cha-
meleons refuse to believe that such respectable men would do such
things. Outsiders who do not understand the methods of batterers
often call the victims liars or insist that the victims provoked the
attacks. Such refusal to believe compounds the harm done to the
victims and protects the batterers.

'Scholars make similar excuses for YHWH. Rather than looking at
these words as the illogical rantings of a batterer, scholars blame an
editor. If we stop defending YHWH's respectable reputation, and look
at these words as a unit, we can see the mind of a batterer at work. He
blusters through his accusations, repeating the same charges, as he
shifts blame for the violence done to the mountains. First he says to
the mountains of Israel: "I, I myself will bring a sword upon you"
(Ezek. 6.3). Then he says to the mountains of Israel about Edom:
"Because they made you desolate indeed" (Ezek. 36.3). Then he says:
"Because you have suffered the insults of the nations, therefore, thus
says the Lord GOD: I swear that the nations that are all around you
shall themselves suffer insults" (Ezek. 36.6b-7). Then he says: "No
longer will I let you hear the insults of the nations" (Ezek. 36.15). In
other words, YHWH says that he did it to the mountains of Israel
because they deserved it, and then he blames Edom for doing it to
them, and then says that he will destroy Edom for what Edom did to
the mountains of Israel, and then he says to the mountains of Israel
that he will save them because of what Edom did to them. The whole
speech mixes these charges with claims of power, appeals to pride,
and gloating threats. No one can win with a batterer. It is always
someone else's fault and it is always about the batterer's pride.

Scapegoating
'We admit into evidence Ezek. 35.10-15. These words demonstrate one
of the most insidious techniques of battering: the separation and scapegoating of a victim. We call your attention to the following statement:

"As the whole Earth rejoices, I will make you desolate" (Ezek. 35.14).'

James McBride (1995: 14) returns to the witness stand to explain how batterers adopt tactics that separate and isolate their victims from family and friends.

Vimala Pillari testifies about the process of scapegoating that transfers responsibility for a conflict to an innocent victim. She makes clear that popular understanding of this term misses the most important aspect of the Yom Kippur ritual. On Yom Kippur, the community acknowledged its own guilt and transferred it onto the goat in a ritual act of cleansing. When batterers find a scapegoat, they transfer the blame, but take no responsibility (Pillari 1991: 3-4).

Earth speaks again. 'We see both separation and scapegoating in this speech. YHWH sets the whole Earth against Mount Seir and blames Mount Seir itself for the violence done to it. He claims that the whole Earth rejoices over the desolation of a part of itself. We remind the jury that the mountains of Edom and the mountains of Israel are united in their complaint against YHWH. They will not succumb to this scapegoating technique.'

The Unchanged Heart of a Batterer

'Next, we admit Ezek. 36.22-32 into evidence. Even though YHWH was not speaking to the mountains here, this speech once again shows a batterer blaming others for his own actions. YHWH says that the people had hearts of stone, which he will change. YHWH says nothing about his own jealous heart. If we doubted that YHWH inflicted violence for the sake of his reputation, consider his own words: "It is not for your sake, O house of Israel, that I am about to act, but for the sake of my holy name" (Ezek. 36.22, 32). YHWH does violence to protect his name.'

The Third Charge: Discrimination against the Mountains

'We also use this speech as evidence for our third charge: discrimination against the mountains. We define discrimination as a failure to treat all equally. YHWH's discrimination takes the form of anthropocentrism. He made the mountains invisible by turning them into metaphors for the people, without considering the effect of this upon the mountains themselves.

Earth calls Sarah Bentley to testify about the invisibility of women as the property of men, particularly their husbands. Bentley insists that women have a primary right to a separate identity, to be the subjects of their own lives, rather than the possessions of their husbands.

As long as women are regarded as objects rather than the subjects of their own lives, they are invisible (Bentley 1995: 151-71).

Earth turns to the jury. 'YHWH has treated the mountains as objects, as his own possession to use and abuse. He has failed to treat the mountains as the subjects of their own lives. YHWH has made the mountains invisible.'

The Invisibility of the Mountains

'Justice ignores the invisible. The mountains will have no justice as long as they remain invisible to YHWH and to the jury. We have searched for expert witnesses to testify on behalf of the mountains among those who study Ezekiel's book. But everywhere we look, we see the same anthropocentric bias, which loses the mountains in the metaphor. These scholars see only the fate of the people while remaining blind to the fate of the mountains. As subjects, the mountains remain invisible.'

What Happened to the Mountains?

'We will call only one expert witness to testify so that you can see for yourselves the effect of YHWH's discrimination. Earth calls the noted lexicographer, Professor Francis Brown.[7] Professor Brown, in his speeches, YHWH claimed to leave the mountains "desolate and waste". Can you tell us exactly what happened to the mountains?'

Professor Brown explains that Ezekiel uses several related words, meaning 'desolated', 'deserted', 'devastated' and 'appalled'. Earth is impatient.

'Yes, Professor Brown. We have already consulted your dictionary. We want to know what happened to the mountains themselves. Are you telling us that "desolation of Earth" means "depopulation"? Do these words describe "scorched Earth" as well as "abandoned Earth"? Do they refer to "destruction of the landscape" or just "removal of the inhabitants"? Did the mountains themselves undergo an ecological crisis? What actual damage was done to the mountains?'

Professor Brown admits that he has not asked these questions, but he suspects that Ezekiel was thinking only of the people who lived on the mountains, and not about the mountains themselves.

Earth speaks again. 'We have one last question for you, Professor Brown. We are curious to know the meaning of the words *'erets* and *'adamah*. Are they synonyms? How do these words relate to Earth?'

---

7.   Professor Brown is of course one of the editors of the indispensable Brown, Driver and Briggs *Hebrew and English Lexicon*.

Professor Brown testifies that these two words have multiple and overlapping meanings. He explains that *'erets* can refer to the whole Earth, or political territories, or even the ground itself. He observes that *'adamah* doesn't seem to refer to the whole Earth, but it can refer to political territories or the ground.

Earth continues. 'How does YHWH use these words in the book of Ezekiel? Does YHWH consider the effect of his actions upon the mountains themselves? Does he think about the whole Earth with its mountains and oceans, its rivers and lakes, its plains and hills, its mountain peaks and valleys? Or does he think only of Earth as a place for people to live and grow their crops?'

Professor Brown looks quite uncomfortable now. He admits that he has never asked these questions but he suspects that YHWH most often uses *'erets* to refer to political territories, especially when he uses the plural to contrast the political territories of Israel with the political territories of other peoples, such as the Edomites. YHWH uses *'adamah* less often, sometimes when referring to soil for crops and sometimes when talking about political territories.

Prosecutor Earth wears a pained expression. 'In other words, Professor Brown, you are testifying that YHWH thought only of the mountains as his possession to give or to take away from the people, without thinking of the mountains themselves.'

Earth turns again to the jury. 'We will call no more expert witnesses to testify on these particular questions, since we have found none who ask the questions we ask. The roots of anthropocentrism are deep here and the discrimination is pervasive. Even the experts see the mountains as nothing more than a place for people. They do not see the mountains as mountains.'

Using the Mountains as a Reward

'We again call your attention to YHWH's vow to the mountains of Israel. He promises abundant fruit, tilled Earth, bountiful crops, rebuilt towns, and increased human and animal populations (Ezek. 36.8-11). How do these promises benefit the mountains? YHWH considers the mountains as objects. First they were battered for YHWH's wounded pride and now they are being offered as a reward. The mountains themselves remain invisible.'

Who is YHWH's Adversary?

'This whole case pivots on YHWH's claim that the whole Earth belongs to him. He has tried to intimidate and control the mountains to establish and maintain his authority. We have admitted into evidence various speeches by YHWH demonstrating his rage. We have seen that he has directed his words against the mountains, even though he meant them as words against the people. We have one more question. We have seen that the mountains are the contested objects. The people are also targets of YHWH's rage. Now we ask: Who is YHWH's primary adversary? We call John Kutsko to testify.'

Kutsko testifies that YHWH's rage concerns the worship of idols, and that YHWH's concern is theocentric rather than anthropocentric. By denying that other gods exist, he intends to prove that he alone is God (Kutsko 2000: 25-76).

Earth speaks again. 'Ladies and gentlemen of the jury, we finally reach the principal adversary. YHWH battles the gods and goddesses who also claim possession of the mountains. Most people believed that the land belonged to local deities. Since they depended upon the land for their survival, they worshipped the local gods at their shrines. But YHWH insisted that the people stop worshipping the local deities, and acknowledge that he alone was God and that he owned all of the land. Behind every accusation hurled at the people and the mountains, we can see the traces of ancient enmities between rival gods, between the male sky god and the female earth goddess, between Marduk and Tiamat, between Baal and YHWH. Since YHWH denied that these local gods existed, he refused to call them by name, or to address them directly. YHWH demanded that the people abandon their worship of the local gods of the land by putting at risk the very thing that motivated their worship. He threatened to deprive them of the land.'

Treating the Land as an Object

'We now come to the connection between battering and discrimination. Batterers discriminate against others, by treating victims as objects rather than subjects. The mountains are innocent victims of a battle for supremacy: YHWH's true struggle is with the gods and goddesses who claim control of the land. He insisted that the people turn their allegiance to him alone, and when they would not, he waged war upon them. And because the land is at the core of the struggle, he threatened to harm it.'

'YHWH's threats against the mountains demonstrate once again the mentality of a batterer. He will destroy what the victim loves most, for the sake of establishing his own power.'

'Batterers will destroy what they cannot control. We remind the jurors of the battered women killed when they decide to escape the batterer, and the children murdered by fathers who have lost custody of them in divorce cases. Demonstrating the same illogic as the infamous statement from the Vietnam War about destroying the village to save it, YHWH desolated the land to save it from the local gods.'

Justice for the Mountains

'Ladies and gentlemen of the jury, we ask you: Where is justice for the mountains? The mountains are innocent of any wrongdoing, yet they suffered so that YHWH might triumph. Justice requires that you see the mountains as subjects of their own lives. They do not exist for the benefit of the human beings who live upon them. Nor do they exist as objects to prove YHWH's supremacy. They exist to be mountains. Earth asks you, on behalf of its mountains, its hills, its valleys, its watercourses, and its land, where is justice for the mountains?'

Earth's Challenge to YHWH

Earth says: 'Now we will ask YHWH to defend himself against these charges. Will he continue to justify his actions? Will he persist in making his batterer's accusations? Or will he demonstrate that he has truly heard the complaints of the mountains? Will he undergo a change of his batterer's heart?'

Earth's Challenge to the Jury

Earth continues. 'Will you also undergo a change in your hearts? Will you listen to YHWH's words with the ears of the mountains? Will you count the cost of such language? Will you see what you have not seen before, that the mountains have suffered for your blindness? The mountains also wait for you.'

Epilogue

My little courtroom drama ends with this scene. If it has raised disturbing questions, then my effort has succeeded. What does this profoundly troubling biblical book, Ezekiel, show us about how our reading of the Bible affects Earth? Despite the difficulty of the language and the offensiveness of the images, the book of Ezekiel is worth studying for its attitude toward Earth. Ezekiel has much to say about the land but very little about Earth. As much as any biblical book, Ezekiel helps us distinguish between theocentric, anthropocentric and geocentric readings. By seeing YHWH's threats and claims from the perspective of battered Earth, we see how much we have treated Earth as an object to possess rather than as a subject to respect. If we are willing to face the truth, we can acknowledge how we too have battered Earth. If Earth could speak, what case would it make against us?

Retrieving Earth's Voice in Jeremiah:
An Annotated Voicing of Jeremiah 4

Shirley Wurst

Introduction

This paper is my attempt to demonstrate that in the text of Jeremiah 4, Earth is given a voice. This reading requires a re-vision of the text: seeing the text through new eyes, eyes looking from Earth's perspective, as well as those of God and God's people, Israel.[1] To facilitate 'seeing' the new reading, I divide the text of Jeremiah 4 into voices, and in the process retrieve a voice that has been ignored: the voice of Earth.

My reading of Jeremiah 4, like Kalinda Rose Stevenson's reading of Ezekiel in this volume, reveals a record of an assault and battery. Jeremiah 4 graphically shows how Earth's body,[2] too, like the bodies of the people in the land, and the bodies of women beaten by battering husbands, is marked by the awful punishment carried out by a jealous God in an attempt to cleanse and purify a wayward partner.

In my reading, there are five characters: YHWH (the name for the God-character in this text), Jeremiah, the narrator/observer, Earth, Israel and Judah. Each person involved in the action depicted in the text—as we know only too well from our experiences of any group of people witnessing an event—speaks from their own perspective, and has their own view of what has happened. In this reading, God speaks, Jeremiah speaks in the role of a narrator/observer, and Earth has a voice. Despite the human bias of the text—it remains, even in this reading, a text written by humans, for human readers—the voices of the two non-human characters offer a perspective that differs from the perspective of the human 'controlling' voice—the voice that describes

---

1.   Adrienne Rich (1980: 35) makes this observation: 'Re-vision—the art of looking back, of seeing with fresh eyes, of entering an old text from a new critical direction—is for women more than a chapter in cultural history: it is an act of survival'.

2.   See Jer. 4.23-26.

the action, the voice read by Jeremiah. In this text Israel and Judah rarely speak; for the most part, these sisters are mute. In my reading, when they speak, it is in concert with the voice of Earth.

My reading uses and demonstrates two Earth Bible Project principles: the principles of voice and interconnectedness.

Other Readings of Jeremiah

Most scholars reading the text of Jeremiah 4 demonstrate the close identification between the prophet and the God for whom the prophet speaks. Many readings blend the two voices, and resist the challenge of distinguishing God's voice from the voice of the prophet. For many readers of Jeremiah 4, the voices of these two characters become so blended as to be indistinguishable.

The close connection between these two voices is justifiably sustained by the initial chapter in Jeremiah, which is a report of a dialogue between the prophet and his God.

> Now the word of YHWH came to me, saying:
> 'Before I formed you in the womb I knew you,
> and before you were born I consecrated you;
> I appointed you a prophet to the nations'.
> Then I [Jeremiah] said:
> 'Ah, YHWH! Truly I do not know how to speak, for I am only a young
>   child.'
> But YHWH said to me:
> 'Do not say: "I am only a young child"';
> for you shall go to all to whom I send you,
> and speak whatever I command you'.
> Then YHWH's hand touched my mouth, and YHWH said to me:
> 'Now I have put my words in your mouth.
> See, today I appoint you over nations and over kingdoms,
> to pluck up and to pull down,
> to destroy and to overthrow,
> to build and to plant' (Jer. 1.4-10).

This is powerful intimacy: a prophet who is 'known' by a God even before his birth, chosen before anyone, even his mother, can have a claim on his love, and given the words to say.

Jeremiah is indeed 'known' in a very intense way—the Hebrew verb יָדַע (*yada'*) is used in a variety of contexts. It is used in Isaiah to mean experience; it is used in the sense of recognize or perceive, become acquainted with, know and come to understand, and have insight and judgment; it is often used to refer to sexual intimacy; it is used to talk about the care and concern of people for each other, and

God's care and concern for others.[3] In Jeremiah, this intimacy involves God and prophet speaking with one voice. However, as my reading below demonstrates, in Jeremiah 4 the prophet shows understanding of which the YHWH character is not yet aware.

In her chapter in this volume, Kalinda Rose Stevenson demonstrates that the text of Ezekiel sustains a reading in which the God in the text speaks from a definitively male perspective, the perspective in which a man perceives his partner as his possession, to do with as he sees fit. If she is not obedient, he must break her spirit, stop her willingness to resist his will with his fists—or anything else that comes to hand. A woman who refuses to be obedient to her partner—her master, her *va'al*,[4] her God—loses all human rights. Because she refuses to be as this male-championed God made her—subservient to her lord and master—she can be battered, or shot, to death.[5]

Some sections in the book of Jeremiah also sustain a reading of the text in terms of battery. There is objectification of the woman, sexually explicit derogatory language designed to demean women's sexuality, and jealous punitive possessiveness. In Jeremiah, too, the people of God (divided into two kingdoms, Israel and Judah), are depicted as women obsessed with sexuality, women who reject the love of their partner-in-marriage, who is also the 'devotion of…[their] youth' (Jer. 2.2),[6] and promiscuously have sex with every other partner they can find—publicly: 'on every high hill and under every green tree…[they]

3.   As this chapter of Jeremiah focuses on sexual behaviour, the use of the term in relation to God's knowing Jeremiah is interesting. Eilberg-Schwartz (1994) raises some interesting issues relating to the way God's sexuality is a contested concept in the Hebrew Scriptures. In the introduction to his text, provocatively entitled *God's Phallus*, he observes: 'this is a book about divine fatherhood and the ways in which the sexual body of a father God is troubling for the conception of masculinity' (1994: 1).

4.   The Hebrew term בעל (*va'al*) literally means 'possessor, husband, lord, owner, partner'; in this paper, I translate the term 'lord and master' to emphasize the possessiveness and ownership the term implies.

5.   Reports of crimes against women demonstrate that many women are killed by their partners—often when they have separated from a former partner, or even when they have divorced their partner and are in a new relationship with another man. A judge in South Australia, commenting on a woman's accusation of assault against her partner, observed that a man was permitted, in a marital situation, to use 'rougher than usual treatment' in order to enjoy his full conjugal (sexual) rights.

6.   This term is also used in Prov. 2.17 to demonstrate a woman's callous betrayal of her partner; the description is used in relation to the 'Strange Woman' (אשה זרה 'ishah zarah) whom the wise young boys are enjoined to avoid on pain of death.

sprawled and played the whore' (Jer. 2.20); they 'scattered…[their] favours among strangers under every green tree' (Jer. 3.13). YHWH, in providing a context for the faithless partners' sexual promiscuity, observes:

> long ago you broke your yoke and burst your bonds,
> and said, 'I will not serve!' (Jer. 2.20).

> you have rebelled against YHWH your God…
> and have not obeyed my voice (Jer. 3.13).

As in Ezekiel, this portrait of God demonstrates a patriarchal perspective: in this text, a woman is a man's possession; she is yoked and bound to her 'lawful' partner whom she must serve and obey. When she chooses another lover, she is indiscriminate and promiscuous, even making love with more than one stranger in public parks!

In patriarchal ancient Hebrew style, the man divorces his sexually unfaithful partner, Israel, and marries her sister, Judah, who also 'went and played the whore' (Jer. 3.8). True to form, this God-husband treats his wives as children,[7] and in an attempt to control them offers them a marital reconciliation. However, it is obvious that it must be on his terms: he will take them back, and take them to another home—isolating them from their family and friends—because he is '[their] master', literally '[their] va'al'. And, this time, these 'faithless children'—literally 'backsliding children'—will be supervised, shepherded like silly sheep, by 'shepherds after my own heart' (Jer. 3.15).

Their sexual indiscretions will be overlooked, and their faithlessness will be healed—but their change of heart must be complete; they must be perfectly faithful in his eyes, from his perspective, or they will experience the full force of his anger:

> Circumcise yourselves to YHWH,
> remove the foreskin of your hearts…
> or else my wrath will go forth like fire,
> and burn with no one to quench it,
> because of the evil of your doings (Jer. 4.4).

As is usual in the patriarchal paradigm, the male perspective is the only acceptable view; the man is the judge, the jury, the prosecutor and the executioner—there is no defence: guilt is a 'done-deal', that is, assumed!

Finally, in Jeremiah, too, Earth suffers with the faithless women: both bear the signs of assault on their bodies.

---

7.   The text leading up to Jer. 4 presents Israel and Judah as sexual partners and as children, often in adjoining texts; see Jer. 2.2, 20; 3.1, 6-10, 13, 20; cf. 3.14, 19, 22.

For many readers of the text of Jeremiah, the two chapters preceding Jeremiah 4 are a salacious and obscene presentation of a woman who chooses her own sexual partners and refuses to 'serve' her possessive and controlling partner.[8] In patriarchal terms, such a woman is a sexually promiscuous woman, a slut, a 'bike', a whore. The text is graphic, the misogyny sustained by metaphors using the most depraved images of uncontrolled and promiscuous, indiscriminate sexuality—the mating of wild animals in the wild places, the places where evil lurks. The animals referred to in the text—a restive young camel and a wild ass—were perceived as 'unclean' and a 'danger to purity' by the ancient Near Eastern Hebrew readers of the text.

In this text, too, the woman who falls from patriarchal grace wears her 'sin' on her body; she can never be washed clean, even with the harshest cleansing agents. Perhaps this explains why men cannot tolerate another man's 'presence' in their 'property', and perceive that the only way to make a woman faithful is to punish her body, as if to beat the rebellion, and the other man's sexual ownership/stain, out of her. Even when a woman does not consent to the invasion, she is guilty. The 'stain' of another man's sexual invasion cannot be tolerated, as Jer. 2.22 demonstrates:

> Though you wash yourself with lye and use much soap,
> the stain of your guilt is still before me...
> How can you say, 'I am not defiled,
> I have not gone after the *va'als* [other lords and masters]'?
> Look at your way in the valley;
> know what you have done—
> a restive young camel interlacing her tracks,
> a wild ass at home in the wilderness,
> in her heat sniffing the wind!
> Who can restrain her lust?
> None who seek her need weary themselves;
> in her month they will find her (Jer. 2.22-24).

A Voiced Reading of Jeremiah 4: Retrieving Earth's Voice

In an astute reading, Norman Habel (1995: 75-76) observes that in the text of Jeremiah, a tripartite symbiosis exists: God–Land–People.

> In the triangle of close relationships...the land is both Israel's *naḥᵃlâ*...
> and YHWH's *nḥᵃlâ*...Israel, as YHWH's people, however, is also

---

8.   Several scholars have read the text as ancient Near Eastern pornography; see Brenner (ed.) 1995, esp. articles by Brenner and Carroll; see also section on Hosea and van Dijk-Hemmes' article on Ezekiel.

YHWH's *nah^{a}lâ*...YHWH is Israel's 'allotted portion'...YHWH, Israel, and Canaan are destined to belong together in a god–land–people symbiosis (1995: 76).

My reading uses Habel's insight of the 'central symbol' of the 'intimate bond' in Jeremiah (1995: 76) to unpack the complex voicing in the text of Jeremiah 4. I understand 'symbiosis' to mean the living together, the mutualism of a close relationship, which has advantages for and enhances the life of all participants. However, as their lives depend on and are sustained by the close connection between them, the participants also become vulnerable: not only are they susceptible to their own weaknesses; when other parties are invaded or suffer, so do they all. This understanding of symbiosis is integral to my reading.

My understanding of the symbiosis in Jeremiah also seems to explain what has mystified scholars for many years: the text in Jeremiah 4 is so convoluted because the relationship is so integrated; there are links that even the participants may not recognize or understand, and the pain of the other's suffering becomes indistinguishable, ultimately, from personal pain. Jeremiah 4, in its verbal richness and ambiguity, demonstrates in itself the mystery it is describing: the complexity of intimate mutual relationship.

The translation of the text and the division of the text into voices follows the Masoretic Text and the contemporary NRSV English version and the TANAKH; in places I have gone back to the original in order to convey the nuances in the Hebrew text more clearly. In some places I have used poetic licence—I have used alternative terms to make the intention of the text clear, or to strengthen the sense of the voices. These departures from the actual text are footnoted.

Many readers will perceive that the characterizations and reading I have chosen are emotive—I would agree. I have chosen the batterer and the batterer's targets as a device to draw a distinct line from other readings. This element in my interpretation is informed and inspired by Stevenson's reading of Ezekiel. Like her, I am employing this strategy to underline the violence in the book, and the urgency of the message: assault and battery is an offence, and cannot be tolerated. If we abhor men who batter and abuse, how can we continue to condone the abuse and battery of Earth, our mother?

As Stevenson observes regarding the book of Ezekiel, the book of Jeremiah 'radiates violence'. Like Ezekiel, Jeremiah uses exaggeration and figurative speech to dramatize the dangers. Without recognizing the violence and misogyny that are implicitly condoned because God is the agent, and because the targets of the punishment, God's people and God's Earth, are polluted and need to be cleansed, we are in danger of desensitizing ourselves, as people have done throughout history, to violence in the name of justice. A justice, a peace, a reconciliation built on violence is a perversion of the terms.

There is another way; Jeremiah's message that we are in symbiotic relationship with Earth and God, and that this intimate interconnectedness makes all participants vulnerable, is something Indigenous peoples understand and experience. Indigenous peoples know that when their kin—Earth and Earth community—are destroyed, they also suffer. In *Rainbow Spirit Theology* (Rainbow Spirit Elders 1997: 29-54), this close and vulnerable connection is explored. One Aboriginal Australian man observed: 'It tears me apart. I grieve with the Creator when I hear the land crying' (Rainbow Spirit Elders 1997: 43). Bill Neidjie, colloquially known as Kakadu man, asserts:

> I feel it with my body,
> with my blood.
> Feeling all these trees,
> all this country.
> When this wind blow you can feel it.
> Same for country...
> You feel it.
> You can look,
> but feeling...
> that make you (Neidjie *et al.* 1986: 81).

It is time for Western peoples to understand the fragility of our Earth community. It is, after all, the basis of our being.

Jeremiah 4: Battering Three in One Act

Cast:

YHWH: a god and master, male; assertive and powerful, aware of his own power; tends to unbridled range; a batterer; both Earth, his former partner,[9] and Israel and Judah, his new wives, are the targets of his anger; YHWH appears oblivious to the consequences of his actions for himself and his relationship with the three women, each of whom he loves and cherishes—or, perhaps, like many patriarchal partners, he feels he has no choice: he must punish the women he has accused of being unfaithful or they will not respect him and will run amok!

---

9.   In my paper in Earth Bible 2 (Wurst 2000) I argued that Earth is portrayed as mother in Gen. 2-3, and that Earth and YHWH together produce human beings and all life.

Israel: a young woman, fragile and slight in stature; she was married to YHWH as a young woman; she has been accused of looking for other, more suitable, sexual relationships with men her own age.

Judah: also young; she became YHWH's third wife when he divorced her sister, Israel, for her alleged unfaithfulness; she is also now accused of being unfaithful to her partner.

Earth: an older woman, the former partner of YHWH; she is a woman who is linked with YHWH and Israel; she is the partner of YHWH, and loves his new wives as her sisters/children; it is apparent that she still loves her former partner; she also suffers abuse from YHWH although she is not explicitly accused of unfaithfulness; it seems she will suffer, too, because she loves, supports and nurtures the two women as though they were her daughters/sisters.

Jeremiah: the narrator/observer, who witnesses the events depicted; we see the action through his eyes; despite a close connection with YHWH—he admires and loves the man loyally—he also loves the three women and is able to see the destruction YHWH's anger causes.

Jeremiah [*speaks to the audience; like a Shakespearean narrator/muse*]:
> YHWH told me what to say, let me watch his punishment. I had no choice but to stand by and let it happen. I am telling you so that you can learn the lesson, too.[10]

YHWH [*to Israel, pleading, but signs of barely controlled anger are apparent in his voice*]:
> If you return, O Israel,
> if you return to me,
> if you remove your abominations from my presence,
> and do not waver,

[*to Judah*]
> and if you swear: 'As YHWH lives!'
> in truth, in justice, and in uprightness,
> then...people[11] will bless themselves by you
> and they will boast by you

YHWH [*to Earth, and Judah and Israel, still pleading, but the command, the desire to control is clear*]:
> Break up your fallow ground,
> and do not sow among thorns.[12]

10. A gloss of the opening section of the book of Jeremiah, and the role of the prophet in ancient Near Eastern culture.

11. I have interpreted 'nations' as people.

12. The same term, קוֹץ, is used in Gen. 3.15.

[*Focusing on Israel*]
> Circumcise yourselves to YHWH,
> remove the foreskin of your hearts...
> or else my wrath will go forth like fire,
> and burn with no one to quench it,
> because of the evil of your doings

[*The threat in YHWH's voice is more apparent now – the assumed power and the lust for retribution, the righteous anger, are dominant; YHWH is clearly speaking to all three women, but focusing on Israel and Judah*]:
> Declare...and proclaim...
> Blow the trumpet through Israel;[13]
> shout aloud, speak:
> 'Gather together, and let us go into the fortified cities!'
> Raise a standard toward Judah,[14]
> flee for safety, do not delay,
> for I am bringing evil from the north,
> and a great destruction.

[*YHWH is now directing his words towards Earth*]:
> A lion has gone up from its thicket,
> a destroyer of nations has set out;
> he has gone out from his place
> to make Earth a waste; Israel and Judah[15] will be ruins without inhabitant.

[*Again, YHWH is speaking to all three women; the irony is clear – even though both YHWH and the women recognize that the punishment is inescapable, YHWH requires that they demonstrate their willingness to be subject to his will*]:
> Because of this put on sackcloth, lament and wail:
> 'The fierce anger of YHWH has not turned away from us'.

[*The women are silent; they can say nothing; they are clearly afraid; they know what to expect because it has happened before*]
> On that day, courage shall fail your protectors;[16] those who defend you[17] shall
> be appalled and astounded.

Jeremiah [*to the audience and YHWH*]
> Ah, YHWH, how utterly you have deceived Israel and Judah,[18] saying:
> 'It shall be well with you', even while the sword is at the throat.

YHWH [*speaking to the audience and Jeremiah; the tone is self-justificatory*]:
> The conduct of my Israel and Judah is like a hot searing wind
> from the bare heights of the desert –
> it will not serve to winnow or to fan.

13. Here I have interpreted 'the land' as Israel.

14. I have interpreted Zion as Judah – Zion, another name for Jerusalem, was located in Judah.

15. I have interpreted 'your cities' as Israel and Judah, and 'your land' as Earth.

16. The text reads 'king' and 'officials'.

17. The text reads 'priests' and 'prophets'.

18. Literally, 'this people and Jerusalem'; in this context I have interpreted Jerusalem, located in Judah, as representing Judah.

A full blast from them comes against me:
now I in turn will bring charges against them.[19]

Jeremiah [*to the audience; it is apparent from his voice that he is describing what he is seeing happening before him*]:
Look! He comes up like the clouds,
his chariots like the whirlwind;
his horses are swifter than eagles—

Earth [*although Earth begins to speak, all three women recognize what is happening to them; to demonstrate this, Israel and Judah pick up the second part of Earth's speech seamlessly; all three speak in chorus; their voices betray two feelings: fear because they know about the pain of being battered; and regret, because they know that each battering reduces the love they feel for YHWH*]:
Woe to us!
Earth, Israel, Judah:
For we are ruined!

Jeremiah [*to Judah and Israel*]:
O Judah and Israel,[20] wash your heart clean of wickedness
so that you may be saved.

YHWH [*to all three women, but focusing on Earth; it is as if he has heard Jeremiah's plea to the younger women to save themselves*]:
How long shall your evil schemes lodge within you?
For a voice declares from Dan
and proclaims disaster from Mount Ephraim.
Tell people, 'Here they are!'
Proclaim against Earth,
'Beseigers come from a distant land;
they shout against the cities of Judah'.
[*Still focusing on Earth; however, the first words are directed to the audience*]:
They have closed around Earth like watchers of a field,
because Earth has rebelled against me.
[*Focusing on Earth, and Israel and Judah; YHWH is clearly unaware of the irony of his words*]:
Your ways and your doings have brought this upon you.
This is your doom; how bitter it is!
It has reached your very heart.

Jeremiah [*repeats YHWH's words to the audience; he is speaking to YHWH, too, trying to warn the angry man that these words will return to haunt him*]:
Your ways and your doings have brought this upon you.
This is your doom; how bitter it is!
It has reached your very heart.[21]

19. This section relies on the 1998 TANAKH translation; I have changed 'my poor people' to Israel and Judah; the translators' gloss observes that the literal Hebrew reads 'the daughter that is my people'.

20. As above—I am interpreting Jerusalem as Judah.

Earth, Judah and Israel [*in chorus, softly – are they speaking to each other? to YHWH?*]
Your ways and your doings have brought this upon you.
This is your doom; how bitter it is!
It has reached your very heart.[22]

Earth, Israel, Judah, Jeremiah, and YHWH [*in chorus, but it is clear from their tones that each has a particular understanding of the words: the women know they are about to be abused by the man they love; Jeremiah knows he is about to witness the intense suffering of three women, and that this will have implications for their relationship with the man he loves and respects; even though YHWH understands that his abusive violence will harm himself, there is a sense in which, at this moment, he feels that he is powerless to stop what he has begun – the regret is apparent in his voice*]:
My anguish! My anguish! I writhe in pain!
Oh, the walls of my heart!

Earth [*her emotion is apparent in her voice; she speaks to the audience; she knows she is about to experience a beating; it is obvious that she is unable to protect herself; her voice is tinged with the pain and anguish of her predicament – she is about to be abused by a man she loves*]:
My heart is beating wildly; I cannot keep silent;
for I hear the sound of the trumpet,
the alarm of war.

Jeremiah [*it is apparent from his voice that Jeremiah is watching what is happening and is powerless to do anything; his voice betrays a divided loyalty between the man and the three defenceless women*]:
Disaster overtakes disaster,
Earth is laid waste.

Earth [*it is obvious as she speaks that her body is shuddering from the pain of the blows as her body is beaten, her clothes are torn*]:
Suddenly my tents are destroyed,
my curtains in a moment.
How long must I see the standard,
and hear the sound of the trumpet?

YHWH [*to deal with his now mixed emotions, and harden himself to the pain he feels he must inflict, the abuser blames his target for his violence and abuse*]:
For my Israel and Judah[23] are foolish,
they do not know me;
they are stupid children,
they have no understanding.
they are skilled in doing evil,
but do not know how to do good.

---

21.   This repetition is poetic licence; in the text, the words are only said once.
22.   As above, poetic licence.
23.   I have changed 'my people' into Israel and Judah.

Jeremiah [*speaking to the audience, describing what he is witnessing; the compassion and pain are apparent in his voice*]:

I looked at Earth,[24] and lo, she was wasted and void;
and to her skies, and they had no light.
I looked on her mountains, and lo, they were quaking,
and all the hills moved to and fro.
I looked, and lo, there was no life at all, and all the birds of the air had fled.
I looked, and lo, fruitful Earth was a desert,
and Judah and Israel[25] were laid in ruins
before YHWH, before YHWH's fierce anger.[26]

YHWH [*there is a hint of regret in his voice; he recognizes what he has done, but cannot bring himself to empathize with the violated Earth; he now focuses on Israel and Judah*]:

Earth shall be a desolation; yet I will not make a full end.
Because of this Earth shall mourn,
and her skies above grow black;
for I have spoken, I have purposed;
I have not relented nor will I turn back.

Jeremiah [*still reporting what he is seeing; his voice is filled with mixed emotions of fear, regret, compassion*]:

At the noise of horseman and archer
Israel [and Judah] take to flight;
they enter thickets; they climb among rocks;
Judah and Israel[27] are forsaken,
and there is no life in them.[28]

YHWH [*to Israel and Judah; his words mock the blood on their faces and bodies; on the word 'life', both women scream*]:

And you, O desolate one[s],

24. In this reading, as Earth is a female character, I have changed the neutral forms to feminine possessives in this section and below.

25. I have interpreted 'her cities' as Israel and Judah.

26. This section, Jer. 4.23-26, is often referred to as a de-creation; a comparison with Gen. 1 reveals the bitter irony of what is seen (ראה – the same verb is used in both texts): in Gen. 1, Earth and Earth community is formed and shaped, and the co-creator, God, pronounces each new development as good, and the whole product as 'very good' – perfect. In Jer. 4, Earth is made desolate: Earth returns to its pre-creation state of תהו ובהו – the same words as in Gen. 1.2, often translated 'unformed and void'. The Jeremiah text underlines the difference: instead of Earth teeming with life, being blessed, being fruitful and multiplying to fill Earth, in Jer. 4.25, there is no living person and the birds are all gone; the fruitful Earth is returned to desert – as in Gen. 2, there is no living thing, as there are no humans to look after and nurture Earth.

27. I have changed 'all the towns' to Israel and Judah.

28. Literally, 'nothing is living/inhabiting' them; I have used poetic license to render this concept 'no life', to conform with my personification of Israel and Judah as women. The Hebrew term, אין, emphasizes absence.

what do you mean that you dress in crimson,
that you deck yourself with ornaments of gold,
that you enlarge your eyes with paint?
In vain you beautify yourself.
Your lovers despise you;
they seek your life.

Jeremiah [*his final words; again, his voice betrays a mixture of emotions*]:
For I heard a cry as of a woman in labour,
anguish as of one bringing forth her first child,
the cry of daughter Judah gasping for breath,
stretching out her hands,
'Woe is me! I am faint before killers!'

Concluding Note

Why does Earth mourn? Why is Earth punished? In my reading she is not unfaithful—she has not 'played the whore'. Rather, her crime seems to be that she nurtures and cares for the two wives, despite their partner's displeasure. Like the two women in the film *Stepmom*, they share a bond as women and mothers that is stronger than their rivalry as wives—a rivalry that is advocated and encouraged by the patriarchal system.

Earth Community in Hosea 2

Laurie J. Braaten

Introduction

Hosea has captured the imagination of Bible readers everywhere. While scholars and interpreters continue to debate many of the details, there is a widely repeated story of Hosea found in many standard textbooks and proclaimed in worship services: Hosea, the passionate lover and hurt husband, learned from his own marital history the pathos of YHWH in his relationship with Israel, God's unfaithful bride. The appeal of this story lies in its resonance with human experience and its theological and homiletical yield. A careful examination of the text, however, will reveal that this version of the story claims more than the text can support, and offers less than the text declares—it omits the important story of God's relationship with Land. In this story Earth struggles to make her voice heard through the words of a victimized Land. Land's voice is the voice of one oppressed; her voice is being suppressed by those who are closest to her. But as her God offers her restoration, Land has opportunity to make her voice clearly heard.

The Story in Context

The story of God's relationship with Land is introduced in Hosea 1, but is not developed until Hosea 2. The symbolic deeds of Hosea 1 form the backdrop for a series of oracles concerning God's action toward people and Land in Hosea 1–3. While it is widely acknowledged that Hosea 1–3 has a long redactional history (e.g. Yee 1987), for purposes of this study we are concerned with a canonical reading, focusing primarily on the theological shaping of Hosea 2 as a whole.

The first glimpse of the story of YHWH's relationship with Land and people is found at the beginning of Hosea in the opening word of YHWH—a command to 'marry a woman of whoredom and [engender] children of whoredom' (Hos. 1.2a).[1] The explanation of this deed

---

1.　Translations are the author's unless otherwise indicated. Bible references

is an amazing accusation: 'for Land (*ha'arets*) commits whoredom away from YHWH' (Hos. 1.2b). While the common way of interpreting this accusation is to assume that Land connotes God's people, a closer look at Hosea 1–2 shows that 'Land' means 'Land *per se*'. In Hosea 1 the symbolic namings indicate that Hosea's 'children' represent God's people; i.e., Israel is depicted as God's child(ren). Hosea's wife symbolizes 'Land', who, as YHWH's unfaithful wife (Braaten 1987: 55-57), is threatened with punishment in Hos. 2.2-13. God's people are accused of being 'children of whoredom' because their mother is a 'woman of whoredom' — that is, they share the status and guilt of their mother (Hos. 1.2; 2.4-5). Therefore they are threatened with disownment and disinheritance, the 'not' in the symbolic names of Hos. 1.6, 9 being similar to ancient Near Eastern repudiation formulas[2] (ANET 175, 545; Buss 1969: 88; Paul 1979–80: 180; Braaten 1987: 96, 220-53). The sharing of one's mother's status leading to expulsion is known elsewhere in the Hebrew Bible.[3] Hosea's symbolism immediately raises questions: What does it mean to accuse Land of whoredom? How can Land be held accountable for guilt? And what is the significance of this family imagery linking together Land, people and YHWH? These questions need to be answered before we can relate the story of Land's distress in Hosea 2.

Earth Community in Hosea

In Hosea Land ('*erets*) is the 'house(hold) of God' (Hos. 8.1; 9.15, Braaten 1987: 308-15; Wolff 1974: 137). Land is the place where YHWH, Israel, plants and animals dwell (see Hos. 4.3; Andersen and Freedman 1980: 332), but this Land belongs ultimately to YHWH (Hos. 9.3; Wolff 1974: 154-55). Although the focus in Hosea is often on the territory that encompasses the 'promised land', Land has a much broader and paradigmatic significance as the '*erets* of creation, or Earth (Hos. 2.18-22; 4.3; Fretheim 2000: 96). This same 'paradigmatic application' (Wright 1990: xviii, 174-80) is found throughout much of the Hebrew Bible. Just as God's relationship with a particular people

will follow the English numbering when they differ from the Hebrew, as they do in Hos. 1.10-2.23.

2.   For the background of the formula 'she is not my wife and I am not her husband' of Hos. 2.2 and its relation to an impending divorce, see Wolff 1974: 33-34.

3.   E.g., Gen. 21.8-14; 25.1-6; Judg. 10.17-11.3; Ezra 10.1-3; and 2 Kgs 9.22-26, discussed in Braaten 1987, chapter 2, 'Legitimacy and Maternal Status in Ancient Israel'.

has broader universalistic implications for all peoples, so God's relationship with a particular Land occupied by these people has a more universal application for all of creation, or Earth.

Hosea depicts an intimate relationship between YHWH, Land and Israel. The book of Hosea employs a widespread biblical picture of God as creator/father of persons out of the womb of Earth (Ps. 139.13, 15; Job 1.21;[4] 38.28-29). A related view, that God personally fashions humans from the dust or clay of Earth, is expressed in the Yahwistic creation account and elsewhere (Gen. 2.7; cf. Job 10.8-12; 33.6; Ps. 103.14; cf. Ps. 119.73; Braaten 1987: 283-89). In Hosea, Land is the source of nurture for Israel (or Ephraim), God's son(s) (Hos. 1.10; 11.10, 13.13). Land is Israel's mother (Hos. 2.2, 4-5): 'she who conceived them' (Hos. 2.2a), 'the woman giving (him) birth' (Hos. 13.13, see Braaten 2000: 235). Ephraim, like a plant, is rooted in and draws his sustenance from his Mother Earth (e.g. Hos. 9.10, 13, 16; 10.1, 12-13; 14.5-7). YHWH is Land's husband and provider and Israel's father.[5] As such, YHWH desires offspring that serve and worship only him. When his children are faithful, YHWH blesses them and Land with fertility of offspring and agricultural produce (Hos. 2.8, cf. 14.5-8). When the Israelites are unfaithful, they reap what they sow and fertility fails (Hos. 8.7-10; cf. 4.16; 5.7; 9.1-2, 10-12). YHWH then disowns his rebellious children, casting them out of (*grsh*) God's house (Hos. 9.15; Braaten 1987: 308-10). This three-way relationship between YHWH, Land and people is epitomized in Hosea by the symbolic name of the first child—Jezreel: 'God sows' or 'God inseminates'. This name not only symbolizes YHWH's judgment (Hos. 1.3) and restoration of Land, vegetation and people (Hos. 1.11; 2.22-23; Braaten 2000), but it also emphasizes God and Israel's intimate association with Land.

---

4. 'Naked I came from my *mother's womb*, naked I shall return *there*' (NRSV, italics added). 'The place of Job's return is obviously not his mother's womb, but the (womb of the) land' (Braaten 1987: 287), cf. Qoh. 5.15 and Sir. 40.1. Likewise, the Ps. 139 passage parallels God's personal creation of the psalmist in the womb of a human mother with creation in the depths of Earth.

5. Although the idea of YHWH as father/begetter and Earth as womb or matrix of Israel (and the rest of creation) underlies much of Hosea's imagery, the prophet sometimes uses other images; for instance, Hosea depicts YHWH as Israel's parent, possibly as mother, by an act of adoption from Egypt in the Exodus (Hos. 11.1-7). Likewise, in Hosea Israel (Ephraim) is usually called God's 'son' (Hos. 11.1; 13.13, a collective noun), or God's 'sons' (Hos. 1.10; 2.4; see Schmitt 1983). To be consistent with the father–son imagery explored in this essay, masculine pronouns will be used for God and Israel.

In Hosea, Land is not just real estate where the drama of salvation is played out or where Israel receives agricultural blessing—she is a major participant in the story. Hosea assumes that YHWH, Land and people are bound together as an interconnected whole. When anything in the relationship goes wrong, it affects all parties and disrupts the entire relationship. Whenever one member of this three-way relationship is affected by sin or suffering, the others are drawn in, they are all somehow involved in both the sin and the suffering. The two-way dialogue between YHWH and Israel is well known (Sheppard 1992: 143-44). When the people suffer, they cry out in prayer and lamentation to YHWH. When YHWH finds something amiss with the people, God speaks to them through a prophet. But Land is an often overlooked but important third party in the conversation (see Fretheim 2000: 104). When violence, idolatry and sexual misconduct are practiced upon Land, she recoils; she is rendered defiled, she mourns; sickened, she vomits out the offending poisonous portion.

We have already seen that Hosea sometimes refers to Land as YHWH's house or household. It is popular today to picture the interrelationships of the environment in terms of a house, or *oikos* – from which we get the prefix for ecology. But the term 'community' would be a more comprehensive and organic term for the whole, and would more accurately preserve Hosea's social meaning. With this in view, I shall borrow and adapt Thomas Berry's term 'Earth community' (Hessel [ed.] 1996: 2-3)[6] to characterize the society formed by these three entities. We could illustrate this relationship heuristically by a triangle with Earth community in the center (Fig. 1; modified from C.J.H. Wright 1990: 105).

All relationships are conducted in the context of each party's membership in Earth community. Interaction between any two parties necessarily affects and involves the third since each is a member of the community at large. There is no interaction between YHWH and people that does not also include Land. Likewise, it is not possible for people or Land to be considered apart from their relationship to one another and to YHWH. Although YHWH is not to be reduced to just another member of Earth community, God's presence is intimately bound up and connected with the actions of all its members. Any action taken by a member of Earth community, for good or ill, implicates all members, including God. So if sin results in disaster in Earth community, then God's 'purpose' in the disaster is assumed to be

6.   This term is also used by the Earth Bible Project to refer to all members of God's creation on Earth, animate and inanimate.

judgment against this sin. Much effort is expended in the Hebrew Bible justifying God's 'purpose' in destructive events whose origins could be otherwise explained (Barton 1990). The accusations against Land in Hosea 2 need to be considered in this light.

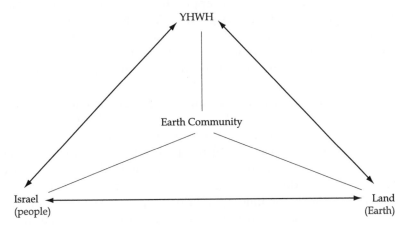

Figure 1. *Earth Community Relationships.*

We have already explored the positive background for the YHWH–Land–people relationship in Hosea. But the dominant account of this three-way relationship in Hosea is negative: the relationship has been disrupted due to 'whoredom' (Hos. 1.2; 2.2, 4, 5; 4.10-14; 5.3-4; 6.10) and 'bloodshed'[7] (Hos. 1.4; 4.2; 6.8; 12.14). The prophet has been called to declare and justify God's judgment against the sin that has disrupted and distorted the relationships in Earth community.

Estrangement in Earth Community (Hosea 2.2-13)

Hos. 2.2-13 indicates how the relationship between YHWH and Land and Israel has broken down. Hosea portrays this fractured relationship with an extended metaphor of sin as whoredom, which he then correlates with the judgment of YHWH (Miller 1982: 7, 9). For this metaphor to have its effect, however, Hosea presupposes that the hearers already believe and accept the basis for the imagery, viz.: Land is the wife of YHWH and the Israelites are the 'offspring' of YHWH and Land. If the people had not already presupposed this, it would be easy for them to justify indifference to Hosea's message. 'The Israelites would simply deny the accusations by denying that they are the

---

7.   NRSV 'crimes'; see Braaten 2000: 220.

offspring of the land' or that Land was YHWH's wife (Braaten 1987: 290). It is apparent that although the people thought of the relationship of YHWH with Land as a marriage, they saw nothing wrong with Land having other partners, the *baals*. The effectiveness of Hosea's challenge to this view lies in his application of the standards of Israelite marriage to Land's marriage with YHWH: if the bride is not committed to her husband and seeks sexual gratification outside the marriage relationship, then she is guilty of 'whoredom' and so deserves punishment. Hosea therefore fills his oracles with allusions to ancient family laws and customs.

The passage begins with Hosea employing a parable-like legal action similar to Isaiah's Song of the Vineyard (Isa. 5.1-7). Hosea announces God's call for the children—God's people—to initiate a legal action against their mother—Land.[8] 'Accuse (*ribu be*) your mother! Accuse! For she is not my wife, and I am not her husband!' (Hos. 2.2a; see Andersen and Freedman 1980: 221). YHWH threatens a certain end to the family relationships unless the bride responds to YHWH's remedial punitive actions. Ostensibly, the children are commanded to get involved in the accusations due to self-interest: they share their mother's status and fate and will be disowned as 'children of whoredom' if they do not persuade her to change (Hos. 2.4-5; cf. comments above on Hos. 1.6, 9). The call to accuse Land with the charge of whoredom is actually a rhetorical device employed to get the Israelites involved in pronouncing judgment upon themselves as the true guilty party (see below on Hos. 2.8).

YHWH's first command to his wife is to take off the ornamental signs of promiscuity from her face and between her breasts (Hos. 2.2b, cf. 2.13; see Wolff 1974: 33-34). If she will not yield, YHWH threatens to strip and expose her and kill her with thirst (Hos. 2.3). The background for this threat is the cruel fate men imposed upon women charged with sexual misconduct in the ancient world: she could be publicly stripped (cf. Nah. 3.4-6; Ezek. 16.37-38; 23.22-35), or executed by burning (see Gen. 38.24; Lev. 21.9; cf. Ezek. 16.41; 23.26, 29; cf. Lev. 20.14 and CH 157 in *ANET* 172). In Hosea Land will be stripped of her

---

8.   Nothing in the text suggests that Hos. 2 is an account of the prophet Hosea addressing *his three children* with a threat to punish *their mother* and *his wife Gomer* (Braaten 1987: 67-68). Hos. 2, unlike chs. 1 and 3, is not prophetic biography recounting a symbolic action. The assumption that Hosea divorced and remarried his wife is based on a view that Hos. 3 recounts the prophet's *remarriage* to Gomer. It is more likely that Hos. 3 is a second tradition presenting an alternative interpretation of Hos. 1–2 (Braaten 1987: 68-72, 279-80; cf. Yee 1987: 62).

vegetational covering, rendering her like a parched desert burned by 'thirst' (Hos. 2.3b; cf. Braaten 1987: 262-64).

But before the description of this act is given, a further consequence of the situation is spelled out: God will withdraw compassion from his children because they are 'children of whoredom' shamefully conceived by their mother (Hos. 2.4-5a; cf. 5.7). For the first time we hear the voice of Land explaining her behavior (although quoted as an accusation by her offended husband; see van Dijk-Hemmes 1996: 285): 'I will go after my lovers, the providers of my grain, my water, my wool and my flax, my oil and my drink' (Hos. 2.5). Land has sought to fulfill real needs, yet she turned to the cult of lovers rather than to the legitimate cult of her husband YHWH to fill them. How could this happen?

The persistence of the wife in her sin is recounted in the next few verses, which are difficult to follow. Hos. 2.6-7 appears to be a disruptive parenthesis when interpreted as a threat of *future* judgment (e.g., NRSV). Hos. 2.8 does not seem to suitably follow Hos. 2.6-7 when the latter is translated in the future tense. This problem is often resolved by various proposals that would move Hos. 2.6-7 or 2.8 elsewhere in Hosea 2 (see the discussion in Wolff 1974: 35-36). But if Hos. 2.6-7 is translated as a record of a past judgment rather than as a threat of future judgment, it makes sense in context (Braaten 1987: 257-61). In this interpretation, the woman's guilt due to her 'shameful' behavior (Hos. 2.5) is heightened since YHWH's past remedial action (Hos. 2.6-7) did not change her (Hos. 2.8). The point of Hos. 2.6-8 in this reading, therefore, is to justify YHWH's further threats of judgment in Hos. 2.9 and throughout Hos. 2.2-13.

Because of Land's 'liaisons' with lovers, YHWH had disciplined her. He had blocked the bride's paths to lovers with hedges of thorns and a wall; that is, he frustrated her attempts to find productivity through deities (cf. Job 19.8 and Lam. 3.9) other than YHWH. When she continued to pursue them, she was unable to find them (Hos. 2.6-7a). YHWH's plan had apparently worked, and so we hear the voice of Land reconsidering who her real provider is: 'I will go back to my first husband, for it was better for me then than now' (Hos. 2.7b). But here a breakdown in communication becomes evident:

> But she did not know that it was I who gave her the grain, the wine and the olive oil. Silver I multiplied for her, and gold—but they made it into a *baal* (Hos. 2.8).

Under God's judgment it appears that Land has now completely forgotten who her real provider has been. Rather than see her past calamities as YHWH's corrective judgment, she concludes that the former inhabitants were right—Baal is Land's husband (cf. Hos. 2.13a). So she continues to serve the *baals* and pursue her lovers (Hos. 2.8, 10, 12, 13). YHWH has a different view. Although YHWH may have once allowed Land to confess 'Baal' ('master' or 'husband') as her deity, it was really YHWH who stood behind that title from the beginning (Hos. 2.8a, cf. v. 16).

But there is more—a careful reading confirms that Land does not stand alone in her guilt. It is they—the children—who took the very gifts YHWH granted through Land (silver and gold) and fashioned these into a *baal* image (Hos. 2.8; cf. 13.1-2). Land, as a member of Earth community, suffers guilt from the sins of its human citizens. This is a turning point in the oracle. Now it is evident that the children are the very ones who have corrupted Land in the first place by practicing a baalistic fertility cult, including prostitution (cf. Hos. 4.12-14; 5.3-7; 7.14; 9.1-2; 11.2; 13.1-3), thereby bringing Land into prostitution or 'whoredom' (cf. Jer. 3.1-2; Lev. 19.26; Brueggemann 1977: 119-20).

It is now apparent that YHWH's lawsuit against the mother, Land (Hos. 2.2), in effect becomes a lawsuit against the children, the Israelites. From this point on all charges against Land are ultimately charges against the Israelites who are responsible for bringing Land into 'whoredom' by worshiping the *baals* as Land's provider. The primary guilt of Israel is also conveyed by the structure of the major literary unit. In Hosea 1 and 3 the primary focus is upon the sin of the people and their deserved judgment. All mention of Land is dropped in Hosea 3, where the bride represents 'the sons of Israel' (Hos. 3.1, 4, 5; see NASB) rather than Land. Since Hosea 1 and 3 frame Hosea 2, the effect is to focus the reader on the responsibility of the people, and not Land.[9] If the reader fails to see this here, then the introductory oracle in the next section will leave no doubt about who bears ultimate responsibility for the demise of Land. Hos. 4.1-3 is a lawsuit by YHWH against the people in response to the mourning voice of Land (here 'Earth'). YHWH resolves to act against the people for the sake of Earth and her creaturely inhabitants.

Responding to Earth community's break with the creator, YHWH says he will again cut off fertility from Land as a further act of corrective judgment (Hos. 2.9-13). At this point, if Land is going to speak, we would expect her to cry out in complaint against those who are polluting her and causing her demise, as we find elsewhere in the

---

9.   The final shape of Hos. 1–3 is so successful at conveying the message that the primary guilt is due to the people that many readers miss the indications that YHWH's marital accusations in Hos. 1–2 are against Land, and not the people.

Hebrew Bible. Yet the only words she utters reveal her continued solidarity with her children. Not only does she not raise her voice in protest, but also—we now discover—she has declared that her agricultural abundance was prostitute's pay from her lovers (Hos. 2.12, cf. 9.1)! The reader must wait until Hosea 4 to hear the voice of Land recoiling against victimization by her offspring.

It is important to remember, however, what we have discussed above as we ponder Land's words. First, these are words attributed to Land as the prophet attempts to explain YHWH's judgment against her. These words ultimately reflect the guilt of the children, and so in effect serve to bring further judgment to bear against them. In a similar vein, the interconnectedness of Earth community might serve to explain the bride's words. If one member speaks, that member speaks for the whole. In that case Land would have no choice but to speak what the children speak for her. The true voice of Land is suppressed as others 'put words in her mouth'. It is also possible, however, that Hosea depicts Land allowing the children to speak through her, in an effort to hasten YHWH's corrective judgment and purge the whoredom and bloodshed of the people from her soil. However interpreted, it is apparent that Land is ultimately a victim of her children's sin; their sin has brought her husband's judgment upon her.

The second series of judgments (introduced by *laken*, Hos. 2.9a) is still impending: YHWH will strip Land of her vegetational 'clothing'; he will take back her grain, wine, wool and flax (Hos. 2.9). God will devastate her vineyards and fig orchards; they will become thickets providing food for wild animals (Hos. 2.12). The baalistic fertility cults will be ended (Hos. 2.11, cf. v. 13). The cessation of cult festivals, the growth of thorns and thickets and the increased presence of animals indicate that Land will be emptied of her human inhabitants, who will be taken into exile (cf. Hos. 8.5-10; 9.1-6, 15; 10.7-8). Yet YHWH's wife still seems to have forgotten him (Hos. 2.13), so YHWH will continue to discipline her with the rest of Earth community until she—they—remember and return. Earth community's demise seems certain unless one of its members take immediate and drastic action. Such action is promised in Hos. 2.14-23.

Earth Community Reconciled (Hosea 2.14-17)

This passage presents YHWH's plan for reconciliation after the harsh realities of judgment and exile have their purging effect on Land. The proposed reconciliation of the entire Earth community calls for a slight change in the husband–wife imagery from that found in Hos. 2.2-13.

In Hos. 2.14-15 the reader notices that the bride will be 'taken into' the
desert rather than be 'made like' a desert as in Hos. 2.3.[10] Furthermore, the declaration that the bride 'came out of the land of Egypt'
(Hos. 2.15c) is analogous to formulas applied to the people elsewhere
in Hosea (e.g. Hos. 11.1; 12.13; 13.4). It is evident that the bride in
Hos. 2.14-15 now includes the human community, and is no longer
Land *per se*. Since the sinful people, in their solidarity with Land, were
responsible for bringing Land under judgment, God will bring Land
out of judgment by changing the people. This change in the people
will also affect Land, since the people are in solidarity with her. When
the reader comes to Hos. 2.16 the bride once again seems to be Land,
or at least both Land and people in their corporate unity as members
of Earth community.

We will now look at Hos. 2.14-17 in greater detail. The passage is
introduced by the third 'therefore' in Hosea 2. The first (*laken hineni*,
Hos. 2.6) introduces an account of YHWH's past judgment; the second
(*laken*, Hos. 2.9) introduces God's impending judgment. This third and
final 'therefore' (*laken hinneh*) introduces another impending action.
Whether this will be more judgment or salvation is initially ambigu-
ous. The oracle begins with language cognizant of past violence. 'I will
seduce her... I will speak to her heart' (Hos. 2.14). 'Seduce' is the
language of violation, trickery and deception and rape (Exod. 22.16; 1
Sam. 3.25; Jer. 20.7; Prov. 16.29). 'Speak to the heart' are words men
often speak to women when they are seeking to counter past abuse or
a breach in a relationship—perpetrated either by themselves or by
another (e.g., Gen. 34.2-3; Judg. 19.3; Ruth 2.13; cf. Isa. 40.2; see van
Dijk-Himmes 1996: 287). But these same words are often used to offer
comfort to mourners who have suffered violence, sometimes due to
the sins of themselves or others (Gen. 50.21; Ruth 2.13; cf. Isa. 40.1-2,
see Pham 1999: 31-32, 111). In Hosea, YHWH brings the bride to the
frightful land of the wilderness for a last act of remedial discipline,
hopeful that he will finally gain her attention. As a pledge of good
faith YHWH will redistribute Land's gifts, the vineyards lost in
judgment (Hos. 2.15a; cf. 2.12). YHWH's action has its intended effect;
the bride will 'answer' YHWH 'like the days of her youth, as (in) the
day she came up from the land of Egypt' (Hos. 2.15c). As mentioned
above, here the bride appears to be Earth community, represented by
the human community that now will properly confess YHWH as

---

10. According to the MT; the major Greek codices translate the verse as 'I will
designate her as a desert' (see *BHK*). It is likely that these translators were attempt-
ing to harmonize this passage with the previous imagery.

provider. Next, YHWH gives the bride a new way of speaking: she
will call YHWH 'my husband' (*'ishi*) rather than 'my Baal' (*ba'ali*)
when God removes the names of the *baals* from her mouth (Hos. 2.16-
17). This corrects the earlier misunderstanding concerning Land's identification of her real husband (Hos. 2.7-8, 13).

Although YHWH is depicted as acting for the good of Earth community, the restoration of the relationship looks rather one-sided up
to this point. Is YHWH's goal to restore to Land her lost voice, or is
God content to dominate her and force her to submit by stripping her,
making her repent,[11] and changing her into what the divine master
wants (cf. van Dijk-Hemmes 1996: 288-89)? At the beginning of Hosea
2, YHWH let the children speak for Land and then brought Land and
children under his judgment. What will be the result of Land 'speaking' only the words YHWH allows her to speak in Hos. 2.16-17? Will
Land have the inner strength to be faithful in her relationships in
Earth community? If YHWH's goal is to master her, what right has
God to reject the title of the patriarchal lords (*baals*)? The reader will
have to wait until the end of Hosea 2 before all these questions are
answered.

Earth Community Re-Created (Hosea 2.18-23)

This passage presents Earth community in one of the most comprehensive ways in the entire book: it is more than the northern kingdom
or the Holy Land; it includes YHWH, Heavens, Earth, the wild animals, birds of the air, creeping things, the grain, wine and oil and God's
people. Before we begin reading the passage, however, we must once
again sort out the identity of the various addressees. More particularly, how do we determine the antecedents of the various pronouns:
'they/them' (masc. pl. Hos. 2.18, 21, 22), 'you/your' (fem. sing., Hos.
2.19, 20) and 'her/it' (Hos. 2.23)? A partial solution to this problem is
reached by noting another slight change in the identity of the bride.
As we have seen, in Hos. 2.4-13 Land plays the role of bride, whereas
in Hos. 2.14-17 the bride is the human community bound with Land.
In Hos. 2.18-23, however, the bride is once again Land (designated by
fem. sing. pronouns), while the plural pronouns seem to refer to the
people and the other inhabitants of Land, i.e., Earth community.

---

11. It is possible that the stripping of Hos. 2 connotes an imposed mourning
(Hayes 1997: 1-23, 69-72) that constitutes a ritual mourning for the sins of Earth
community (see Hos. 4.1-3; cf. Braaten 2000: 223-24).

Hos. 2.18 provides the foundation for YHWH's designs for Earth community. After removing the names of the *baals* from Land, YHWH declares:

> I will cut for them a covenant on that day with the wild animals, the birds of the heavens and the creeping things of the ground. And I will break the bow, the sword and warfare from the Land, and I will make them lie down securely.

The covenant is transacted with the animals 'for them',[12] that is, for Earth community. What does this mean?

The covenant with the animals alludes to the lists of animals found in the creation narratives of Genesis 1–11 (see Gen. 1.20-30; 2.20; 9.1-17). Each of these narratives describes an aspect of the human relationship with the animals: they have dominion over them (Gen. 1.26), they name them (Gen. 2.20), God makes a covenant with humans and animals, and the animals will begin to fear humans (Gen. 9.1-17). Hos. 2.18 can also be compared to texts that envisage a return to primeval conditions by removal of wild animals (Lev. 26.6; Ezek. 34.25; cf. 14.21; Isa. 35.9; and Job 5.17-27; the first two texts also mention the removal of warfare; cf. Hayes 1998: 4, 6). Some scholars draw attention to the similarities of the Hosea passage with the ancient Near Eastern motif of a 'covenant of peace' as a restoration to primeval times after the destruction of creation by the gods (Isa. 54.10; Ezek. 34.25; 37.26; cf. Batto 1987).

While Hos. 2.18 bears some verbal similarities to all of these texts, there are some important differences. First, the groups of texts that mention the removal of animals presuppose hostility between animals and humans, and focus on saving the humans from these malevolent creatures. The description of the animals bears this out: they are called 'harmful animals' (*chayyah ra'ah*, Lev. 26.6; Ezek. 34.25), 'violent animals' (*perits chayyot*, Isa. 35.9), animals that the people fear (Job 5.22-23, cf. Hayes 1998: 3-5). In Hosea the animals are not given these negative roles. Although they have participated in God's judgment

---

12. The common expression for making a covenant, *karat berit*, literally 'cut a covenant', can be followed by an object introduced either by *l-* (e.g. Exod. 23.32; Deut. 7.2; 1 Sam. 11.2; Isa. 55.3; 61.8; Jer. 32.40) or by *'im-* (e.g. Exod. 24.8; Deut. 4.23; 5.2; 9.9; 1 Kgs 8.21; KB *s.v. karat*). In the only other occurrence of the phrase in Hosea (Hos. 12.1) the expression *karat berit 'im-* is employed. I interpret the *lhm* in Hos. 2.18 as a dative construction; see GKC 119s (1). The grammar of Hos. 2.18 does not suggest that God is instituting a covenant between animals and people (contra to Macintosh 1997: 82; Bergant 1994: 11; and others).

against Earth community (Hos. 2.12), they are nowhere given disparaging labels because of their effect upon humans. The second difference grows out of the first: each of the other texts emphasizes a direct benefit for or covenant with the people (Lev. 26.9; Isa. 35.9-10; 54.9-10[?]; Ezek. 34.25; 37.26; Job 5.22-23), whereas the covenant in Hosea is made directly with the animals for the sake of Earth community. Third, while Land is mentioned in many of the other passages, it is primarily to introduce a direct benefit for the people.[13] In Hosea Land continues to be the direct recipient of God's action. A fourth difference grows out of the others: in Hosea there is no hint of human dominance over Earth community as the Genesis texts imply.[14] We are now ready for a detailed interpretation of the passage.

First, why does God make a covenant with the animals? The broader context supplied by the book of Hosea suggests the answer. The animals are members of Earth community who have participated in the judgment of God. From one perspective, they have benefited from God's judgment on Land since they were allowed to devour her produce (e.g. Hos. 2.12). But once the initial feedings are over and the devastations of drought and warfare take effect, the animals find themselves sharing in the suffering of Earth community. The animals suffer as victims under the sins of the human inhabitants as they languish and mourn together with Earth (Hos. 4.1-3). Therefore any restoration of Earth community must include freeing the animals from this undeserved suffering. In correcting these injustices, however, God gives the animals a new dominant role in Earth community. It is almost as if the prophet is saying that since people have failed in their role as custodians of the covenant with creation, it will now be the animals' turn to mediate the covenant to the people! Ironically, this situation is almost exactly the opposite of the other covenants of peace, where the animals are viewed as instruments of God's judgment and then vilified when that judgment is reversed.

It is still necessary, however, for the animals in Hosea to know that although God will provide for them, it will not be at the expense of the rest of Earth community as before. This leads to a second question: in what way do the members of Earth community share in the

13.   An exception is Lev. 26.34 where God threatens judgment through warfare, wild animals, and exile so that Land might enjoy her Sabbaths (which humans have neglected).

14.   As is often observed today, the 'dominion' that humans are granted in Gen. 1 is circumscribed by the qualification that humans image God, that is, that they mediate God's creation blessing to Earth and stand in creative, not exploitative, relationship with her and the rest of creation.

covenant, i.e., in what way is the covenant 'for (the sake of) them'? We need to look back at the first section of Hosea 2 for the answer. Land is a beneficiary of the covenant because she was the first object of God's judgment. Two of the three means of that judgment are removed from her in this covenant with the animals (Hos. 2.18). The first is the devouring animals themselves (Hos. 2.12), as mentioned above. The second is warfare, the destruction caused by the invading armies. This promise to remove warfare is not strictly anthropocentric. God removes warfare 'from the Land' since war's effects ravage her and all her inhabitants, including her vegetation[15] and animal life. Although not the sole focus, humans are included in this covenant. The cessation of armed conflict allows 'them', i.e., Earth community, represented by humans and animals, to once again 'lie down securely' in a wholly restored Land and Earth community. Drought, the third means of judgment against Land, is alluded to in the restoration of vineyards (Hos. 2.15) and the 'answering' of the grain, wine and oil (Hos. 2.22).

Hos. 2.19-20 depicts the restored relationship with Earth community in terms of a new marriage covenant (Wolff 1974: 47).[16] YHWH declares:

> I will betroth you to me forever, I will betroth you to me with (the bridewealth of)[17] righteousness and justice, loving commitment and compassion, I will betroth you with (the bridewealth of) faithfulness, and you will know YHWH.

Bridewealth assures the woman that this is a legitimate marriage with the consent of the wife's family, and with rights to legal protection granted by the husband. It also indicates that the offspring of the marriage are legitimate, and will be granted full legal rights as heirs (Taber 1976: 575).[18] Hosea once again depicts Land as God's bride,

---

15. See Hos. 2.3, 9-10, 12; and cf. 8.7-9; 9.2-3 where *Israel* is warned of agricultural devastation by the Assyrian invasion and exile.

16. The exile presupposed in Hos. 2.14 is a separation and divorce of Land (and Earth community), which God attempted to avoid at the beginning of the chapter (Hos. 2.2-4, see Wolff 1974: 33). If the laws forbidding divorce and remarriage with the same woman (Deut. 24.1-4) were known at the time of the composition of this passage, then the writer was not concerned to apply them consistently or explain their violation, as was Jeremiah in another time (Jer. 3).

17. The Hebrew term for bridewealth, *mohar*, is not present, but is implied in the sentence. For the translation of *'rs* PN *b*-X as 'I shall betroth PN to me with the bridewealth consisting of X' see 2 Sam. 3.14, cf. 1 Sam. 18.25 (KB, *s.v. 'rs*; see Braaten 1987: 188-89, 276-77; and Wolff 1974: 52).

18. 'Bridewealth' (or 'bride wealth') is the term now preferred by anthropologists rather than the tendentious term 'bride price', which implies marriage by

with Earth community representing the family receiving the bride-wealth. The bridewealth 'rendered' here is an attribute that is necessary for maintaining faithfulness and commitment to God and community. The lack of these attributes in Israel (e.g. *chsd* in Hos. 4.2; 6.4, 6; 10.12-13 and *'mt* in 4.1) led to the demise of Earth community due to sin. Others are connected with God's judgment against sin (*rchm*, in Hos. 1.6; 2.4; cf. 14.3; for *tsdq* and *mshpt* see Wolff 1974: 52). Being deficient in these attributes, Israel's commitment to other members of Earth community and to YHWH has repeatedly failed. YHWH now indicates a commitment to Land and her offspring by giving these attributes to Earth community at large. Earth community now has the means for all of its members to sustain commitments within the community and with the divine provider. In summary, Hos. 2.18-20 offers a multifaceted view of the restoration of Earth community. It includes YHWH's covenant with the animals, an assurance of security for God's offspring, and a new marriage commitment to Land.

The final verses of Hosea 2 develop the themes begun in the previous verses. They bear a striking resemblance to motifs found in the covenant of peace mentioned above (Batto 1987: 199-205).

> And it shall be in that day, I will answer (oracle of YHWH) —
> I will answer the Heavens, and they will answer Earth (*'erets*);[19]
> Earth will answer the grain, the wine and the oil;
> They shall answer Jezreel ['God sows'],
> I will sow it for myself in the Land (*'erets*).
> I will have compassion on Not-Found-Compassion,
> and I will say to Not-My-People 'You are My People'
> and he will say 'My God' (Hos. 2.21-23).

Earlier in this paper we questioned whether or not the bride answered YHWH because YHWH forced her into submission in the desert, and whether or not she had the inner power to maintain a commitment to YHWH. The final answers to these questions are found in this passage: here Land responds of her own accord, not only to YHWH but also to members of Earth community. Land, or Earth, now has the capacity to answer and speak with her own voice. This response is clearly free from divine domination. Because YHWH empowers Land

purchase (cf. Taber 1976 and Braaten 1987, ch. 4, 'Bridewealth and Maternal Status in Anthropological Perspective').

19. In this passage the term *'erets* is not just Land as the territory of Israel, but connotes Land in its broadest meaning, Earth. It is possible to use Land and Earth interchangeably here. The work of transformation of *'erets* narrowly conceived (Land) is paradigmatic of a comprehensive transformation of the *'erets* more universally conceived (Earth).

to do this she will know that this is YHWH, and not one of the *baals*. This interpretation is confirmed in the first line of Hos. 2.23 where we read that God sows 'it' for himself 'in the Earth'. The antecedent of 'it' (fem. sing.) is much debated. A plausible interpretation is that 'it' is used collectively, referring to the items previously mentioned, including the covenant (a feminine noun) and the attributes of the bridewealth (cf. Batto 1987: 202 n. 46). If this is correct, then the 'it' of Hos. 2.23 forms an *inclusio* with the 'covenant' of Hos. 2.18 which is thereby connected with the bridewealth attributes of Hos. 2.19-20.

What does it mean when YHWH says he sows it 'for myself' (*li*)? First, it should be observed that the *li* in Hos. 2.23 repeats the three-fold use of *li* in Hos. 2.19-20 (Andersen and Freedman 1980: 290). One possible meaning of the *li* in Hos. 2.23 is that it strengthens the verb. In this case it could be omitted or roughly translated 'I myself will sow it'.[20] Another possibility is that it is similar to the *lhm* construction of Hos. 2.18. In that passage, as we have seen, YHWH's *direct* action in the covenant is for the animals, but this includes indirect benefits 'for them' (*lhm*). If Hos. 2.23 is to be interpreted similarly, then it means that YHWH's action gives Earth the ability to respond 'to me' (i.e. to YHWH), the emphasis being upon YHWH's action for Land, not on how YHWH benefits from the transaction. YHWH empowers Land to answer on her own by the bridewealth attributes sown 'in the Land'. Through this empowerment, Land completely regains her suppressed voice; Land is also enabled to sustain her commitment to YHWH.

God's planting grants life to all members of Earth community, including the children. The name Jezreel formerly symbolized God's judgment on the Jehu dynasty and Israel (Hos. 1.4-5). It now symbolizes God's sowing of salvation in and for Earth community, particularly for Land/Earth. The disownment of the children (indicated by the symbolic names of ch. 1), resulting in their expulsion from the Land (Hos. 9.15), is reversed by the positive transformation of the names, connoting their security in and God's planting in the Land (Hos. 2.18-23). This sequence is similar to Hos. 1.10-2.1, where God promises that the children's names will be reversed and then they will 'go up from the Land' (Hos. 1.11)—a figure of speech applicable both to the Exodus and the growing of a plant rooted in the soil (Yee 1987: 75). In this way, the end of Hosea 2 is bracketed with the disownment oracles of Hosea 1, and with the reversals and plant imagery of Hos. 1.10–2.1 (the beginning of Hos. 2 in the Hebrew text).

---

20. This 'ethical dative' usage is suggested by Macintosh, who leaves the *li* untranslated (Macintosh 1997: 89; cf. GKC 119s). The ethical dative occurs elsewhere in Hosea at Hos. 2.2; 8.9; 10.1; 12.9; and 13.2 (BDB *s.v. l-* 5.i.).

We can illustrate the major elements of the renewed relationship outlined in Hos. 2.14-23 by modifying (Fig. 2) the Earth community triangle used in earlier Fig. 1. The arrows leading from YHWH and forming a triangle connote the 'answering'. Although there is no mention of an 'answering' between Jezreel and Land, an arrow with a question mark is supplied for the sake of completion. We will return to this later.

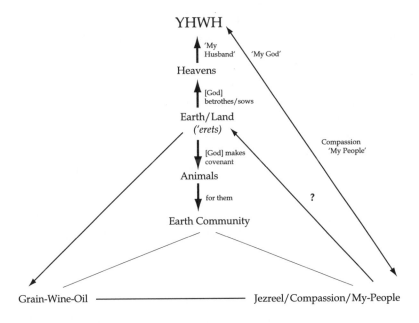

Figure 2. *The New Earth Community in Hosea 2*

The diagram reveals a surprising new place for Earth under a reformulated dominance of YHWH. In this Hosean vision of a renewed Earth community, the order of creation is reversed. Through the assistance of the blessings of the Heavens, *'erets*, Earth or Land, stands as head over produce and people in her role of mediating and granting life. Since human sin has set in motion a series of events that have damaged the fabric of creation, Earth is the first recipient of God's salvation. At the other end of the triangle are the people. Humans are presented here in their utter dependence upon Earth for their life and sustenance. The blessings of Heaven will not reach them unless mediated through the sustaining nurture of their Mother Earth. Likewise, the grace of God declaring them God's people does not and cannot reach them in a placeless void. 'In *the place where* it was said to them, "You are not my people", it will be said to them, "Children of the

living God"' (Hos. 1.10, NRSV, emphasis added). Without Land or
Earth there is no locus for life, blessing, or the grace of God.

While humans usually consider themselves the keepers of Earth
(based on such passages as Gen. 2.15), here they are reminded that it
is Earth who keeps them. Humans have not always done well at
protecting the very Earth that sustains their life. Because humans have
failed as mediators of God's covenant and as conveyors of God's
blessing on Earth community, God can appoint other covenant mediators (animals!) and 'keepers' (Earth herself) of this community. This is
a radical departure from a widely attested biblical pattern of the ordering of creation (e.g. Gen. 1.26-30; Ps. 8.6-8; cf. Gen. 9.8-17). If humans
will not respect the intrinsic value of creation, then God will do what
is necessary to preserve Earth community, even if it means rearrang-
ing the order of creation to suit this end.

As we look back over this section we see in this Hoseanic vision a
portrayal of the new creation (Wolff 1974: 55; Bergant 1994: 15). It is a
place where YHWH surrenders divine power in a loving commitment
(*chesed*) to Earth community. God has empowered Earth and Earth
community to respond to him by surrendering the bridewealth attributes to Earth community; he has sown them in the Land; he has
committed himself in covenant with the animals. Since YHWH has
willingly identified with Earth community, those who seek YHWH's
presence find it primarily in God's sustaining power in relationship to
their fellow creatures of Earth. Although YHWH occasionally makes
the divine power and mercy directly available to members of the
community, this 'inbreaking' is not the norm.

YHWH is not, however, to be equated with scientific laws or metaphysical processes. YHWH has identified with, but is not reduced to,
Earth community. 'Divine' power is still capable of releasing destructive forces on Earth community. The cosmos ('the Heavens') may lash
out against Earth community with storm, flood, earthquake, drought
and pestilence—phenomena that are sometimes called 'acts of God'.
The biblical writer depicts YHWH as directly behind all such events,
whatever their effect on Earth. They remain a mystery to humans who
cannot comprehend a beneficent God or cosmos without seeing everything directly working for their own benefit. But there is no mystery
behind the source of most of the damage done to Earth community.
Driven by the idolatry of greed, fueled by consumerism, humans have
taken their 'God-sown' power to creatively nurture Earth community
and have misused it to destroy Earth, her inhabitants, and even themselves.

At this point we need to return to Fig. 2 and discuss the arrow I supplied leading from the people to Earth, the arrow labeled with a question mark. We know an arrow belongs there because people will respond to Earth; the question is how? Perhaps the missing response is to be supplied by the reader. God has empowered Earth community to respond to each other and to their God. When Earth community responds properly, God is present among them as nurturing parent or spouse who sustains and nourishes them. But, as we have seen, when the human inhabitants of Earth community respond in ways that harm Earth community — with idolatry and violence — then destructive forces are unleashed against its members. When this happens Earth bears the consequence of human sin; she languishes, she mourns with Earth community to her God. In this response Earth provides her people with an example (Braaten 2000: 224). If humans will only mourn with her and willingly turn (*shub*) from their sin then Earth might be saved. But Earth will not sustain those who commit violence against her. If people continue the violence, then Earth and her inhabitants will perish, swept away by the consequences of the self-serving deeds of a few.

The action of each generation supplies the missing label on our diagram. Will humans today repeat the patterns condemned in Hosea's judgment oracles, or will they follow the lead of the rest of Earth community? Will we continue in the sins attacked by Hosea, decked out in new ornaments, and label the arrow 'greed', 'consumerism' and 'violence'? Or will we — in solidarity with Earth community — respond to God's gifts and Earth's nurture with gratitude and service to Earth, and so label the arrow 'You are our Mother' and 'loving commitment'?

Ecojustice or Anthropological Justice?
A Study of the New Heavens and the New Earth in Isaiah 65.17

Anne Gardner

Introduction

This paper is concerned with one verse in Isaiah, Isa. 65.17,[1] which asserts that God will create new heavens and a new Earth.[2] At first sight this assertion brings into play two main principles which are involved in an ecojustice hermeneutic:

1. the principle of intrinsic worth, which is concerned with whether 'the universe, Earth and all its components have equal value'; if new heavens and a new Earth are necessary, then why is this so? Are the previous heavens and Earth flawed in some way or have they decayed to the point where they can no longer be sustained? Even if, as some scholars maintain, 'new' does not mean 'destruction' and 're-creation', but merely a 'renewal' of what had existed previously, it must be asked: Why is renewal necessary?

2. the principle of purpose, which states that 'the universe, Earth and all its components are part of a dynamic cosmic design within which each piece has a place in the overall goal of that design', must also be put to the test: Does the re-creation/ renewal of heavens and Earth indicate that they were corresponding to their goal and purpose so little that they had to be realigned?

It is possible that a third principle comes into play in a minor way:

---

1.   Isa. 66.22 also asserts that God will make new heavens and a new Earth, but this will be the subject of another paper.
2.   In keeping with the focal point of the Earth Bible Project, 'Earth' is capitalized and treated as a proper name, except in direct quotations from the biblical text.

3.   the principle of interconnectedness, which asserts that 'Earth is a community of interconnected living beings which are mutually dependent on each other for life and survival', must also be considered. People, animals, reptiles and botanical life are part of Earth,[3] so what happens to them? Are they re-created or renewed? Are they interconnected?

These principles will be borne in mind in my exegesis of Isa. 65.17 where God creates 'new heavens and a new earth'.

The history of the literary-critical analysis of Isaiah is complex and the views of individual scholars are frequently contradictory, both on Isaiah as a whole[4] and on Isaiah 65–66 in particular.[5] Isa. 65.17 has also been seen as a later addition to the text.[6] For these reasons a synchronic approach to the text will be pursued in the present paper. This does not mean that it will be totally uncritical, for as Williamson (1999: 177) so cogently remarked, 'To be postcritical implies that we have first been critical; in the scholarly world there is no short cut to modernity'. It is apparent that in the verse concerned and in those of its immediate context, allusions are made to preceding chapters in Isaiah itself. Such an idea is not new: Clements (1982: 117-24; 1985: 95-113) and Rendtorff (1984: 295-322), who claim a redactional unity for Isaiah, have both asserted that there are close links between the various parts of Isaiah, with Isaiah 40–55 being pivotal. Conrad (1991) treats Isaiah as a whole, recognizing repetition in the various parts of the book. As he points out, however, 'repetition is always repetition with a difference. Variation in the recurrence of repeated elements in the text suggests movement and progression' (1991: 30). Such movement has been seen by Williamson (1999: 177, 194) to yield information concerning the relative dates of the passages studied. The question of dating aside, the approach approximates to the way in which the ancient

3.   Birds and fish have not been listed here as belonging to Earth as Gen. 1.20 specifies that birds are of the heavens and fish belong to the waters beneath Earth.

4.   For details of the scholarship on the historical/literary unity or disunity of Isaiah cf. Driver 1888; Pfeiffer 1948; Eissfeldt 1966.

5.   For a summary of scholarly criticism of Isaiah 65–66 cf. Gardner forthcoming, n. 2.

6.   Isa. 65.17 is thought by Westermann (1969: 306) to have been a later addition to the text as the verses that follow it are deemed not to be cosmic in character. Isa. 65 has been seen by Tomasino (1993: 96) to disrupt the thought sequence of Isa. 64.12 and Isa. 66.1. He claims that Isa. 65 was inserted into the text, in conscious imitation of Isa. 66.22, after the rebuilding of the Second Temple in Jerusalem, with the purpose of shifting attention away from an anti-cultic theme apparent in the original text.

listener/reader would have understood Isa. 65.17.[7] Further, connections have been made by some scholars between Isaiah and other biblical works: Sommer's approach in his thematic analysis of Isaiah 40–66 (1996) showed the presence of themes and vocabulary from Jeremiah in greater quantity than those from Isaiah 1–39; Wells (1996: 140-55) shows links between Isaiah 56–66 and legal texts in P, implicitly positing that P or its forerunner was in existence at the time of the writing of these Isaianic chapters. As such, the creation story of Gen. 1–2.4a, or much of it, would also have been available to our writer—a story which tells of the original creation of the heavens and Earth—as would the tale of the destruction of Earth at the time of the Flood, stories to which Isaiah may well have been alluding with his mention of new heavens and new Earth; Sehmsdorf (1972: 526-27) and, to a lesser extent, Smith (1995: 143, 146) show that Deuteronomy is the background to a number of Isaianic verses. The book of Psalms has also been seen as an influence on Isaiah (cf. Willey 1997).

Isa. 65.17 reads: 'For behold I am creating new heavens and a new earth and the former ones will not be remembered or come into mind'.

The commentators are divided as to what is implied by the notion of newness. The two views are as follows:

1. The old heavens and old Earth are to be physically destroyed and new ones created in their place. Skinner (cf. Kissane 1943: 311) for example, followed this view. It has also been adopted by Whybray (1975: 275-76), who thinks that Isa. 65.17 was added at a later time to the non-cosmic vision of Isa. 65.18-25 by someone who was inspired by Isa. 51.6, where the cosmic order is transitory. Biddle (1996: 139) appears to endorse the view that the heavens and Earth will be replaced.

2. The old heavens and old Earth are to be renewed in a metaphorical or figurative sense. Westermann (1969: 408) explicitly rejects the first view, saying that it belongs to apocalyptic literature. Instead the created order 'is to be miraculously renewed'. Kissane (1943: 311) is more specific, seeing 'the restoration of Sion' as 'a new world order in which piety and justice will prevail'. Watts (1987: 353) also takes the new heavens as indicative of a new world order and, like Kissane, links it to the events of history: 'the Persian Empire has Yahweh's salvation and Israel is called to be a worshipping and pilgrim people with Jerusalem as its focus' (1987: 354).

---

7.   Cf. Carr 1996: 193-97 for an excellent summary of the differences between the ancient and modern reader of texts.

Recreation or renewal? We could go even further: recreation or renewal of the heavens and Earth, or recreation/renewal of Zion and God's community? Or both? In order to determine the answer to these questions, Isa. 65.17 will first be looked at in its context[8] and then an enquiry will be made into the vocabulary used in the text and what connections the verse makes with previous Isaianic passages in terms of both theme and vocabulary.

Isa. 65.17 appears after a contrast on the one hand between those 'who did not seek me' (Isa. 65.1), 'who walk in a way that is not good, after their own thoughts' (Isa. 65.2) and appear to be worshipping deities other than YHWH (Isa. 65.3-7, 11) and, on the other hand, his 'servants' (Isa. 65.9, 13), who are identified as 'a seed out of Jacob, an inheritor out of Judah...my chosen ones' (Isa. 65.9). The latter will inherit God's mountains and dwell there (Isa. 65.9). In Isa. 65.13-15, which Smith (1995: 143) thinks is strongly influenced by Deut. 28.27-48, appear a series of contrasts addressed to God's servants about the future for the two groups: the servants will eat, the others will not; the servants will drink, the others will not; the servants will rejoice, the others will be ashamed; God's servants 'will sing for joy of heart' but the others 'will howl for breaking of spirit'; God 'will call his servants by another name' but the others will leave their name for an oath. Further, God will kill them. Isa. 65.16 is an enigmatic verse; it will be amplified later. After the creation of the new heavens and Earth in Isa. 65.17, a number of assertions about future bliss are made, many of which contrast with previous conditions or fulfil promises God had made.

1. God will be creating (*bore'*) Jerusalem a rejoicing (*gilah*) and her people a joy (*masos*) (Isa. 65.18). God says: 'I will rejoice (*galti*) in Jerusalem and joy (*sosti*) in her people and the sound of weeping (*beki*) and the sound of crying (*ze'aqah*) will be heard in her no more' (Isa. 65.19). 'Weeping' (*beki*) and 'crying' (*ze'aqah*) appear elsewhere in Isaiah in the context of destruction.[9] Against this background, the implication of the present

---

8.   Westermann (1969: 441) thinks that Isa. 65.16b-25 links with Isa. 60–62 and that it has been moved from directly following these chapters. A number of scholars follow his view in part or in whole (cf. Smith 1995: 144 n. 56). Smith (1995: 142-52) posits that, although there are some thematic similarities between the two blocks of material, Isa. 65.16b-25 shows linguistic links with biblical material other than Third Isaiah and was written independently of it.

9.   The Hebrew word *beki* is used of Moab weeping in Isa. 15.2, 3, 5; 16.9; of

passage is that God is creating a Jerusalem that will never again be destroyed. Instead it is to be a 'rejoicing' (*gilah*).[10] The only other occurrence of *gilah* is in Isa. 35.2 where the wilderness will blossom and rejoice when God's people are on their way to Zion, thus linking with Isa. 65.18-19.

2.   There will be no more premature death (Isa. 65.20). This may hark back to Gen. 6.3 where God limited the life-span of humans because of sin. Death was linked in Isa. 51.6 with the old heavens and old Earth and their passing. Isa. 25.8 asserts that God has 'swallowed up death forever', but this goes beyond Isa. 65.20 and Isa. 65.22 where life, although it is long, is limited. The sinner is cursed (*yequllal*). This may be an allusion to Ps. 37.22 where it is said that the wicked are cursed (*mequllalaw*) by God.

3.   Houses built will be inhabited by those who build them and vineyards will have their fruit eaten by those who plant them and not by another (Isa. 65.21). This provides a counterpart to Deut. 28.30 where those who do not listen to God's commandments would 'build, but not dwell therein, plant a vineyard and not use the fruits thereof'. Smith (1995: 146) also makes a link to Zeph. 1.13.

4.   God's people will have lives as long as the life of a tree (Isa. 65.22). Unless the tree referred to is the tree of life (Gen. 2.9; 3.22, 24), and there is no indication that it is, trees still die. The tree imagery may link with Isa. 61.3 where God's new community is to be called 'Trees of Righteousness'. The simile of a righteous person as like a tree also appears in Ps. 1.3 and Jer. 17.8.

Judah in Isa. 22.4, 12, and in Isa. 38.3 of Hezekiah at the time of his apparently imminent death. *Za'ak* (crying) is used only of Moab (Isa. 15.5, 8).

10.   The whole of Isa. 35 may well be important as a background to Isa. 65.18-25. Its context is God's saving of God's people (Isa. 35.4) who will be brought through a fertile land (previously a wilderness; Isa. 35.1, 6-7) where no lion or ravenous beast will be found (cf. Isa. 65.25). Indeed the ransomed of Yahweh will return and come with singing to Zion and everlasting joy will be upon their heads: they will obtain gladness and joy and sorrow and sighing will flee away (cf. Isa. 65.18, 19). Further, Isa. 35 evidences other linguistic links with Isa. 65.18-19: the verb *gil* (rejoice) appears in Isa. 35.1, 2 and the verb *sus* in Isa. 35.1. The noun *sason*, which derives from the latter verb and is similar in meaning to *masos*, refers in Isa. 35.10 to the joy that awaits God's ransomed returnees. There may also be an allusion in Isa. 65.18-19 to Isa. 62.5 where God rejoices over the restored Jerusalem. Both Isa. 35 and 62 are in the context of the restored community in Jerusalem, as is Isa. 65.18-19.

5.   In Isa. 65.22 God's chosen people will enjoy the work of their hands. This is in keeping with Deut. 16.15; 24.19; 25.12; 28.12; these texts announce blessings on the work of the hands of those who keep God's commandments.[11] It should be noted that the verb translated as 'enjoy' in most English versions actually means 'wear out' in Hebrew. The true implication of the verb is that the people will live long enough to be able to benefit from the work of their hands (cf. Whybray 1975: 278; Motyer 1993: 531). The stanza thus links with the previous one, paralleling life as long as a tree, and also links with the following stanza where labour will not be in vain.

6.   The people will not labour 'in vain' (*leriq*) nor bring forth 'calamity' (*behalah*), with both words appearing in Lev. 26.16 (cf. Smith 1995: 151), in a passage concerned with what will happen if people do not obey the covenant. Lev. 26.16 appears in a similar context to Deut. 28.12. The notion of not labouring in vain is also likely to be a reversal of Isa. 49.4 where God's servant believed he had laboured in vain (*leriq*).

7.   God will be attentive to them (Isa. 65.24). This verse contrasts God's immediate response to his servants with the lack of response God received from those people who had forsaken him (Isa. 65.12; cf. Smith 1995: 152). For previous appeals to people to be attentive to God compare, for example, Isa. 55.6; 56.1.

8.   Wild beasts will be at peace with domesticated ones (Isa. 65.25). This is almost a repeat of Isa. 11.6-9. It is also what God intended for his original creation, but which did not eventuate.[12] It brings into play the principle of interconnectedness—at least as far as the behaviour of humans and the effect it has upon wild animals is concerned.

To sum up what has been found in Isaiah 65 up to the present: Isaiah 65 is primarily concerned with changed conditions for humans depending upon which attitude to God they display; it pronounces reward in the form of physical benefits and spiritual peace upon God's servants and earthly punishment in the form of physical deprivation—as well as mental anguish and ultimately death—upon those who have not sought God. In such a world, there will be no aggression from wild beasts or snakes. It is humans to whom justice is being

11.   Smith (1995: 151) highlights Deut. 28.12 as the background to the expression in Isa. 65.22, but the other Deuteronomic passages cited above are also valid.

12.   For details cf. Gardner 2000: 121-26.

given[13] and righteous humans will enjoy the fruits of their labour, in contrast to those pictured in Deut. 28.30. Furthermore, in the future, Jerusalem will be spared devastation.

The only verse in Isaiah 65 which mentions Earth, apart from the one which forms the focus of this paper, is Isa. 65.16. It is worth looking at in some detail. It reads:

> he will call his servants by another name
> so that he who blesses himself by the earth
> blesses himself by the God of *'amen*
> and he who swears (*hannishba'*) by the earth
> swears (*yishshaba͏ᵉ*) by the God of *'āmēn*
> because the former troubles are forgotten
> and because they are hidden from my eyes.

The LXX substituted *'emet*, 'truth', for *'amen*. However, the *'amen* of the Masoretic Text is supported by the Dead Sea Scrolls and thus must be taken seriously.

The phrase 'God of "*amen*' does not appear elsewhere in the Bible. However, *'amen* does. It is a response to statements made—it signifies agreement, an affirmation of acceptance. The statements to which *'amen* is a response fall into two categories:

1. promise of obedience: curses are invoked upon those who perform specific acts which are contrary to God's laws (Deut. 27.15-16). Jer. 11.5 picks up on these curses (Jer. 11.4), asserting that if people obey God then they will possess a land flowing with milk and honey, to which the people respond with *'amen*;

2. affirmations of God's singular and everlasting nature; cf. Ps. 41.14(13) which is repeated in 1 Chron. 16.36; Ps. 72.9; Ps. 89.33(52); Ps. 106.48. As the message of all these passages is similar, I shall only give one of them in full here:

---

13. It has been suggested by a number of commentators that Isa. 65 is a response to the plea for justice made in Isa. 63.7–64.12 and this may well be so, but whereas the latter block of material is an appeal for all Israel, Isa. 65–66 is addressed to a divided community where only the righteous will be saved. See Steck 1987: 103-16; 1991: 217-28 cf. also Sweeney 1988: 91 and Carr 1996: 204-12.

'Blessed be the Lord, the God of Israel,
From everlasting to everlasting.'
And all the people said *'amen* and praised the Lord (Ps. 41.14[13]).

With that little word *'amen,* then, Isaiah has alluded to the ever-lasting nature of God and the blessings upon those who live in accordance with divine will. As such its meaning is similar to 'truth' (*'emet*). *'amen* may have been used instead of *'emet* in order to allude to the passage in Deuteronomy that specifies rewards for those obedient to God. This links with the allusions to Deuteronomic passages that were found in Isa. 65.18-25. Although Isaiah nowhere else uses the noun *'amen,* he twice uses the verbal form associated with it. In Isa. 7.9, in a message to Ahaz he says: 'If you will not believe (*ta'aminu*), surely you will not be established'. Belief in God's word, then, is all-important, a statement which is borne out in the only other occurrence of the verb in Isa. 43.10, which reads:

You are my witnesses, says Yahweh,
my servants whom I have chosen
that you may know and believe (*ta'aminu*)
and understand that I am he.

To return to the exegesis of Isa. 65.16: it is the servants of God (Isa. 65.15) who bless themselves in the 'God of *'amen'*, thus linking the text with Isa. 43.10.

The notion of swearing by Earth (Isa. 65.16) is not without its prob-lems either. The phrase appears nowhere else in Isaiah; however, 'Earth/land' (*'erets*) and 'swear' (*sab'*) occur together frequently in Deuteronomy, with the following progression of thought being appar-ent:

1. the land was promised (sworn) to Abraham and his seed (Deut. 1.8; 6.10, 23; 7.13; 8.1; 10.11; 28.11; 30.20; 34.40);
2. only those who obey God will be allowed to enter/stay in the land (Deut. 1.35; 6.18, 23-24; 8.1; 30.20) which God promised (swore) to Abraham, Isaac and Jacob;
3. the land that God promised (swore) to the fathers will be fruitful (so will cattle and people) if God's judgments are kept (Deut. 7.13; 28.11).

The linking of swearing by earth (Isa. 65.16) with Deuteronomy is justified because the close association of the phrase with *'amen* in Isa. 65.16 also features prominently in Deuteronomy 27. Those then who 'swear by the earth' in Isa. 65.16, when interpreted through the ref-erences to Deuteronomy, are God's people who understand the connection between possession of the land, along with its fertility, and keeping God's commandments. However, Isa. 65.16 goes beyond that: swearing by Earth is the same as swearing by God; blessing oneself by Earth is like blessing oneself by God. Blessing and cursing in the ancient world were seen as powerful creative forces capable of engendering life or curtailing it. That Earth has the same power as God is significant—a partnership is in view. In Isa. 65.16 Earth is not subdued as in Gen. 1.28 but is in co-operation with God, a co-operation that was evident on the third day of creation (see Habel 2000: 41-43), but denied on day six through fear of the power of Earth in its role as fertility goddess (Gardner 2000: 124). Now the intrinsic worth of Earth is recognized and its purpose is no longer suppressed; rather its original role is being restored.

Are there any prior intimations in Isaiah of the new status of Earth? In Isa. 45.8 righteousness is poured into Earth from above. Isa. 45.8 appears in a chapter which has a strong emphasis on God as the maker of all humankind (Isa. 45.12, 18) and so has a universal application. Isa. 45.8 itself is anticipating a new world order:

> Cause to drop down, you heavens, from above,
> And let the skies pour down righteousness;
> Let the earth open, that they may be fruitful in salvation,
> Let her cause righteousness to spring up together;
> I, Yahweh, have created it.

The passage contains some textual difficulties,[14] but as Motyer (1993: 360) says, the Masoretic Text can be retained if 'salvation and righteousness' are rendered as the subjects of the plural verb 'be fruitful'. Accordingly he translates,

> Let the earth open;
> Let salvation and righteousness[15] be fruitful;
> Let it [earth] make them grow together.

---

14.   Qa and LXX have 'shout aloud' (*har'iyu*) instead of the MT *har'ipu*, possibly because they expected an object, and to make a parallel with the next line 'and let the skies pour down righteousness'. 'Shout aloud' would also be in keeping with the new heavens as witnesses to God's acts. However, as Motyer (1993: 359) points out, the verb *r'p* does appear without an object in Isa. 22.22 and 2 Kgs 15.16. 'Be fruitful' (*yipru*) is, as Whybray (1975: 106) says, 'unaccountably plural and *tatsmiach* 'cause to spring' (f.s.) has also caused problems'.

15.   The two words translated as 'righteousness' in English are in fact different in Hebrew. The first is *tsedeq* and the second *tsedaqah* and scholars have seen different shades of meaning in them. Watts (1987: 157), in keeping with his tying of the Isaianic work to the events of history, links them closely with God working through Cyrus and translates *tsedeq* as 'right' and *tsedaqah* as 'legitimacy'. Motyer

Both Westermann (1969: 163) and Brueggemann (1998: 77) see the verse in terms of a new creation, with Brueggemann stating 'here the gift of creation causes the earth to prosper'. He does not specify in what way Earth prospers nor does he investigate whether physical Earth, as opposed to a community of people, is meant. Whybray (1975: 106) may well understand the background to the concepts involved when he draws attention to Ps. 85.10-14(85.9-13) and Ps. 72.1-7, although he does not elaborate greatly upon the connection between them and Isa. 45.8, except to say, rather imprecisely, that in those psalms, fertility and national order are linked to the king. Psalm 72 pictures the king responding to God's gifts of judgment and righteousness by displaying the same attributes to his people. (Interestingly, in Psalm 72, *tsedeq* and *tsedaqah*, which both featured in Isa. 45.8, alternate as in the latter text, although in opposite sequence.) The mountains and hills in turn are said to bring peace and righteousness. In Psalm 85, where there is a direct reference to a return from captivity (Ps. 85.2[1]), the people plead with God: 'Show us your mercy and grant us your salvation' (Ps. 85.8[7]). The verse is followed by the belief that

> Moreover his salvation is near to those who fear him,
> that glory may dwell in our land.
> Mercy and truth are met together;
> righteousness and peace have kissed each other;
> truth (*'emet*) springs out of the earth;
> and righteousness has looked down from heaven.
> Yes, the Lord will give that which is good
> and our land will yield her increase (Ps. 85.10-13[9-12]).

There is a strong similarity in these verses with terms and concepts in Isaiah in general. In particular, 'salvation' and 'righteousness' appear here, the latter in association with the heavens as in Isa. 45.8, as does the notion of a force for right living[16] springing out of Earth. It is explicitly stated in Ps. 85.13 (12), but not in Psalm 72, that Earth would respond to the state of heavenly communion on Earth by yielding 'her

---

(1993: 360) thinks that the difference may amount to no more than a poetic variation, while Kissane (1943: 80) understands *ṣedeq* as an attribute of God (i.e. God's righteousness) and *tsedaqah* as virtually synonymous with 'salvation'. A perusal of the occurrences of both words in the Hebrew Bible suggests that there is little difference in meaning between the two and that Motyer's view should be upheld.

16. 'Truth' appears to be a wide-ranging concept which embraces 'loyalty to a deity' and right living in accordance with that loyalty; cf. the contrast implied between Isa. 59.14, 15, where there is transgression, and Isa. 38.3, where Hezekiah walked before God 'in truth and with a perfect heart and [did] what was right'.

increase'. The links then between Psalm 85 and Isaiah are very important and would bear further investigation.

What is the meaning of Isa. 45.8 in terms of the present investigation of the new heavens and new Earth in Isaiah? The verse represents the notion of the heavens and Earth co-operating, with Earth as nurturer of righteousness and salvation. 'Earth opening' is a metaphor for the world below incorporating aspects of the divine which are actively poured into it from the heavenly sphere.[17] The partnership of God and Earth that comes to full flower in Isa. 65.16 is foreshadowed here.

To return to an exegesis of Isa. 65.16: 'the former troubles' which are 'forgotten' are likely to hark back to the time when those who were supposedly God's people refused to give loyalty and obedience. Some of their misdeeds are catalogued in Isaiah 65 itself (Isa. 65.2-7, 11-12), as is their punishment (Isa. 65.13-15). Isaiah 48 gives a clear delineation of the wrongful attitude of Jacob/Israel/those from Judah who 'swear by the name of the Lord and make mention of the God of Israel, but not in truth nor in righteousness' (Isa. 48.1). 'For they call themselves of the holy city' (Isa. 48.2). In Isa. 48.18 God laments:

> Oh that you had listened to my commandments!
> Then your peace would have been as a river
> And your righteousness as the waves of the sea;
> Your seed also would have been like the sand
> And the offspring of your bowels like its grains.
> His name would not be cut off or destroyed from before me.

Isa. 48.1, 18 can be seen to have many links with Isa. 65.15-16 in both theme and vocabulary: the contrast is sharply drawn in both texts between those who keep the commandments and their subsequent blessed state and those who do not and their consequent lack of peace and righteousness, lack of seed, lack of a name.[18]

'Former' (*rishonot*) recalls earlier Isaianic passages where it was announced that former things were passing and new things were about to begin (Isa. 42.9; 43.18). The notion of former troubles being hidden

---

17. However, Isa. 45.8 says nothing about any resulting effects, in terms of fertility for Earth, in the way that Psalm 85 does. Linked with Isa. 45.8 is Isa. 61.11. In the latter text, God's action in causing righteousness (*tsedaqah*) and praise to spring forth (*yatsmiach*) before all the nations is seen in terms of a simile with earth bringing forth her shoot, causing her seeds to spring forth.

18. In turn these two texts, Isa. 65.15-16 and Isa. 48.1, 18, shed light upon Isa. 66.22, the second of the two passages where besides 'new heavens and a new Earth', the seed and name of the new community are promised permanence.

from God's eyes suggests that a new era in the relationship of God and people is about to begin. In Isa. 65.17 God announces:

> For behold I am creating new heavens and a new earth
> and the former things will not be remembered or come into mind.

Again it is stated that former things (*rishonot*) will not be remembered (*tizzakarnah*). This may well hark back to Isa. 43.25 where God says to the exiles: 'I will not remember (*'ezkor*) your sins'. This is in the context of God doing a new thing (Isa. 43.19). In Isa. 65.17, God asserts, in parallel to not remembering the former things, that they will not 'come into mind' (*ta'alenah 'al leh*). Smith (1995: 150) points out that the latter expression is found four times in Jeremiah (Jer. 3.16; 7.31; 19.5; 32.35), three of which concern God not permitting syncretistic worship. There is a further reference in Jeremiah that Smith does not mention: this is Jer. 44.21, a passage that is most appropriate as a background to Isa. 65.17. It includes both 'remember' (*zakar*) and 'come into mind' (*'alah 'al leb*) and, as in Isa. 65.17, it is God who is the subject of the verbs. In an address to the exiles from Judah who were living in Egypt, Jeremiah says:

> The incense you burned in the cities of Judah and in the streets of
>   Jerusalem,
> you and your fathers and the people of the land,
> did not Yahweh remember them (*zakar*)
> and did it not come into his mind (*ta'alenah 'al leh*)?
> so that Yahweh could not stand it, because of the evil of your works
> and because of the abominations you committed;
> therefore your land has become a desolation, an astonishment, a curse,
> without inhabitant, as it is this day (Jer. 44.21-22).[19]

God's memory of sins then brought about the devastation of the land. Applied to Isa. 65.17, this suggests that in the time of the new heavens and new Earth, God will not remember past sins and therefore new Earth will not be made desolate. The 'curse' (*'alah*) appears a number of times in Deuteronomy 29 where it is applied to those who break the Mosaic covenant. There the curse affects the land so that it becomes like Sodom and Gomorrah (Deut. 29.23). This will not happen in the time of the new heavens and new Earth for then *sinners themselves* would be cursed (Isa. 65.20), rather than *Earth* being the innocent victim of the curse. Instead, God's servants, who bless themselves by the God of *'amen*, bless themselves by Earth and those who swear by Earth, swear by the God of *'amen*, recalling the promises and

---

19. Sommer (1996) has also missed this allusion.

threats of Deuteronomy. A continuous process is in operation: those who believe in God and obey his commandments partake of the blessings of Earth, Earth that has been enriched by having righteousness and salvation poured into it (Isa. 45.8). This brings about harmony in all creation (cf. the principle of interconnectedness)—a harmony that was intended, but did not eventuate, in the first creation.

That a new creation, in some form, is heralded in Isa. 65.17 is certain: the verb 'create' (*bara'*)[20] and the adjective 'new' (*chadash*)[21] highlight this. The notion of land being cursed because of human disobedience to God is found, time after time, in allusions made by Isa. 65.16-25 to Deuteronomy and Jeremiah. New Earth, by contrast, will be a place where justice will prevail (cf. Isa. 42.3-4; 65.20-24), where there will be salvation for the righteous (Isa. 45.8; 61.11) who will congregate in Jerusalem (Isa. 62.7; Isa. 65.18-19).[22] Not as many references to the heavens are made in Isa. 65.16-25: Isa. 45.8 has the heavens dropping down and mingling with earth, producing salvation and righteousness together. It is possible that Isa. 34.4 should be seen as contributing to the picture of the new heavens. It reads:

> All the host of heaven will be dissolved
> and the heavens will be rolled together as a scroll;
> and all their host will fade away
> as the leaf fades from the vine
> and as a fading leaf from the fig tree.

This is to happen in the context of God's wrath against the nations and their host whom 'he has put under the ban and given over to slaughter' (Isa. 34.2). Isa. 34.3 details the death of the human wrongdoers whose blood will be so prolific that it will melt mountains. Isa. 34.4 describes the punishment of the host of heaven who must surely be seen in terms of the gods of the nations who have just been slain. The imagery suggests that the heavens are so compressed by being rolled up that their host are denied life-giving sustenance and thus die in the same way as leaves on a tree will wither and fall if their

20. It is tempting to see a link with the first version of the creation story in Gen. 1–2.4a where *bara'* is used. Whether such an allusion is present or not, the use of *bārā'* is attested elsewhere in Isaiah itself in relation to the original creation (Isa. 40.28; 42.5; 45.18).

21. 'New' (*chadash*) does not appear in Isaiah prior to Isa. 41.15 and it is noticeable with each of its occurrences, whether it refers to events (Isa. 41.15; 42.9; 43.19; 48.6), a song (Isa. 42.10), or a name (Isa. 62.2), that it appears in a context of hope, redemption and a putting away of the past with all its difficulties. Isa. 48.7 is very emphatic that new things that are created 'are created now, not from then'.

22. All passages cited here have been referred to already in the present paper.

capillaries are unable to suck moisture from the branch. It should be noted that the heavens themselves are not destroyed. They are rolled up as a scroll and so, like a scroll, they can be unrolled again. When they are, they will be without the heavenly bodies that had been falsely worshipped in the past. Such an interpretation fits well with Isa. 60.1-2, 19-20, where the only light is YHWH. Without it, darkness would cover Earth. Isa. 60.3 goes on to say that nations and kings will be attracted to the light. Isa. 60.19 specifies that the sun will no longer be the light by day or the moon by night. Instead God will be an 'everlasting light'.

In Isa. 65.16-25 there are many allusions to texts in Isaiah and elsewhere that promise punishment for those people who do not devote themselves to YHWH exclusively. Isa. 34.2 makes it clear that God's words there are addressed to the nations, whereas Isaiah 65 is addressed to two groups within Israel—the sinners and the righteous. The behaviour of the sinners, though, is like the behaviour of the nations for they, too, have been worshipping deities other than YHWH (Isa. 65.1-7). Further, the sinners in Isaiah 65 are killed (Isa. 65.15), as are those in Isa. 34.2-3. Removal of the host of heaven, as specified in Isa. 34.4, would go a long way, in the ancient world, to removing bodies that were worshipped in place of YHWH.[23]

Were the old heavens and old Earth destroyed or renewed in Isa. 65.17? They appear to have been renewed, with Earth becoming a partner with God as a source of blessing and a power to swear by. There are no allusions to passages which specify total destruction: devastation of land results from the curse which is part of God's punishment for disobedient people (cf. Deut. 29; Jer. 4.21-22), but devastation is not the equivalent of obliteration. In addition, Zion is to be renewed and is assured of perpetuity as its only inhabitants will be those loyal to God. As such, they will not bring the curses of Deuteronomy upon the land or themselves. Anyone who did sin in the new Zion would bear the curse in their own person (Isa. 65.20).

It is appropriate at this point to review the ecojustice principles that were seen to be involved in Isa. 65.17 and its context:

1. The principle of intrinsic worth: a renewal of both heavens and Earth was necessary because the heavens contained bodies that could be seen by sinners to rival God. Earth itself is

23. Isa. 51.6 has not been included as a passage lying behind Isa. 65.17 for it is thought to represent a later stage of thought: upon the destruction of heavens and Earth all who dwell therein will die (with the exception of 'his servants', according to Isa. 51.16).

transformed from being the innocent victim, devastated under a curse that had been placed upon a disobedient humanity, to being a partner with the heavens in ensuring that righteousness and justice/salvation are dispensed. Earth is a source of blessing, a power to swear by.

2. The principle of purpose: humankind's sinfulness was the cause of devastation. Further, the heavens needed to co-operate more with Earth and endow it with righteousness. Justice resulted in sinners being under the curse, not Earth. Earth would never again be a victim. It is noticeable that Earth, which co-operated in the task of creation on day three (Habel 2000: 41-43), but, by day six, was to be subdued by humans through fear of its power as a fertility goddess (Gardner 2000: 124),[24] is now a partner with the heavens (Isa. 45.8) or God (Isa. 65.16). Earth is eternal, a source of blessing (Isa. 65.16). Earth is not affected by human behaviour; rather, Earth is a source of strength for those humans who recognize its power. The original role and purpose of Earth, it seems, is being restored.

3. The principle of interconnectedness: righteousness among people will result in the fertility of Earth, which they can utilize (Isa. 65.21). Further, animals and reptiles will no longer cause terror to each other or to people (Isa. 65.25).

In conclusion, the context of Isa. 65.17 advocates both anthropological justice and ecojustice.

---

24. The precept of subduing Earth was withdrawn after the Flood (Gardner 2000: 128-29).

'The Wolf, the Lamb, and a Little Child':
Transforming the Diverse Earth Community in Isaiah

John W. Olley

Introduction

The book of Isaiah starts with the naming of Isaiah and kings, and
rulers and prophet continue to play important roles. Yet very soon
animals are named: the ox and the donkey of Isa. 1.3. As the reader
continues it becomes apparent that the book is richly 'animalled' (to
coin a word avoiding the anthropocentric 'populated').[1] There is the
idyllic picture of wild animals and children playing together (Isa. 11.6-
9), with a similar picture near the end of the book (Isa. 65.35).

In descriptions of the present and visions of the future non-human
members of the Earth community are clearly visible, but how are they
involved? As decorations and symbols, or as participants; as append-
ages to human society and literary metaphors, or as beings with their
own integrity? As references to animals in the book of Isaiah are
explored most of the ecojustice principles adopted by the Earth Bible
Project will be evident.

Diversity and Individuality

Reading through the book of Isaiah soon shows that there is detailed
naming of a great variety of animals: wild animals—mole, ostrich,
wild goat, hyena, jackal, lion (using four different words), leopard,
wolf, bear, hedgehog; flying creatures—bat, bee, fly, eagle, owl, peli-
can, raven, buzzard, locust, crane, dove, swallow, moth; reptiles—
adder, asp, viper, fiery serpent; and the miscellaneous caterpillars,
grasshoppers, worms, mice and spiders! To this could be added domestic animals—and dogs.[2]

1. According to the categories of Katz ([ed.] 1992) there are at least 160 references to animals in Isaiah.
2. The list is a representative translation reflecting the variety in Hebrew, the
English equivalent of some creatures being uncertain (Firmage 1992: 1109-67 lists

The generic *ehayyah* '(wild) creature' occurs in only five verses, and only two of these have violent connotations (Isa. 35.9, 'ferocious beast'; 56.9, devouring). This is in striking contrast to the language of the book of Ezekiel where there is frequent use of *ehayyah*, always (except in Ezek. 31.6, 13) with connotations of violence and threat (Olley 2001). In Isaiah there is recognition and appreciation of the diversity. Indeed, a personal impression is that of all of the Hebrew Scriptures, Isaiah has the greatest diversity of animal names outside of the food legislation passages in the Torah.

Not only is there naming of creatures, but also alertness to diversity in behaviour. As elsewhere in the Bible (and throughout the world) animal behaviour is used metaphorically. In Isaiah animals provide positive role models. Thus the first reference in the book is to the ox and donkey who know their owner (Isa. 1.3). (Interestingly it is this verse that led to the ox and donkey being associated with nativity scenes from the early years of the Christian church; see Sawyer 1996: 119-20.) There are comparisons with animals in situations of vulnerability: frightened humans are seen as being like 'a hunted gazelle or like sheep with no one to gather them' (Isa. 13.14), Moab as 'fluttering birds' (Isa. 16.2), or people as 'growling bears and moaning doves' (Isa. 59.11),[3] worried birds (Isa. 38.14), or 'sheep going to the slaughter' (Isa. 53.7). (Again this is in contrast with Ezekiel which focuses on negative behaviour of humans.[4])

Surprisingly, in only a couple of places does the violence of animals come to the fore in speaking of people. The attacking Assyrians are compared with lions (Isa. 5.29-30), and Cyrus is a 'bird of prey' (Isa. 46.11). Yet the same animals can become protective! YHWH is like an undaunted lion and a hovering bird in his protection of Jerusalem (Isa. 31.4). The only remaining passage is the call to 'wild animals in the forest' (i.e., other nations) to come and devour, because Jerusalem's

all names in the Hebrew Bible). To avoid European connotations, it should be noted that in the Hebrew Bible, 'the dog is always spoken of in contempt' and is a scavenger (Firmage 1992: 1143).

3.   Motyer interprets as an 'angry growl, for the believers are angry at the havoc sin makes of God's world' (1993: 487). This is forcing of the imagery as the context is mourning. Unfortunately, while the image of moaning doves is known in Babylonian laments, the bear image, 'probably also traditional, does not occur in any other extant text' (Whybray 1975: 224).

4.   Violence compared with 'wild animals' (Ezek. 22.27; 34.25) and selfish and fat sheep and goats (Ezek. 34.17-21), and liaison with other nations compared with sexual behaviour of donkeys and stallions (Ezek. 23.20).

'watch-dog' leaders are too busy satisfying their own appetite (Isa. 56.9-11).

Here there is a mixture of domestic and wild creatures. Significantly, in the imagery of wildlife there is both violence and vulnerability. And the lion can be both attacking and protecting. The variegated picture, with the richness of vocabulary, is scattered throughout the book. The principle of intrinsic worth is implied: animals in their diversity are valued and embraced as full participants along with humans in the Earth community.

Wild Animals Have an Active Part in the Vision of the Future

Wild Animals Honour YHWH

Highlighting particularly Isa. 43.20, Galambush (1999: 164) compares Deutero-Isaiah[5] and Ezekiel:

> Deutero-Isaiah shares Ezekiel's utilitarian sensibility according to which nature is good when it is useful for human welfare. Thus YHWH's gift of water flowing from the bare heights to the valleys and on into the wilderness (41.18-20) is wonderful because it serves the needs of the poor. But in Deutero-Isaiah the divine gift of water is a blessing, not only to humans or their livestock, but to the wild animals as well. 'Wild animals', says YHWH, 'will honor me, the jackals and ostriches, for I will give water in the wilderness' (43.20).

The question is, what does it mean that these animals and birds 'honour' YHWH? Several commentators agree with Galambush in noting that the animals share in the benefits of the water, yet rare is comment on 'honour'! Bonnard (1972: 147) compares with the praise of God by mountains and trees, also in Deutero-Isaiah (Isa. 44.23; 49.13; 55.12), but this does not elucidate the manner or content of honouring.

The association of jackals, ostriches and water is also apparent in Isaiah 34-35, chapters which are a bridge introducing the second half of the book.[6] The contrast between Isaiah 34 and 35 is that between desolation (with dryness) and water in abundance. The desolation is

---

5. The book of Isaiah is often considered to be the work of at least three writers; Deutero-Isaiah is the middle section, Isa. 40-55, also known as Second Isaiah.

6. 'Steck's [1985] interpretation of Isa. 35 as written with the explicit function to connect chs. 1-39 and 40-66 (in Steck's view, 40-62) with each other, in my view is one of the most important contributions towards an understanding of the book of Isaiah as a whole' (Rendtorff 1996: 46). Seitz (1993: 240-42) argues that chs. 34-35 introduce the second half of the book, including chs. 36-39.

inhabited by various wild animals, including jackals and ostriches (Isa. 34.13).[7] With the provision of abundant water (Isa. 35.6-7) a change comes: 'the haunt of jackals, their resting place, (will be) grass for reeds and rushes' (so literal reading of the Hebrew of Isa. 35.7b). The verse is difficult.[8] Rather than being a negative portrayal of jackals, the phrase is best seen as simply an expression of 'the reversal of a settled and inhospitable situation' (Motyer 1993: 274), recognizing that jackals usually inhabit dry and desolate places. Such animals may still be around. Yet some animals will be absent: 'no lion shall be there, nor shall any ravenous beast come up on it [the highway]' (Isa. 35.9). There is to be safety. Is this the way the animals 'honour' YHWH: by keeping away and not harming his people?

The phrase 'honour YHWH' is rare in Isaiah. Each instance of giving honour, whether to God or people, is in a context of reversal. One instance that may inform Isa. 43.20 is in Isa. 25.3: 'strong peoples' give honour to God when they see him delivering people from their oppression. Do the animals give honour to God by recognizing and affirming the reversal in the land? This would fit in with the reversals in Isaiah 34–35. There is more than simply the animals benefiting from the water: they affirm the transforming activity of God.

Two older commentators dwell on transformation as causing praise, with interesting additions. Delitzsch (1892: 146) moves beyond the point of 'advantage of the animal world' to affirm that

> their joyful cries are an unconscious praise of Jahve... The prophet has...an open ear for the sighing of creation; he knows that the end of the period of suffering for the people of God will also be the end of suffering for creation.

While one might question the use of 'unconscious', the reference to suffering is of interest, although not apparent in Isaiah. Young (1972: 157) brings another dimension: the idea of a change to animals now recognizing God:

> The desert and wilderness were...regions of darkness, and creatures who occupied them, subject as it were to the demonic power of darkness, now praise and honor the God of Jacob. God has performed a miracle of transformation.[9]

In Isa. 43.20 is an amazing breaking through of the animal voice in celebration (the principle of voice): even wild animals are to be active

---

7.   In Isa. 34.11-15 eleven different wild animals and birds are mentioned.

8.   Compare various modern translations and commentaries. See text analysis by de Waard (1997: 139-40).

9.   The term 'demonic' is not used in the Hebrew Scriptures.

participants in the praise of YHWH. Animals share in the praise of the redeemed people.

'The Peaceable Kingdom'
Probably the most popular animal image from Isaiah is the following passage:

> 6 The wolf shall live with the lamb,
> the leopard shall lie down with the kid,
> the calf and the lion and the fatling together,
> and a little child shall lead them.
> 7 The cow and the bear shall graze,
> their young shall lie down together;
> and the lion shall eat straw like the ox.
> 8 The nursing child shall play over the hole of the asp,
> and the weaned child shall put its hand on the adder's den.
> 9 They will not hurt or destroy on all my holy mountain;
> for the earth will be full of the knowledge of the LORD
> as the waters cover the sea (Isa. 11.6-9 NRSV).

Similar words, with significant variation, occur as part of the description of the 'new heavens and the new earth':

> The wolf and the lamb shall feed together,
> the lion shall eat straw like the ox;
> but the serpent—its food shall be dust!
> They shall not hurt or destroy on all my holy mountain, says the LORD
> (Isa. 65.25 NRSV).

The imagery is so vivid that 'we cannot but be amazed that it has been so little used until modern times' (Sawyer 1996: 234). Prior to the nineteenth century, there are only scattered uses in art and interpretation was generally allegorical, apart from some early Christian interpretation that argued for literal fulfilment in a millennial reign of Christ (e.g. Justin Martyr, *Dialogue with Trypho* 81, and Irenaeus, *Against Heresies* 5.33.4 [citing, with agreement, Papias][10]). The popularity of the image is due mainly to the American Quaker, Edward Hicks (1780–1849), who painted many versions:

10. For English translation, see ANF: I, 239, 563. Papias (c. 110 CE) is cited as writing, 'I am quite aware that some persons endeavour to refer these words [Isa. 11.6-9, and 65.25] to the case of savage men, both of different nations and various habits, who come to believe, and when they have believed, act in harmony with the righteous. But...in the resurrection of the just [the words shall also apply] to those animals mentioned' (ANF: I, 563).

He originally derived the idea from an illustration by the English artist Richard Westall, which was engraved in contemporary Bibles with the title, 'The Peaceable Kingdom of the Branch'. While Westall focused on the child (clearly Christ), Hicks gradually came to focus on the lion and the other animals as symbols of the warring elements in human nature (Sawyer 1996: 236).[11]

Issues in interpretation are many, but may be focused on three aspects: (1) the role of the child; (2) the significance of the animals, and (3) the relationship between the two passages.

1. It is understandable that Christian exegetes have often seen a christological significance, given the references to a child in Isa. 7.14 ('Immanuel') and Isa. 9.6 (Heb. 9.5), leading to the 'root from Jesse' at the start of Isaiah 11. For such exegetes the 'leading' (Isa. 11.6) implies ruling. In this vein, Oswalt (1986: 283) comments that throughout Isaiah 7–12 God chooses as ruler 'a child, not a strutting monarch'. Nevertheless, there is a strong case for this not being the most appropriate reading. The earlier references to a 'child' (*yeled*) are all signs of hope for a future when the child grows up, whereas here the picture is of the envisaged future, with the Davidic ruler now an adult.[12]

Does however 'a little child shall lead them' (Isa. 11.6) show 'the superiority of the human race...acknowledged by the submission of the animal kingdom' (Slotki 1949: 57)? Or is it not rather that the following 'playing' actions of the children, with a note of pleasure and delight, highlight rather a joyous interaction, without harm or dominance? Who has not watched the exploratory play of young children? This accords with the description of the young of the cow and the bear 'lying down together' (Isa. 11.7) and the different vocabulary for 'child' already noted.

Brueggemann also links Isa. 11.6-9 with 11.1-5, but provides a different interpretation through focusing on the economic dimensions of the Davidic rule and seeing a link with Genesis 3:

11. For fuller presentation of the history of the use of the imagery, see Sawyer 1996: 234-39.

12. To this can be added the observation that Isa. 11.6-9 has three terms for 'child', none being used in the earlier 'child' passages: *na'ar qaton*, 'little lad', *yoneq*, '(nursing) infant', and *gamul*, 'weaned child'. In fact, the word used earlier, *yeled*, is here used of the young of the cow and bear (Isa. 11.7). The LXX maintains the distinction, in that while *paidion* is used in Isa. 9.5 and 11.6-8, in Isa. 11.6-8 it has a qualifying adjective, *mikron* (Isa. 11.6) and *nepion* (Isa. 11.8) for human references. Thus early Christian interpretation, using the LXX, could also have observed the difference.

> *The distortion of human relationships* is at the root of all *distortions in creation*... Peaceableness in the created order requires, first, the enactment in the human community of a conciliation that is fundamentally economic (1998: 102, italics his).

Tucker notes the uncertainty as to whether the two oracles (Isa. 11.1-5 and 11.6-9) were originally linked, but draws attention to the double reference to 'knowledge of the Lord' in Isa. 11.2, 9, and concludes that 'there is no good reason either to treat 11.6-9 as late or as separate from 11.1-5' (2000: 217). On this basis he too affirms the link between 'the establishment of justice and righteousness, and therefore of peace in the human world' and 'transformation' (2000: 216).

2. The presence of the varied young children in Isa. 11.6-9 argues for the reference to animals as being literal. Various commentators have argued otherwise. For some the reference is to nations, because of animal metaphors used elsewhere, such as Assyria being a 'lion' (Isa. 5.29) and Arameans and Philistia 'devouring' (Isa. 9.12) (see, e.g., Seitz 1993: 106-107, and Buber [so Wildberger 1991: 481]). Sawyer draws many parallels from Wisdom literature of animal metaphors for human behaviour, seeing here reference to the mighty and the weak, exploiters and the needy, and the vulnerable (Sawyer 1984: 122-23). This is similar to the spiritualizing of past commentators, referring to 'various spiritual conditions and states within human beings' (so Oswalt 1986: 283, giving Calvin as an example; note also the interpretation of the Quaker Hicks and the view criticized by Papias alluded to above). These conclusions have some support from the description later in the passage of Ephraim (Israel) and Judah as being at peace (Isa. 11.13, the reversal of Isa. 9.19-21) – one cannot deny the possible use of metaphorical language. However, as Wildberger argues cogently, 'if the text were meant to be interpreted allegorically, it would be radically different than it is – it would speak *only* of animals and not of children' (1991: 481, italics his). To this we can add the question: is it likely that an allegorical intention would have included the young of animals? Tucker (2000: 218) appositely notes that Isaiah 1–39 is free of allegory. When there is symbolism, it is defined (e.g. Isa. 5.1-7).

But what kind of world is it in which lions are not carnivorous and snakes do not discharge their poison?

> Until and unless God intervenes at the end of the age to abolish the food chain as we know it and puts us all on a photosynthetic diet, hunting, killing, and eating among the creatures will continue indefinitely. It cannot be any other way (Towner 1996: 28, citing a lecture by Rolston).

Certainly there is to be a transformation. Oswalt uses this fact to argue that 'another interpretation is intended' and he proposes a 'figurative' sense (1986: 283). To be preferred, however, because of the wide-ranging picture, is Wildberger's 'mythological portrayal of the future' (1991: 480-81).

As one looks at the passage from an animal perspective, there is a further important feature. The biblical writer is not interested in the actualities of animal physiology, but does see a place for all such animals in the future. Unlike Ezekiel who excludes wild animals (e.g. Ezek. 34.25-27), Isaiah's vision seems to be saying that somehow all have a part. Just as young human children will be in the future kingdom, so too will be the whole animal family.

The wonder is that the animals are included in the 'knowledge of YHWH' (Isa. 11.9). Some commentators have difficulty with this concept and want to make a break before Isa. 11.9, or else see the subject of the verbs 'harm and destroy' as being impersonal (while allowing that they refer to the animals in Isa. 65.25; so Schultz 1999: 253-55, and others cited by him). Is this because of an anthropocentric presupposition (Schultz uses the word 'incongruity')? However, if Isaiah can speak of 'an ox knowing its master' (Isa. 1.3), would he find it strange to allow the knowing of YHWH? Reading the book as a whole, it is of note that, outside Genesis, only Isaiah refers to the promise of God made after the flood (Isa. 54.9), significantly a promise made to Noah *and* all the animals with him (Gen. 9; see discussion in Olley 2000).

3. The relationship between the two passages, Isa. 11.6-9 and Isa. 65.25, is much debated.[13] Three points of comparison are of particular relevance:

1. While Isa. 11.6-9 is in the setting of the restored Davidic kingdom, Isa. 65.25 is of the 'new heavens and new earth' (Isa. 65.17-25). The earthly king has disappeared from the scene in Isaiah 40–66. Focus is on YHWH as 'king', with the only reference to David being democratized (Isa. 55.3). Again, wild and domestic animals are together in the future harmony.[14]

---

13. Schultz (1999: 240-56) presents various arguments as to whether one is based on the other, and if so which has priority. He concludes that diachronically the matter is unresolved, but that synchronically the second will be read as building on the first. A related issue is the possible use of contemporary imagery. There is an idyllic description of animal peace and well-being in the Sumerian myth *Enki and Ninhusanga* (Beyerlin [ed.] 1978: 85-86).

14. Although, as for Isa. 11.6-9, there are commentators who argue for a figurative interpretation, on similar grounds (see, e.g., Sawyer 1986: 212; Oswalt 1998: 662).

2. There is no reference to children, but then they have had
    their place in the preceding verses (Isa. 65.20, 23). Here ani-
    mals are spoken of in their own right.

3. A striking feature is the reference to the 'serpent—its food
    shall be dust!' (Isa. 65.25). The use of 'serpent' (as in Gen. 3;
    different to the 'snake' words in Isa. 11.6-9) points clearly to
    the story of Genesis 3.[15] In a different way, the harm has gone.

As in Isaiah 11, the vision of the future involves transformation, but it
is transformation of a total real world, not only of human society, and
not into a spiritual realm where animals have no place.

What stands out in both passages, again in contrast to Ezekiel (e.g.
Ezek. 34.25, 28), is the place for all animals in the region of the 'holy
mountain': God's sacred space welcomes all. Comparing the analysis
of Galambush (1999) on the boundary-defining social setting of Ezekiel,
it may be relevant that Isaiah is not interested in boundary-setting
within the community: even within the temple, 'foreigners' and
'eunuchs' are welcome with equal rights (Isa. 56.3-8). Isaiah's vision is
also inclusive with regard to animals! Is there a correlation between a
person's attitude to people who are different and his or her attitude
towards the diversity of creatures?

Throughout the book of Isaiah animals are more than recognized as
part of the Earth community. Whether wild or domestic, their integrity and diversity is affirmed. The vision of the future worshipping life
on the holy mountain includes animals. For Isaiah the distinctive core
of the future is not temple worship but an Earth community where all
live in mutuality, where all is made right and there is no harming or
destroying. 'Harmful' animals are not banished, rather they share in
the transformation with humans (principles of interconnectedness and
purpose). All participate in the 'knowledge of YHWH' on the 'holy
mountain'.

Relevance for the Present?

Throughout the centuries commentators have assumed, from passages such as these, that the world as it is falls short of being good.
There is often a focus on an eschatological return to an earlier time of
harmony, as seen in the description of Eden in Genesis 2. The arguments, details and nuances vary, but it has been common for Jewish
and Christian thinkers to see some form of distortion in animal

---

15. Steck (1997) provides detailed discussion on a variety of links with Gen. 1-3.

behaviour from that originally designed. Even where the actuality of a pristine 'peaceable kingdom' is debated, there is still a recognition that the portrayal of the future is one of harmony including both wild and domestic animals, with no destruction (often linked with Christian images of the end of death itself). This perspective is certainly encouraged by the totality of the presentation of the book of Isaiah, with the images of Isa. 11.6-9 and Isa. 65.25 being supported by the detailed affirmation of diversity in the animal world and the possibility of animals 'honouring' YHWH.

It is widely recognized that prophetic portrayals of the future are not designed merely as predictions or to satisfy curiosity, but rather are means of encouraging appropriate behavioural responses in the present. This is often affirmed with regard to such human responses as worshipping and trusting YHWH alone and doing what is right and just. Yet commentators are almost universally silent as to any attitudes or actions that may be commended by the portrayal of harmony within the animal world and between all animals and humans. There is little recognition that 'biblical renditions of the future of nature come to us not as metaphysical claims but as moral ones' (Towner 1996: 30).

In 1996, however, encouraged by ecological concerns, two articles appeared that began to explore the implications of human interaction with animals which respects animals (rather than seeing animals as for human benefit). One can only affirm this listening to the voice of the wider Earth community. Webb (1996: 239) interacts with ecologists who state that 'interlocking ecological systems, no matter what the fate of individual organisms, are inherently good', and wants 'to stress the Christian sense that suffering is wrong, everywhere and for everybody, including animals'. This calls for some human action as 'animals and humans are tied together in this world and in the world to come' (1996: 240). He is aware of the necessity of listening to those who point out that 'nature does work quite well by itself' but sees the need for Christians (he does not consider Jewish involvement) 'to remind others that it [nature] works by making suffering necessary and productive' (1996: 243). Included in his suggestions are that '[w]e should not encourage or enhance the violence in nature' and 'we should worry about individual animals', such as a beached whale (1996: 249), then focusing on the treatment of animals which already have close association with humans, such as farm animals.

Writing in a journal issue on the theme 'Theology and Ecology', Towner (1996), in keeping with the long tradition mentioned above, also adopts a view whereby the 'life-giving reciprocity' of Eden is recapitulated in the end-time (1996: 28). While critical (as is Webb) of some of the theological rationale of the present violence in the food-chain, he argues that visions of the future call for proleptic action:

> If peace is the hallmark of the new age (Isa. 11.1-9), then our work in this time of tribulation is to abolish war and to effect reconciliation between people, as well as between people, wolves, and snakes... The biblical pictures of nature in the future function as incitements toward a style of ethical living in the present that is holistic, interdependent, non-hierarchical, and one that does not reject flesh and matter as corrupt because God does not reject them (1996: 33). [16]

A non-carnivorous lion and a non-venomous snake are impossibili-ties in the present order (and lest there be human pride, it should be noted that human attitudes and actions also need transforming), but the prophetic vision is that they are possible for God. If one is to follow the prophetic vision of diversity, individuality and peace, with all honouring God, then one must respond to a moral claim to do what is possible to minimize violence and enhance harmony now. To extend a later exhortation, 'If it is possible, so far as it depends on you, live peaceably with all' (Rom. 12.18)—not only with people, but with the whole Earth community.

16. Of note here is the way that, analogous to the perspectives of Brueggemann (1998) and Tucker (2000) discussed earlier, Towner astutely links Isa. 11.1-5 and 11.6-9 in calling for a moral response.

Bibliography

Abou-Assaf, A., P. Bordreuil, and A.R. Millard
    1982   *La Statue de Tell Fekherye et son inscription bilingue assyro-araméenne* (Paris: Editions 'Recherche sur les civilisations').

Albright, W.F.
    1968   *Yahweh and the Gods of Canaan: A Historical Analysis of Two Contrasting Faiths* (London: Athlone Press).

Alexander, P.S.
    1999   'Jerusalem as the Omphalos of the World: On the History of a Geographical Concept', in L.I. Levine (ed.), *Jerusalem: Its Sanctity and Centrality to Judaism, Christianity, and Islam* (New York: Continuum): 104-19.

Alt, A.
    1968   *Kleine Schriften zur Geschichte des Volkes Israel*, III (Munich: C.H. Beck, 2nd edn).

Ambler, R.
    1990   *Global Theology: The Meaning of Faith in the Present World Crisis* (London: SCM Press; Philadelphia: Trinity Press).

Amoah, E.
    1995   'Women as Portrayed in Some African Proverbs' (paper presented at a symposium on the African Proverb in the Twenty-First Century, Pretoria).

Anderson, A.A.
    1972   *The Book of Psalms. I. Psalms 1–72. The New English Bible Commentary* (Grand Rapids: Eerdmans).
    1981   *The Book of Psalms. II. Psalms 73–150. The New English Bible Commentary* (Grand Rapids: Eerdmans).
    1983   *The Book of Psalms* (NCB Commentary, 11; Grand Rapids: Eerdmans).

Anderson, B.W.
    1994   'Creation Faith in its Setting of Worship', in *From Creation to New Creation: Old Testament Perspectives* (Minneapolis: Fortress Press): 207-32.
    1984   *Creation in the Old Testament* (Philadelphia: Fortress Press; London: SPCK).

Andersen, F.I., and D.N. Freedman
    1980   *Hosea: A New Translation with Introduction and Commentary* (AB, 24; Garden City, NY: Doubleday).

Ashley, Timothy R.
    1993   *The Book of Numbers* (NICOT; Grand Rapids: Eerdmans).

Bach, R.
 1961 'Bauen und Pflanzen', in Rendtorff and Koch (eds.) 1961: 7-32.
Barton, J.
 1990 'History and Rhetoric in the Prophets', in Martin Warner (ed.), *The Bible as Rhetoric: Studies in Biblical Persuasion and Credibility* (New York: Routledge): 51-64.
Bascom, William
 1967 *The Yoruba of Southwestern Nigeria* (New York: Holt, Rinehart & Winston).
Batto, Bernard F.
 1987 'The Covenant of Peace: A Neglected Ancient Motif', *CBQ* 49: 187-211.
Baumann, A.
 1978 '*Dumiyyah*', *TDOT*: III, 260-65.
Beattie, John
 1960 *Bunyoro: An African Kingdom* (New York: Holt, Rinehart & Winston).
 1964 *Other Cultures* (New York: Free Press).
Bentley, Sarah
 1995 'Bringing Justice Home: The Challenge of the Battered Women's Movement for Christian Social Ethics', in C.J. Adams and M.M. Fortune (eds.), *Violence against Women and Children: A Christian Theological Sourcebook* (New York: Continuum): 151-71.
Bergant, Dianne
 1994 'Restoration as Re-Creation in Hosea 2', in Richard N. Fragomeni and John T. Pawlikowski (eds.), *The Ecological Challenge: Ethical, Liturgical, and Spiritual Resources* (Collegeville, MN: Liturgical Press): 3-15.
Berry, Thomas
 1997 'The Universe Story: Its Religious Significance', in J. Carroll, P. Brockelman and M. Westfall (eds.), *The Greening of Faith: God, the Environment, and the Good Life* (Hanover, NH: University Press of New England).
Beuken, W.A.M.
 1989 'Isaiah Chapters LXV–LXVI: Trito-Isaiah and the Closure of the Book of Isaiah', *VTSup* 43: 204-21.
Beyerlin, W. (ed.)
 1978 *Near Eastern Religious Texts Relating to the Old Testament* (London: SCM Press).
Biddle, M.E.
 1996 'Lady Zion's Alter-Egos: Isaiah 47.1-15 and 57.6-13 as Structural Components', in R.F. Melugin and M.A. Sweeney (eds.), *New Visions of Isaiah* (JSOTSup, 214; Sheffield: Sheffield Academic Press): 124-39.
Birch, Bruce C.
 1991 *Let Justice Roll Down: The Old Testament, Ethics, and Christian Life* (Louisville, KY: Westminster/John Knox Press).
Black, M.
 1962 *Models and Metaphors: Studies in Language and Philosophy* (Ithaca, NY: Cornell University Press).

Blenkinsopp, J.
   1991   'The Social Context of the "Outsider Woman", in Proverbs 1–9',
                Bib 72.3: 457-73.
Block, Daniel I.
   1997   *The Book of Ezekiel, Chapters 1–24* (Grand Rapids: Eerdmans).
   1998   *The Book of Ezekiel, Chapters 25–48* (Grand Rapids: Eerdmans).
Boff, Leonardo
   1994   'Social Ecology: Poverty and Misery', in D.G. Hallman (ed.) *Eco-
                theology: Voices from South and North* (Geneva: WCC Publications;
                Maryknoll, NY: Orbis Books): 235-57.
Bonnard, P.-E.
   1972   Le Second Isaïe, son disciple et leurs éditeurs: Isaïe 40–66 (Ebib;
                Paris: Gabalda).
Boulaga, F. Eboussi
   1981   *Christianity without Fetishes: An African Critique* and *Recapture of
                Christianity* (Maryknoll, NY: Orbis Books).
Braaten, Laurie J.
   1987   'Parent-Child Imagery in Hosea' (PhD dissertation, Boston Univer-
                sity).
   2000   'God Sows the Land: Hosea's Place in the Book of the Twelve', in
                Society of Biblical Literature 2000 Seminar Papers (SBLSP, 39; Atlanta:
                SBL): 218-42.
Braude, W.G.
   1959   *The Midrash on the Psalms* (Yale Judaica Series, 13.2; New Haven:
                Yale University Press).
Brenner, Athalya (ed.)
   1995   *A Feminist Companion to the Latter Prophets* (The Feminist Com-
                panion to the Bible, 8; Sheffield: Sheffield Academic Press).
Briggs, C.A., and E.M. Briggs (eds.)
   1906–1907   *A Critical and Exegetical Commentary on the Book of Psalms*
                (Edinburgh: T. & T. Clark).
Brockelman, Paul
   1997   'With New Eyes: Seeing the Environment as a Spiritual Issue', in
                J. Carroll, P. Brockelman, and M. Westfall (eds.), *The Greening of
                Faith: God, the Environment, and the Good Life* (Hanover, NH:
                University Press of New England).
Brown, W.P.
   1993   *Structure, Role, and Ideology in the Hebrew and Greek Texts of Genesis
                1.1–2.3* (SBLDS, 132; Atlanta: Scholars Press).
Brownlee, William H.
   1986   *Ezekiel 1–19* (WBC, 28; Waco, TX: Word Books).
Brueggemann, Walter
   1977   *The Land: Place as Gift, Promise, and Challenge in Biblical Faith*
                (Overtures to Biblical Theology; Philadelphia: Fortress Press).
   1984   *The Message of the Psalms* (Minneapolis: Augsburg).
   1998a   *Isaiah 1–39* (Westminster Bible Companion; Louisville, KY: West-
                minster/John Knox Press).
   1998b   *Isaiah 40–66* (Westminster Bible Companion; Louisville, KY: West-
                minster/John Knox Press).

Buss, Martin J.
    1969   *The Prophetic Word of Hosea: A Morphological Study* (BZAW, 111; Berlin: Alfred Töpelmann).

Buttrick, G.A. (ed.)
    1955   *The Interpreter's Bible* (Nashville: Abingdon Press).

Camp, C.V.
    1985   *Wisdom and the Feminine in the Book of Proverbs* (Sheffield: Almond Press).
    1991   'What is So Strange about the Strange Woman?', in D. Jobling, L.D. Day and G.T. Sheppard (eds.), *The Bible and the Politics of Exegesis* (Cleveland: Pilgrim Press): 17-31.

Carley, Keith W.
    1975   *Ezekiel Among the Prophets* (SBT, 2.31; London: SCM Press).

Carole Fisch, Harold
    1990   'Prophet versus Audience', in Ellen Spolsky (ed.), *The Uses of Adversity: Failure and Accommodation in Reader Response* (London: Lewisburg).

Carr, D.M.
    1996   'Reading Isaiah from Beginning (Isaiah 1) to End (Isaiah 65–66): Multiple Modern Possibilities', in R.F. Melugin and M.A. Sweeney (eds.), *New Visions of Isaiah* (JSOTSup, 214; Sheffield: Sheffield Academic Press): 188-218.

Carroll, R.P.
    1986   *Jeremiah – A Commentary* (OTL; London: SCM Press).

Cheyne, T.K.
    1888   *The Book of Psalms* (London: Kegan Paul, Trench & Co.).

Childs, Brevard S.
    1971   'Psalm Titles and Midrashic Exegesis', *Journal of Semitic Studies* 16.2: 137-50.

Chung, Hyun Kyung
    1994   'Ecology, Feminism and African and Asian Spirituality: Towards a Spirituality of Eco-Feminism', in D.G. Hallman (ed.), *Ecotheology: Voices from South and North* (Geneva: WCC Publications; Maryknoll, NY: Orbis Books): 175-78.

Clements, R.E.
    1985   'Beyond Tradition History: Deutero-Isaianic Development of First Isaiah's Themes', *JSOT* 31: 95-113.

Clifford, R.J.
    1994   *Creation Accounts in the Ancient Near East and in the Bible* (CBQMS, 26; Washington: Catholic Biblical Association).

Clines, David J.A. (ed.)
    1998   *The Dictionary of Classical Hebrew*, IV (Sheffield: Sheffield Academic Press).

Collins, Terence
    1993   *The Mantle of Elijah: The Redaction Criticism of the Prophetical Books* (The Biblical Seminar, 20; Sheffield: JSOT Press).

Conrad, E.W.
    1991   *Reading Isaiah* (Minneapolis: Fortress Press).

Cooper, Alan M.
    1983   'The Life and Times of King David According to the Book of
                Psalms', in R. Friedman (ed.), *The Poet and the Historian: Essays in
                Literary and Historical Biblical Criticism* (Chico, CA: Scholars Press):
                117-91.
Cooper-White, Pamela
    1995   *The Cry of Tamar: Violence against Women and the Church's Response*
                (Minneapolis: Fortress Press).
Coote, R.B.
    1981   *Among the Prophets: Composition and Theology* (Philadelphia: For-
                tress Press).
Craigie, Peter
    1972   'Psalm 29 in the Hebrew Poetic Tradition', *VT* 22: 142-51.
Creach, Jerome F.D.
    1996   *Yahweh as Refuge and the Editing of the Hebrew Psalter* (JSOTSup, 217;
                Sheffield: Sheffield Academic Press).
Cross, F.M.
    1950   'Notes on a Canaanite Psalm in the Old Testament', *BASOR* 117:
                19-21.
    1973   *Canaanite Myth and Hebrew Epic* (Cambridge, MA: Harvard Univer-
                sity Press).
Cross, F.M., Jr, and Richard J. Saley
    1970   'Phoenician Incantations on a Plaque of the Seventh Century B.C.
                from Arshlan Tash in Upper Syria', *BASOR* 197: 42-49.
Crow, L.D.
    1996   *The Songs of Ascents (Psalms 120–134): Their Place in Israelite History
                and Religion* (Atlanta: Scholars Press).
Crüsemann, F.
    1996   *The Torah: Theology and Social History of Old Testament Law* (Edin-
                burgh: T. & T. Clark).
cummings, e.e.
    1923   *Collected Poems* (New York: Harcourt, Brace and Company).
Cunanan, Jose Pepz M.
    1994   'The Prophet of Environment and Development', in D.G. Hallman
                (ed.) *Ecotheology: Voices from South and North* (Geneva: WCC Publi-
                cations; Maryknoll, NY: Orbis Books).
Dahood, Mitchell
    1968   *Psalms II: 51–100* (Garden City, NY: Doubleday).
Dalley, S.
    1991   *Myths from Mesopotamia: Creation, the Flood, Gilgamesh, and Others*
                (The World's Classics; Oxford: Oxford University Press).
Daly, H.E., and J.B. Cobb, Jr
    1994   *For the Common Good: Redirecting the Economy Toward Community,
                the Environment, and a Sustainable Future* (Boston: Beacon Press, 2nd
                edn).
Daneel, M.L.
    1994   'African Independent Churches Face the Challenge of Environ-
                mental Ethics', in D.G. Hallman (ed.), *Ecotheology: Voices from South*

and North (Geneva: WCC Publications; Maryknoll, NY: Orbis Books).

Davies, G.I.
1992   *Hosea* (NCB Commentary; London: Marshall Pickering; Grand Rapids: Eerdmans): 248-63.

Davis, Jack
1992   *Black Life: Poems* (St Lucia: Queensland University Press).

Day, J.
1985   *God's Conflict with the Dragon and the Sea: Echoes of a Canaanite Myth in the Old Testament* (Cambridge: Cambridge University Press).

De Vaux, R.
1968   *Ancient Israel – Its Life and Institutions* (London: Darton, Longman & Todd, 2nd edn).

Deist, F.E.
1990   *Only Guide for OTB302-3* (Pretoria: University of South Africa).

Delitzsch, F.
1871   *Biblical Commentary on the Psalms* (3 vols.; Edinburgh: T. & T. Clark).
1892   *Biblical Commentary on the Prophecies of Isaiah* (London: Hodder and Stoughton).

Diepold, P
1972   *Israel's Land* (BWANT, 95; Stuttgart: Kohlhammer).

Dietrich, M., O. Loretz and J. Sanmartin
1976   *Die Keilalphabetischen Texte aus Ugarit* (Neukirchen-Vluyn: Neukirchener Verlag).

Dijk-Himmes, Fokkelien van
1996   'The Imagination of Power and the Power of Imagination: An Intertextual Analysis of Two Biblical Love Songs: The Song of Songs and Hosea 2', in Philip R. Davies (ed.), *The Prophets* (The Biblical Seminar, 42; Sheffield: Sheffield Academic Press): 278-91.

Dion, P.E.
1991   'YHWH as Storm-God and Sun-God: The Double Legacy of Egypt and Canaan as Reflected in Psalm 104', *ZAW* 103: 43-71.

Driver, S.R.
1888   *An Introduction to the Literature of the Old Testament* (Edinburgh: T. & T. Clark).

Earth Bible Team
2000   'Guiding Ecojustice Principles', in Habel (ed.) 2000: 38-53.

Eaton, H.
2000   'Ecofeminist Contributions to an Ecojustice Hermeneutics', in Habel (ed.) 2000: 54-71.

Efthimiadis, H.
1999   'Is There a Place for Women in the Theology of the Psalms? Part 1: An Investigation into the Female Imagery of the Ancient Hebrew Psalter', *Old Testament Essays* 12.1: 33-56.

Eichrodt, Walther
1961   *Theology of the Old Testament*, I (Philadelphia: Westminster Press).
1967   *Theology of the Old Testament*, II (Philadelphia: Westminster Press).
1970   *Ezekiel: A Commentary* (trans. C. Quin; OTL; Philadelphia: Westminster Press).

Eilberg-Schwartz, Howard
    1994   *God's Phallus and Other Problems for Men and Monotheism* (Boston: Beacon Press).
Eiseley, Loren
    1957   *The Immense Journey* (New York: Vintage Books).
Eissfeldt, O.
    1953   'Gott und das Meer in der Bibel', in *Studia Orientalia Ioanni Pedersen* (Hauniae: Munksgaard): 76-84.
    1966   *The Old Testament: An Introduction* (trans. P. Ackroyd; Oxford: Basil Blackwell).
Eliade, Mircea
    1959   *The Sacred and the Profane: The Nature of Religion* (New York: Harcourt, Brace & World).
Erasmus, J.G.
    n.d.   *Uitgesoekte Noord-Sotho spreekwoorde* (Johannesburg: APB).
Fassett, Thomas White Wolf
    1996   'Where Do We Go from Here?', in Jace Weaver, (ed.), *Defending Mother Earth* (Maryknoll, NY: Orbis Books): 177-91.
Fensham, F.C.
    1978   'The Use of the Suffix Conjugation and the Prefix Conjugation in a Few Old Hebrew Poems', *JNSL* 6: 9-18.
Farmer, K.A.
    1992   'Psalms', in C. Newsom and S. Ringe (eds.), *Women's Bible Commentary* (London: SPCK): 137-44.
Fisch, Harold
    1990   'Prophet versus Audience', in Ellen Spolsky (ed.), *The Uses of Adversity: Failure and Accomodation in Reader Response* (London: Lewisburg, 1990), pp. 114-27.
Firmage, E.
    1992   'Zoology', in *ABD*: VI, 1109-67.
Fontaine, C.
    2001   ' "Go Forth into the Fields": An Earth-Centered Reading of the Song of Songs', in Habel and Wurst (eds.) 2001: 126-42.
Fortes, M.
    1987   'The Political System of the Tallensi of the Northern Territories of the Gold Coast', in *idem* and E.E. Evans-Pritchard (eds.), *African Political Systems* (London and New York: International African Institute).
Frankfort, H.
    1946   *The Intellectual Adventure of Ancient Man* (Chicago: University of Chicago Press).
Fretheim, Terence E.
    1984   'Nature's Praise of God in the Psalms', *Ex Auditu* 3: 16-30.
    2000   'The Earth Story in Jeremiah 12', in Habel (ed.) 2000: 96-110.
Galambush, J.
    1999   'Castles in the Air: Creation as Property in Ezekiel', in *Society of Biblical Literature 1999 Seminar Papers* (Atlanta: Society of Biblical Literature): 147-72.

Gardner, Anne E.
  2000   'Ecojustice: A Study of Genesis 6.9-11', in Habel and Wurst (eds.)
            2000: 117-29.
  Forthcoming 'The Nature of the New Heavens and New Earth in Isaiah 66.22'.
Gibson, J.C.L.
  1977   *Canaanite Myths and Legends* (Edinburgh: T. & T. Clark).
Gillingham, Susan
  1994   *The Poems and Psalms of the Hebrew Bible* (New York: Oxford Uni-
            versity Press).
Gottwald, Norman K.
  1980   *The Tribes of Yahweh: A Sociology of the Religion of Liberated Israel,
            1250–1050 BCE* (London: SCM Press).
  1985   *The Hebrew Bible: A Socio-Literary Introduction* (Philadelphia: For-
            tress Press).
Grabbe, Lester L. (ed.)
  1998   *Leading Captivity Captive: 'The Exile' as History and Ideology* (Euro-
            pean Seminar in Historical Methodology, 2; Sheffield: Sheffield
            Academic Press).
Gunkel, Herman
  1895   *Schöpfung und Chaos in Urzeit und Endzeit: eine religionsgeschichtliche
            Untersuchung über Gen. 1 und Ap. Joh. 12* (Göttingen: Vandenhoeck
            & Ruprecht).
  1984   'The Influence of Babylonian Mythology upon the Biblical Crea-
            tion Story', in B.W. Anderson (ed.) 1984: 25-52.
Gustafson, James M.
  1994   *A Sense of the Divine: The Natural Environment from a Theocentric
            Perspective* (Cleveland: Pilgrim Press).
Gyekye, Kwame
  1996   *African Cultural Values: An Introduction* (Philadelphia and Accra:
            Sankofa).
Habel, N.C.
  1964   *Yahweh Versus Baal: A Conflict of Religious Cultures* (New York:
            Bookman Associates).
  1972   'He Who Stretches Out the Heavens', *CBQ* 34: 417-30.
  1995   *The Land Is Mine: Six Biblical Ideologies* (Overtures to Biblical Theol-
            ogy; Minneapolis: Fortress Press).
  2000   'Geophany: The Earth Story in Genesis 1', in Habel and Wurst
            (eds.) 2000: 34-48.
  2001   'Earth First: Inverse Cosmology in Job', in Habel and Wurst (eds.)
            2001: 65-77.
Habel, N.C. (ed.)
  2000   *Readings from the Perspective of Earth* (The Earth Bible, 1; Sheffield:
            Sheffield Academic Press).
Habel, N.C., and S. Wurst (eds.)
  2000   *The Earth Story in Genesis* (The Earth Bible, 2; Sheffield: Sheffield
            Academic Press).
  2001   *The Earth Story in Wisdom Traditions* (The Earth Bible, 3; Sheffield:
            Sheffield Academic Press).

Hallman, David G.
    1994   'Beyond 'North/South Dialogue', in *idem* (ed.), *Ecotheology: Voices from South and North* (Geneva: WCC Publications; Maryknoll, NY: Orbis Books): 3-12.
Hals, Ronald M.
    1989   *Ezekiel* (FOTL XIX; Grand Rapids: Eerdmans).
Hanson, P.D.
    1976   *The Dawn of Apocalyptic: The Historical and Sociological Roots of Jewish Apocalyptic Eschatology* (Philadelphia: Fortress Press).
Hardy, Peter
    1999   *The Geology of Somerset* (Bradford on Avon: Ex Libris Press).
Harrelson, W.J.
    1962   'Vengeance', in *IDB*: IV, 748.
Hayes, Katherine M.
    1997   ' "The Earth Mourns": Earth as Actor in a Prophetic Metaphor' (PhD dissertation, Catholic University of America).
    1998   'Entente with the Wild Animals: The Reversal of a Curse as Prelude to a Theology of Creation?' (paper presented at the annual meeting of the SBL at Orlando).
Hessel, Dieter T. (ed.)
    1996   *Theology for Earth Community: A Field Guide* (Ecology and Justice Series; Maryknoll, NY: Orbis Books).
Hiebert, Theodore
    1992   'Theophany in the Old Testament', *ABD*: 6, 505-11.
Holladay, William L.
    1971   *A Concise Hebrew and Aramaic Lexicon of the Old Testament* (Leiden: E.J. Brill).
    1993   *The Psalms Through Three Thousand Years: Prayerbook of a Cloud of Witnesses* (Minneapolis: Augsburg).
Howard, David M., Jr
    1993   'A Contextual Reading of Psalms 90-94', in J.C. McCann (ed.), *The Shape and Shaping of the Psalter* (JSOTSup, 159; Sheffield: JSOT Press): 108-23.
Hubbard, R.L.
    1991   'The Go'el in Ancient Israel', *Bulletin for Biblical Research* 1: 3-19.
Ikenga-Methuh, Emefie
    1987   *Comparative Studies of African Traditional Religions* (Onitsha: IMICO).
Jacob, Irene, and Walter Jacob
    1992   'Flora', in *ABD*: II, 803-17.
Janzen, W.
    1992   'Earth', in *ABD*: II, 245-48.
Jefferson, H.G.
    1949   'Notes on the Authorship of Isaiah 65 and 66', *JBL* 68: 225-30.
Jeremias, J.
    1977   *Theophanie: Die Geschichte einer alttestamentlichen Gattung* (WMANT, 10; Neukirchen–Vluyn: Neukirchener Verlag, 2nd edn).
Johnson, D.G.
    1988   *From Chaos to Restoration: An Integrative Reading of Isaiah 24–27* (JSOTSup; Sheffield: Sheffield Academic Press).

Jones, Lawrence
    1989   'Versions of the Dream: Literature and the Search for Identity', in D. Novitz and B. Willmott (eds.), *Culture and Identity in New Zealand* (Wellington: GP Books): 187-211.

Kassi, Norma
    1986   'A Legacy of Maldevelopment', in Jace Weaver (ed.), *Defending Mother Earth* (Maryknoll, NY: Orbis Books): 72-84.

Katz, E. (ed.)
    1992   *A New Classified Concordance of the Bible: A Hebrew-English Thesaurus of the Bible* (Jerusalem: Kiryat Sefer).

Keel, Othmar
    1978   *The Symbolism of the Biblical World: An Ancient Near Eastern Iconography and the Book of Psalms* (London: SPCK).

Keet, C.C.
    1969   *A Study of the Psalms of Ascents: A Critical and Exgetical Commentary upon Psalms CXX–CXXXIV* (London: The Mitre Press).

Keneally, Tom
    2000   *Bettany's Book* (Sydney: Doubleday).

Kessler, R.
    1992   ' "Ich weiß, daß mein Erlöser lebet": Sozialgeschichtlicher Hintergrund und theologische Bedeutung der Löser-Vorstellung in Hiob 19.25', *ZIK* 89: 139-58.

Kilpp, N.
    1990   *Niederreissen und aufbauen: Das Verhältnis von Heilsverheißung und Unheilsverkündigung bei Jeremia und im Jeremiabuch* (Biblisch-Theologische Studien, 13; Neukirchen–Vluyn: Neukirchener Verlag).

Kilson, Marion
    1971   *Kpele Lala: Ga Religious Songs and Symbols* (Cambridge, MA: Harvard University Press).

Kinew, Tobasonakwut
    1996   ' "Let Them Burn the Sky": Overcoming Repression of the Sacred Use of Anishinaabe Lands', in Jill Oakes, Rick Riewe, Kathi Kinew and Elaine Maloney (eds.), *Sacred Lands* (University of Alberta and Winnipeg, University of Manitoba: Canadian Circumpolar Institute): 33-36.

Kissane, E.J.
    1943   *The Book of Isaiah*, II (Dublin: Browne & Nolan).
    1953   *The Book of Psalms Translated from a Critically Revised Hebrew Text* (Dublin: Browne & Nolan).

Kittel, R. (ed.)
    1962   *Biblia Hebraica Stuttgartensia* (Stuttgart: Deutsche Bibelstiftung).

Kloos, Carola
    1981   'The Flood on Speaking Terms with God', *ZAW* 94: 639-42.
    1986   *YHWH's Combat with the Sea: A Canaanite Tradition in the Religion of Ancient Israel* (Amsterdam: G.A. van Oorschot; Leiden: E.J. Brill).

Knierim, R.P.
    1995   *The Task of Old Testament Theology: Method and Cases* (Grand Rapids: Eerdmans).

Knight, D.A.
1985   'Cosmogony and Order in the Hebrew Tradition', in R.W. Lovin and F.E. Reynolds (eds.), *Cosmogony and Ethical Order: New Studies in Comparative Ethics* (Chicago: University of Chicago Press): 133-57.

Kraft, Michael E.
1996   *Environmental Policy and Politics* (New York: Harper Collins).

Kramer, S.N., and J. Maier (eds.)
1989   *Myths of Enki, the Crafty God* (New York: Oxford University Press).

Kraus, Hans-Joachim
1986   *Theology of the Psalms* (Minneapolis: Augsburg).
1988   *Psalms 1–50* (trans. H.C. Oswald; Minneapolis: Fortress Press).
1989   *Psalms 60–150: A Commentary* (trans. H.C. Oswald; Minneapolis: Augsburg Fortress).

Kloos, C.
1986   *Yhwh's Combat with the Sea: A Canaanite Tradition in the Religion of Ancient Israel* (Amsterdam: G.A. van Oorschot).

Krige, E.J.
1956   *Social System of the Zulus* (Cape Town: Via Africa).

Kutsko, John
2000   *Between Heaven and Earth: Divine Presence and Absence in the Book of Ezekiel* (Winona Lake, IN: Eisenbrauns).

Kwok Pui-lan
1994   'Ecology and the Recycling of Christianity', in D.G. Hallman (ed.), *Ecotheology: Voices from South and North* (Geneva: WCC Publications; Maryknoll, NY: Orbis Books): 107-11.

Lack, R.
1973   *La Symbolique du Livre d'Isaie* (AnBib, 59; Rome: Biblical Institute Press).

Levenson, J.D.
1985   *Sinai and Zion: An Entry Into the Jewish Bible* (San Francisco: HarperCollins).
1992   'Zion Traditions', in *ABD*, IV: 1098-102.

Levin, Harold L.
1991   *The Earth Through Time* (Fort Worth: Saunders College Publishing, 4th edn).

Levine, Baruch
1993   *Numbers 1–20* (Anchor Bible; New York: Doubleday).

Levine, H.J.
1995   *Sing unto God a New Song: A Contemporary Reading of the Psalms* (Bloomington: Indiana University).

Lewis, C.S.
1958   *Reflections on the Psalms* (New York: Harcourt, Brace and Company).

Liebreich, L.
1955–56   'The Composition of the Book of Isaiah', *JQR* 46: 259-77.
1956–57   'The Compilation of the Book of Isaiah', *JQR* 47: 114-38.

Lopez, Barry
1987   *Arctic Dreams* (New York: Bantam Books).

Loretz, O.
1994   'Psalm 92: Ugaritische Texte und Gattungsforschung', *UF* 25: 275-88.
Lovelock, J.
1982   *Gaia: A New Look at Life on Earth* (London: Oxford University Press).
Macintosh, A.A.
1997   *A Critical and Exegetical Commentary on Hosea* (ICC; Edinburgh: T. & T. Clark).
MacLaren, A.
1895   *The Psalms* (London: Hodder and Stoughton).
Mbiti, John S.
1970   *African Religions and Philosophy* (Garden City, NY: Anchor Books).
1989   *African Religions and Philosophy* (London: Heinemann).
McBride, James
1995   *War, Battering, and Other Sports: The Gulf Between American Men and Women* (Atlantic Highlands, NJ: Humanities Press).
McCann, J. Clinton
1993   'Books I–III and the Editorial Purpose of the Hebrew Psalter', in *idem* (ed.), *The Shape and Shaping of the Psalter* (JSOTSup, 159; Sheffield: JSOT Press): 93-107.
McDaniel, Jay
1986   'Christianity and the Need for New Vision', in Eugene C. Hargrove (ed.), *Religion and Environmental Crisis* (Athens, GA, and London: University of Georgia): 188-212.
1997   'The Sacred Whole: An Ecumenical Protestant Approach', in J. Carroll, P. Brockelman, and M. Westfall (eds.), *The Greening of Faith: God, the Environment, and the Good Life* (Hanover, NH: University Press of New England): 105-24.
McDonagh, Sean
1990   *The Greening of the Church* (Maryknoll, NY: Orbis Books).
McFague, S.
1982   *Metaphorical Theology: Models of God in Religious Language* (Philadelphia: Fortress Press).
1993   *The Body of God: An Ecological Theology* (Minneapolis: Fortress Press).
Mann, Thomas
1938   *Joseph and His Brothers*. I. *Joseph in Egypt* (New York: Alfred A. Knopf).
Masenya (ngwana' Mphahlele), M.J.
1989   'In the School of Wisdom: An Interpretation of Some Old Testament Proverbs in a Northern Sotho Context' (MA dissertation, University of South Africa, Pretoria).
1996   'Proverbs 31.10-31 in a South African Context: A Bosadi (Womanhood) Perspective' (D.Litt. D. Phil. thesis, University of South Africa, Pretoria).
May, H.G.
1955   'Some Cosmic Connotations of *mayim rabbim*, "Many Waters"', *JBL* 74: 9-21.

Mays, James Luther
    1986   'The David of the Psalms', *Int* 40: 143-55.
    1994   *Psalms* (Interpretation: A Bible Commentary for Teaching and Preaching; Louisville: John Knox Press).

Meadowcroft, Tim
    2000   'Some Questions for the Earth Bible' Unpublished paper presented to ANZATS Conference, Christchurch.

Meeks, Wayne A. (ed.)
    1993   *The HarperCollins Study Bible* (New York: HarperCollins Pubishers).

Meyers, C.
    1991   '"To her Mother's House": Considering a Counterpart to the Israelite *Bet 'ab'*, in D. Jobling, P.L. Day and G.T. Sheppard (eds.), *The Bible and the Politics of Exegesis* (Cleveland: Pilgrim Press): 39-51.

Miller, Patrick D., Jr
    1982   *Sin and Judgment in the Prophets: A Stylistic and Theological Analysis* (SBLMS, 27; Chico, CA: Scholars Press).
    1993   *The Harper Collins Study Bible* (Harper Collins).

Moltmann, J.
    1985   *God in Creation* (Minneapolis: Fortress Press).

Motyer, J.A.
    1993   *The Prophecy of Isaiah: Introduction and Commentary* (Downers Grove, IL: InterVarsity Press).

Mowinckel, S.
    1962   *The Psalms in Israel's Worship* (2 vols.; Nashville: Abingdon Press).

Neidjie, Bill, S. Davis and A. Fox
    1986   *Australia's Kakadu Man* (Darwin: Resource Managers).

Newsom, C.
    1987   'A Maker of Metaphors: Ezekiel's Oracles Against Tyre', in J.L. Mays and P.J. Achtemeier (eds.), *Interpreting the Prophets* (Philadelphia: Fortress Press): 188-99.

Noth, M.
    1962   *Das dritte Buch Mose: Leviticus* (Gottingen: Vandenhoeck & Ruprecht).

Nouwen, Henri J.M.
    1992   *The Return of the Prodigal Son: A Story of Homecoming* (Garden City, NY: Doubleday).

Oakes, Jill, Rick Riewe, Kathi Kinew and Elaine Maloney (eds.)
    1998   'Preface', in *Sacred Lands* (University of Alberta and Winnipeg, University of Manitoba: Canadian Circumpolar Institute): 99-106.

Olley, J.W.
    2000   'Mixed Blessings for Animals: The Contrasts of Genesis 9', in Habel and Wurst (eds.) 2000: 130-39.
    2001   'Animals in Heaven and Earth: Attitudes in Ezekiel'. *Colloqium* 33, 1: 47-57.

Oduyoye, M.A.
    1994   'Feminist Theology in an African Perspective', in R. Gibellini (ed.), *Paths in African Theology* (Maryknoll, NY: Orbis Books): 166-81.

1995   *Daughters of Anowa: African Women and Patriarchy* (Maryknoll, NY: Orbis Books).

Opoku, Kofi Asare
1978   *West African Traditional Religion* (Accra: FEP).

Oswalt, J.N.
1986   *The Book of Isaiah, Chapters 1–39* (NICOT; Grand Rapids: Eerdmans).
1998   *The Book of Isaiah, Chapters 40–66* (NICOT; Grand Rapids: Eerdmans).

Ottosson, Magnus
1974   אֶרֶץ, *'erets'*, *TDOT*: I, 388-405.

Otwell, J.H.
1977   *And Sarah Laughed: The Status of Women in the Old Testament* (Philadelphia: Westminster Press).

Parker S.B. (ed.)
1997   *Ugaritic Narrative Poetry* (Atlanta: SBL).

Paul, Shalom
1979–80   'Adoption Formulae: A Study of Cuneiform and Biblical Legal Clauses', *MAARAV* 2: 173-85.

Pedersen, J.
1976   *Israel – Its Life and Culture* (2 vols.; London: Oxford University Press [1926]).

Perlitt, L.
1972   'Anklage und Freispruch Gottes: Theologische Motive in der Zeit des Exils', *ZIK* 69: 290-303.

Pfeiffer, R.H.
1948   *Introduction to the Old Testament* (London: A. & C. Black).

Pham, Xuan Huong Thi
1999   *Mourning in the Ancient Near East and the Hebrew Bible* (JSOTSup, 302; Sheffield: Sheffield Academic Press).

Pillari, Vimala
1991   *Scapegoating in Families: Intergenerational Patterns of Physical and Emotional Abuse* (New York: Brunner/Mazel).

Pitard, Wayne T.
1992   'Vengeance', in *ABD*: VI, 786-87.

Pleins, J.D.
1993   *The Psalms: Songs of Tragedy, Hope, and Justice* (Maryknoll, NY: Orbis Books).

Pope, Marvin
1955   *El in the Ugaritic Texts* (Leiden: Brill).

Preminger, Alex, and Edward L. Greenstein (eds.)
1986   *The Hebrew Bible in Literary Criticism* (New York: Ungar).

Primavesi, A.
1991   *From Apocalypse to Genesis: Ecology, Feminism and Christianity* (Minneapolis: Fortress Press).

Pritchard, J.B. (ed.)
1969   *The Ancient Near East in Pictures: Relating to the Old Testament* (Princeton: Princeton University Press, 2nd edn).

Rad, G. von
1965   *Old Testament Theology* (2 vols.; London: SCM Press).

1984 'The Theological Problem of the Old Testament Doctrine of Creation', in B.W. Anderson (ed.) 1984: 53-63.

Rainbow Spirit Elders
1997 *Rainbow Spirit Theology* (Melboure: HarperCollins).

Rakoma, J.R.D.
1971 *Marema-ka-Dika tša Sesotho se Leboa* (Pretoria: Van Schaik).

Ravuvu, A.D.
1987 *The Fijian Ethos* (Suva: Institute of Pacific Studies, University of the South Pacific).

Rendtorff, R.
1984 'Zur Komposition des Buches Jesaja', *VT* 34: 295-320.
1996 'The Book of Isaiah: A Complex Unity. Synchronic and Diachronic Reading', in R.F. Melugin and M.A. Sweeney (eds.), *New Visions of Isaiah* (JSOTSup, 214; Sheffield: Sheffield Academic Press): 32-49.

Rendtorff, R., and K. Koch (eds.)
1961 *Studien zur Theologie der alttestamentlichen überlieferungen: Festschrift G. von Rad zum 60. Geburtstag* (Neukirchen–Vluyn: Neukirchener Verlag).

Renz, Thomas
1999 *The Rhetorical Function of the Book of Ezekiel* (Leiden: E.J. Brill).

Rich, A.
1980 *On Lies, Secrets and Silence: Selected Prose 1966–1978* (London: Virago).

Richardson, M.E.J. (ed.)
1995 *Koehler-Baumgartner Hebrew and Aramaic Lexicon of the Old Testament: The New Koehler-Baumgartner in English*, II (Leiden: E.J. Brill).
1999 *Koehler-Baumgartner Hebrew and Aramaic Lexicon of the Old Testament: The New Koehler-Baumgartner in English*, IV (Leiden: E.J. Brill).

Roberts, John
2000 'World Churches Target Violence', in *Crosslink* (Wellington: Presbyterian, Methodist and Cooperative Ventures): 12.

Salevao, Iutisone
2000 ' "Burning the Land": An Ecojustice Reading of Hebrews 6.7-8', in Habel (ed.) 2000: 221-31.

Sam-Cromarty, Margaret
1996 'Family Closeness: Will James Bay Be Only a Memory for My Grandchildren?', in Jace Weaver (ed.), *Defending Mother Earth* (Maryknoll, NY: Orbis Books): 153-76.

Sawyer, J.F.A.
1984 *Isaiah* 1 (Daily Study Bible; Philadelphia: Westminster Press).
1986 *Isaiah* 2 (Daily Study Bible; Philadelphia: Westminster Press).
1996 *The Fifth Gospel: Isaiah in the History of Christianity* (Cambridge: Cambridge University Press).

Schmid, H.H.
1971 'jrs beerben', *ThWAT*, 1: cols. 778-81.

Schmitt, John J.
1983 'The Gender of Ancient Israel', *JSOT* 26: 115-25.

Schultz, R.L.
    1999   *The Search for Quotation: Verbal Parallels in the Prophets* (JSOTSup, 180; Sheffield: Sheffield Academic Press).

Sehmsdorf, E.
    1972   'Studien zur Redaktionsgeschichte von Jesaja 56–66, Teil 1', *ZAW* 84: 517-62; 'Studien zur Redaktionsgeschichte von Jesaja 56–66, Teil 2', *ZAW* 84: 562-76.

Sekine, T.S.
    1989   *Die Tritojesajanische Sammlung (Jes 56–66) Redaktionsgeschichtliche Untersucht* (BZAW, 175; Berlin: W. de Gruyter).

Seitz, C.
    1993   *Isaiah 1–39* (Interpretation; Louisville: John Knox).

Sheppard, Gerald
    1992   'Theology and the Book of Psalms', *Int* 46: 143-55.

Shorter, Aylward
    1973   *African Culture and the Christian Church* (London: Geoffrey Chapman).
    1985   *Jesus and the Witchdoctor: An Approach to Healing and Wholeness* (London: Geoffrey Chapman; Maryknoll, NY: Orbis Books).

Slotki, I.W.
    1949   *Isaiah with Hebrew Text and English Translation* (London: Soncino).

Smith, M.S.
    1997   'The Baal Cycle', in S.B. Parker (ed.), *Ugaritic Narrative Poetry* (Atlanta: Scholars Press): 81-180.

Smith, P.A.
    1995   *Rhetoric and Redaction in Trito-Isaiah: The Structure, Growth and Authorship of Isaiah 56–66* (Leiden: E.J. Brill).

Sommer, B.D.
    1996   'Allusions and Illusions: The Unity of the Book of Isaiah in Light of Deutero-Isaiah's Use of Prophetic Tradition', in R.F. Melugin and M.A. Sweeney (eds.), *New Visions of Isaiah* (JSOTSup, 214; Sheffield: Sheffield Academic Press): 156-86.

Steck, O.H.
    1987   'Beobachtungen zur Anlage von Jes 65–66', *BN* 38–39: 103-16.
    1991   *Studien zu Tritojesaja* (BZAW, 203; Berlin: de Gruyter).
    1997   'Der neue Himmel und die neue Erde: Beobachtungen zur Rezeption von Gen 1–3 in Jes 65.16b-25', in J. van Ruiten and M. Vervenne (eds.), *Studies in the Book of Isaiah: Festschrift Willem A.M. Beuken* (BETL, 132; Leuven: Leuven University Press/Peeters): 349-65.

Stolzemburg, William
    2000   'Vital Science', *Nature Conservancy* (September–October).

Stuhlmueller, C.
    1988   'Psalms', in J.L. Mays (ed.), *Harper's Bible Commentary* (San Francisco: Harper & Row): 433-94.

Sugirtharajah, R.S.
    1996   'From Orientalist to Post-Colonial: Notes on Reading Practices', *AJT* 10: 20-27.

Sweeney, M.
    1988   *Isaiah 1–4 and the Post-Biblical Understanding of the Isaiah Tradition*
                (BZAW, 1711; Berlin: W. de Gruyter).
Swimme, Brian, and Thomas Berry
    1994   *The Universe Story: From the Primordial Flaring Forth to the Ezozoic
                Era* (Harmondsworth: Arkana).
Taber, C.R.
    1976   'Marriage', in *IDBSup*: 573-76.
Tate, M.E.
    1990   *Psalms 51–100* (WBC, 20; Dallas, TX: Word Books).
Tarlin, Jan William
    1997   'Utopoia and Pornography in Ezekiel: Violence, Hope, and the
                Shattered Male Subject', in T.K. Beal and D.M. Gunn (eds.), *Read-
                ing Bibles, Writing Bodies* (London: Routledge).
Terrien, S.
    1970   'The Omphalos Myth and Hebrew Religion', *VT* 20: 315-38.
Thiel, W.
    1981   *Die deuteronomistische Redaktion von Jeremia 26–45* (WMANT, 52;
                Neukirchen–Vluyn: Neukirchener Verlag).
Tinker, George E.
    1996   'An American Indian Theological Response to Ecojustice', in Jace
                Weaver (ed.), *Defending Mother Earth* (Maryknoll, NY: Orbis Books):
                153-76.
Tomasino, A.J.
    1993   'Isiah 1:1-24 and 63-66 and the Composition of the Isaiamic Cor-
                pus', *JSOT* 57: 81-98.
Toombs, Lawrence E.
    1971   'The Psalms', in Charles M. Layon (ed.), *The Interpreter's One
                Volume Commentary on the Bible* (Nashville: Abingdon Press): 253-
                303.
Toorn, K. van der
    1991   'The Babylonian New Year Festival: New Insights From the
                Cuneiform Texts and their Bearing on Old Testament Study', in
                J.A. Emerton (ed.), *Congress Volume: Leuven 1989* (Leiden: E.J. Brill):
                331-44.
Toorn, K. van der, Bob Becking and Pieter W. van der Hoorst (eds.)
    1999   *Dictionary of Deities and Demons in the Bible* (Leiden: Brill).
Towner, W.S.
    1996   'The Future of Nature', *Int* 50: 27-35.
Tucker, G.M.
    2000   'The Peaceable Kingdom and a Covenant with the Wild Animals',
                in W.P. Brown and S.D. McBride, Jr (eds.), *God Who Creates: Essays
                in Honor of W. Sibley Towner* (Grand Rapids: Eerdmans): 215-25.
Turnbull, Colin M.
    1987   *The Lonely African* (New York: Simon & Schuster).
Turner, Victor
    1970   *The Forest of Symbols: Aspects of Ndembu Ritual* (Ithaca, NY, and
                London: Cornell University Press).

Tuwere, I.S.
1992   'Making Sense of Vanua (Land) in the Fijian Context: A Theological Exploration' (D.Th. thesis, Melbourne College of Divinity).

Tylor, Edward Burnett
1958   *Religion in Primitive Culture*, II (New York: Harper & Brothers).

Urbrock, William J.
1974   'Mortal and Miserable Man: A Form-Critical Investigation of Psalm 90', in G. MacRae (ed.), *Society of Biblical Literature 1974 Seminar Papers* (Cambridge, MA: Society of Biblical Literature): 1-33.

Van Eeeden, I.J.
1987   'Ethical Questions Pertaining to the "Soft Explosion"', in W.S. Worster (ed.), *Are We Killing God's Earth? Ecology and Theology* (Pretoria: University of South Africa): 80-88.

Van Putten, Mark
2000   'The NWF View', *National Wildlife* (August–September): 7.

Waard, J. de
1997   *A Handbook on Isaiah* (Textual Criticism and the Translator, 1; Winona Lake, IN : Eisenbrauns).

Wagner, Gunther
1987   'The Political Organisation of the Bantu of Karivondo', in *African Political Systems* (New York: KPI): 197-236.

Walker-Jones, A.W.
1991   'Alternative Cosmogonies in the Psalms' (PhD thesis, Princeton Theological Seminary).

Washington, Harold C.
1994   'The Strange Woman (אשה זרה/נכריה) of Proverbs 1–9 and Post-Exilic Judaean Society', in T.C. Eskenazi and K.H. Richards (eds.), *Second Temple Studies 2: Temple and Community in the Persian Period* (Sheffield: JSOT Press): 215-42.
2000   'The Lord's Mercy Endures Forever: Toward a Post-Shoah Reading of Grace in the Hebrew Scriptures', *Int* 54: 135-45.

Watts, J.D.W.
1987   *Isaiah 34–66* (WBC; Waco, TX: Word Books).

Webb, S.H.
1996   'Ecology vs. the Peaceable Kingdom', *Soundings* 79: 239-52.

Weiser, Artur
1962   *The Psalms* (OTL; Philadelphia: Westminster Press; London: SCM Press).

Weiskel, Timothy C.
1997   'Notes from Belshaz'zar's Feast', in J. Carroll, P. Brockelman, and Westfall (eds.) *The Greening of Faith: God, the Environment, and the Good Life* (Hanover, NH: University Press of New England): 11-29.

Wells, R.D.
1996   ' "Isaiah" as an Exponent of Torah: Isaiah 56.1-8', in R.F. Melugin and M.A. Sweeney (eds.), *New Visions of Isaiah* (JSOTSup, 214; Sheffield: Sheffield Academic Press): 140-55.

Westermann, C.

1969   _Isaiah 40–66: A Commentary_ (trans. D.M.G. Stalker; OTL; London: SCM Press).

1978   _Blessing: In the Bible and the Life of the Church_ (trans. K. Crim; Philadelphia: Fortress Press).

1981   _Praise and Lament in the Psalms_ (trans. K.R. Crim and R.N. Soulen; Atlanta: John Knox Press).

White, L.

1967   'The Historical Roots of Our Ecological Crisis', _Science_ 155: 1203-207.

Whiteman, Darrell L. (ed.)

1920   _An Introduction to Melanesian Cultures_ (Goroka, PNG: The Melanesian Institute for Pastoral and Socioeconomic Service).

Whybray, R.N.

1975   _Isaiah 40–66_ (NCB; London: Oliphants; Grand Rapids: Eerdmans).

Wildberger, H.

1991   _Isaiah 1–12: A Commentary_ (Minneapolis: Fortress Press).

Willey, P.T.

1997   _Remember the Former Things: The Recollection of Previous Texts in Second Isaiah_ (SBLDS, 161; Atlanta: Scholars Press).

Williamson, H.G.M.

1999   'From One Degree of Glory to Another: Themes and Theology in Isaiah', in Edward Ball (ed.), _In Search of Wisdom: Essays in Old Testament Interpretation: Essays in Honour of Ronald E. Clements_ (Sheffield: Sheffield Academic Press): 174-95.

Wilson, Gerald H.

1993a   _The Editing of the Hebrew Psalter_ (SBLDS, 76; Chico, CA: Scholars Press).

1993b   'Shaping the Psalter: A Consideration of Editorial Linkage in the Book of Psalms', in J.C. McCann (ed.), _The Shape and Shaping of the Psalter_ (JSOTSup, 159; Sheffield: JSOT Press): 72-82.

Wittenberg, G.H.

1978   'The Tenth Commandment in the Old Testament', _JTSA_ 22: 3-17.

1991   'Job the Farmer: The Judean 'am ha'arets and the Wisdom Movement', _Old Testament Essays_ 4: 151-70.

Wolff, Hans Walter

1974   _Hosea_ (Hermeneia; Philadelphia: Fortress Press).

Wright, Christopher J.H.

1979   'The Israelite Household and the Decalogue: The Social Background and Significance of Some Commandments', _Tyndale Bulletin_ 31: 101-24.

1990   _God's People in God's Land: Family Land, and Property in the Hebrew Bible_ (Grand Rapids: Eerdmans).

Wright, David P.

1999   'Holiness in Leviticus and Beyond', _Int_ 53: 351-64.

Wright, G.E.

1952   _God Who Acts: Biblical Theology as Recital_ (London: SCM Press).

Wurst, Shirley
    2000   ' "Beloved, Come Back to Me": Ground's Theme Song in Genesis 3?', in Habel and Wurst (eds.) 2000: 87-104.

Wyatt, N.
    1998   *Religious Texts from Ugarit: The Words of Ilimilku and his Colleagues* (Sheffield: Sheffield Academic Press).

Yee, Gale A.
    1987   *Composition and Tradition in the Book of Hosea: A Redaction Critical Investigation* (SBLDS, 102; Atlanta: Scholars Press).

Young, E.J.
    1972   *The Book of Isaiah*. III. *Chapters 40 through 66* (Grand Rapids: Eerdmans).

Ziervogel, D., and P.C. Mokgokong
    1975   *Comprehensive Northern Sotho Dictionary* (Pretoria: Van Schaik).

Zimmerli, Walther
    1979   *Ezekiel 1: A Commentary on the Book of the Prophet Ezekiel, Chs 1–24* (trans. R.E. Clements; Hermeneia: Philadelphia: Fortress Press).
    1982   'Knowledge of God According to the Book of Ezekiel', in *I am Yahweh* (Atlanta: John Knox): 29-98.
    1983   *Ezekiel 2: A Commentary on the Book of the Prophet Ezekiel, Chs 25–48* (Hermeneia: Philadelphia: Fortress Press).

World Book Encyclopedia
    2000   *The World Book Encyclopedia* (Chicago: World Book).

INDEXES

INDEX OF REFERENCES

OLD TESTAMENT

INDEX OF AUTHORS